Country
Cookbook

Mary Norwak

Hamlyn

London · New York · Sydney · Toronto

Contents

Acknowledgements
Jacket photograph by courtesy of Syndication International
Line drawings by Ann Rees

Published by
The Hamlyn Publishing Group Limited
London · New York · Sydney · Toronto
Astronaut House, Feltham, Middlesex, England
© Copyright The Hamlyn Publishing Group Limited 1976
Reprinted 1977

ISBN 0 600 31882 6

Printed and bound in Great Britain
by Butler & Tanner Limited,
Frome and London

Useful facts and figures

Notes on metrication

In this book quantities have been given in both metric and Imperial measures. Exact conversion from Imperial to metric measures does not usually give very convenient working quantities and so for greater convenience the metric measures have been rounded off into units of 25 grammes. The following table shows the recommended equivalents.

Ounces/fluid ounces	Approx. g. and ml. to nearest whole figure	Recommended conversion to nearest unit of 25
1	28	25
2	57	50
3	85	75
4	113	100
5 (¼ pint)	142	150
6	170	175
7	198	200
8	226	225
9	255	250
10 (½ pint)	283	275
11	311	300
12	340	350
13	368	375
14	396	400
15 (¾ pint)	428	425
16 (1 lb.)	456	450
17	486	475
18	512	500
19	541	550
20 (1 pint)	569	575

NOTE: When converting quantities over 20 oz. first add the appropriate figures in the centre column, then adjust to the nearest unit of 25.

This method of conversion gives good results in nearly all recipes; however, in certain cake recipes a more accurate conversion is necessary to produce a balanced recipe.

Liquid measures The millilitre is a very small unit of measurement and we felt that to use decilitres (units of 100 ml.) would be easier.

All spoon measures are level unless indicated otherwise.

Oven temperature chart

	°F	°C	Gas Mark
Very cool	225	110	$\frac{1}{4}$
	250	130	$\frac{1}{2}$
Cool	275	140	1
	300	150	2
Moderate	325	160	3
	350	180	4
Moderately hot	375	190	5
	400	200	6
Hot	425	220	7
	450	230	8
Very hot	475	240	9

Notes for American users

This list gives American equivalents for terms used in the book.

British	American
Baked/unbaked pastry case	Baked/unbaked pie shell
Cocktail stick	Wooden toothpick
Deep cake tin	Spring form pan
Frying pan	Skillet
Greaseproof paper	Wax paper
Grill	Broil/broiler
Mixer/liquidiser	Mixer/blender
Muslin	Cheesecloth
Pastry cutters	Cookie cutters
Patty tins	Muffin pans/cups
Piping bag	Pastry bag
Piping tube	Nozzle/tip
Sandwich tin	Layer cake pan

NOTE: The British pint measures 20 fluid ounces whereas the American pint equals 16 fluid ounces.

Introduction

Many people believe that generations of country families have been brought up on lavish meals of roast beef, salmon and trout, with all the traditional trimmings. In fact, country women have always had to manage their budgets carefully, and have had little money to spare for such luxuries. They have learned to make delicious and nourishing meals from a few eggs, a little bit of cheese, a scrap of bacon, vegetables from the garden and fruit in season, and have swopped their surplus produce for other people's chickens, the poacher's rabbit or a jug of cream.

In this book, I have collected together many favourite ways of cooking fresh country produce, together with ideas for preserving a glut of fruit and vegetables, and for making the very best of every scrap of food. Few of us now are lucky enough to own the traditional cottager's pig, to tend a row of hives, milk the house cow or gather the warm brown eggs, but we can still enjoy cooking the country way.

The recipes will give 4–6 servings, according to appetite.

Mary Norwak

Poultry and game

Today's poultry tends to be young, and does not retain the innards after killing for as long as poultry slaughtered in the traditional method does; because of this they are often flavourless. To improve the flavour it is important to see that poultry, particularly chicken, is not overcooked, and that it is helped along with plenty of herbs and other trimmings.

Chicken

For best results when roasting, cook in a moderately hot oven (375°F., 190°C., Gas Mark 5) and allow 20 minutes per lb. ($\frac{1}{2}$ kg.), plus 20 minutes extra. Gravy made from the giblets and a garnish of bacon rolls and sausages will give added flavour. If you want to joint a chicken, use a strong sharp knife, a chopping board and a weight. Remove the giblets and put the bird on the board. With a sharp knife, cut through and along the length of the breastbone. Open the bird out, and cut through along the backbone, removing it completely for convenience. Tap the back of the knife sharply with the weight to cut through the bony sections. Put the halves, skin side up, on the board and divide each piece into half again by cutting diagonally across between wing and thigh. Trim off leg shanks and wingtips for neatness.

Duck

For a really delicious bird which is not greasy, try roasting a duck with $\frac{1}{2}$ inch (1 cm.) water in the tin and some salt on the breast, but no extra fat. Turn the bird halfway through cooking to brown the breast and you will have a duck with a crisp skin and full-flavoured meat. It is not necessary to stuff a duck, but a couple of peeled apples or oranges can be tucked inside during roasting to give a delicious flavour. A good gravy can be made with the pan drippings from the duck if equal quantities of stock and white wine or cider are added and then seasoned with a pinch each of grated orange and lemon rind, the juice of 1 orange and 1 teaspoon lemon juice.

Goose

A goose loses half its weight in dressing and cooking, so this should be allowed for when planning a meal. It needs more cooking for its size than the drier turkey or chicken, but the outside fat must be made crisp without drying the meat. Cook a goose on a rack in a large tin and start the bird in a hot oven (450°F., 230°C., Gas Mark 8) for 20 minutes. Prick the skin with a fork and continue cooking in a moderately hot oven (400°F., 200 °C., Gas Mark 6) allowing 20 minutes per lb. ($\frac{1}{2}$ kg.) and 20 minutes extra. Drain off some fat two or three times during cooking, and baste the bird. Sage and onion stuffing is traditional with goose, and it goes particularly well with red cabbage and baked apples which help to counteract the fattiness.

Turkey

A hen bird gives better results than a cock, and one with a broad breast is best of all. Slow roasting reduces shrinkage, but quick roasting seals the bird and gives better flavour. Try a compromise by putting a turkey into a hot oven (425°F., 220°C., Gas Mark 7) for 20 minutes and then reduce to moderately hot (375°F., 190°C., Gas Mark 5) for the remaining cooking time. For a bird under 14 lb. (6$\frac{1}{2}$ kg.) allow 15 minutes per lb. ($\frac{1}{2}$ kg.) and 15 minutes extra; larger birds need 10 minutes per lb. ($\frac{1}{2}$ kg.) and 10 minutes over.

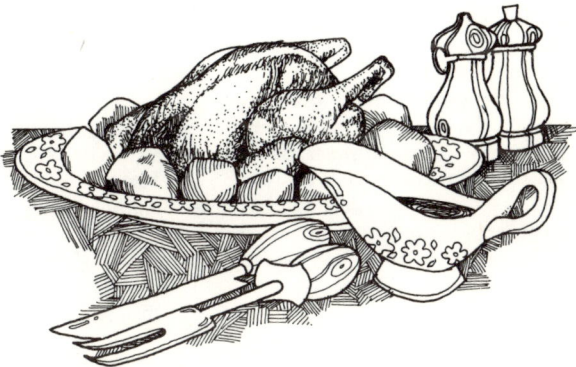

Pressed poultry

IMPERIAL · METRIC	AMERICAN
cold turkey or chicken	cold turkey or chicken
fresh herbs	fresh herbs
salt and pepper	salt and pepper

When the bird has been carved, remove all the remaining flesh in neat pieces. Mix the light and dark meat and pack into loaf tins, pressing under a heavy weight. Break up the carcass and simmer in very little water with plenty of herbs, salt and pepper to make a rich stock. When the liquid is strong and full of flavour, pour it over the meat and press under weights again. Put in a cold place and when firm, cut in slices. This is a useful way of preparing poultry for a cold table for a party. If you want to prepare a bird specially, roast it in foil so it remains very tender.

Christmas pie

IMPERIAL · METRIC	AMERICAN
8 oz./225 g. bacon rashers	½ lb. bacon slices
leftover turkey or chicken	leftover turkey or chicken
pork sausagemeat	pork sausagemeat
stock	stock
leftover poultry stuffing	leftover poultry stuffing

This is a marvellous way of using up a large bird and some of its trimmings. Make the stock from the carcass before you prepare the rest of the dish. The stuffing should be strongly flavoured with herbs.

Remove the rinds from the bacon rashers and make them thin with a wide-bladed knife. Line a pie dish with the bacon. Top with pieces of poultry and sausagemeat. Just cover with stock and bake in a moderate oven (325°F., 160°C., Gas Mark 3) for 3 minutes. Top with the stuffing and bake for 30 minutes longer. Put it into a cold place until firm and turn out to serve. Quantities can be varied to suit the ingredients available.

Chicken with bacon stuffing

IMPERIAL · METRIC	AMERICAN
4 oz./100 g. streaky bacon	¼ lb. bacon slices
1 small onion	1 small onion
1 oz./25 g. butter	2 tablespoons butter
3 oz./75 g. fresh white breadcrumbs	1½ cups fresh soft bread crumbs
2 tablespoons chopped parsley	3 tablespoons chopped parsley
pepper	pepper
3-lb./1½-kg. chicken	3-lb. chicken

To make the stuffing, remove the rinds and cut bacon into pieces. Peel and chop the onion. Cook the bacon and onion for about 4 minutes in the butter. Stir in the breadcrumbs, chopped parsley and pepper. Remove the giblets from the chicken and simmer them in ½ pint (3 dl., 1¼ cups) water for the gravy. Put the stuffing in the neck and body of the bird and roast it in a moderately hot oven (400°F., 200°C., Gas Mark 6) for 1 hour. Serve the chicken with gravy made from the giblet stock.

Aunt Katie's chicken

IMPERIAL · METRIC	AMERICAN
3-lb./1½-kg. chicken, cut into serving pieces	3-lb. chicken, cut into serving pieces
2 oz./50 g. butter	¼ cup butter
1 oz./25 g. plain flour	¼ cup all-purpose flour
½ teaspoon marjoram	½ teaspoon marjoram
½ teaspoon salt	½ teaspoon salt
¼ teaspoon black pepper	¼ teaspoon black pepper
1 tablespoon oil	1 tablespoon oil
¼ pint/1½ dl. double cream	⅔ cup heavy cream

Rub the chicken pieces with half the softened butter and refrigerate for 1 hour. Season the flour with the herb, salt and pepper and use to toss the chicken pieces. Heat the remaining butter and the oil. Brown the chicken on both sides in a heavy frying pan and pour in the cream. Simmer with a lid on for 15 minutes, then uncovered for 15 minutes. Serve with mashed potatoes and a green vegetable.

Chicken with watercress stuffing

IMPERIAL · METRIC	AMERICAN
1 bunch watercress	1 bunch watercress
2 oz./50 g. mushrooms	½ cup finely chopped mushrooms
2 tablespoons fresh breadcrumbs	3 tablespoons fresh soft bread crumbs
seasoning	seasoning
1 egg yolk	1 egg yolk
3½-lb./1¾-kg. roasting chicken	3½-lb. roaster chicken
fat for roasting	oil for roasting
3 streaky bacon rashers	3 bacon slices

Chop the watercress and the mushrooms very finely and mix with the breadcrumbs. Season well and bind with egg yolk. Loosen the skin slightly over the breastbone of the chicken at the neck end and push the stuffing into this space to produce a rounded shape. Fold the loose skin over the opening and secure it under the bird with the wings tucked round. Place the chicken in hot fat in a roasting tin. Put the bacon rashers over the breast and roast in a moderately hot oven (375°F., 190°C., Gas Mark 5) for 1½ hours, until tender and cooked. Serve garnished with plenty of watercress.

Rosemary chicken

IMPERIAL · METRIC	AMERICAN
3-lb./1½-kg. chicken	3-lb. chicken
sprig rosemary	sprig rosemary
salt and pepper	salt and pepper
1 oz./25 g. butter	2 tablespoons butter
¼ pint/1½ dl. stock	⅔ cup stock

Put the chicken giblets inside the chicken, together with the rosemary. Put the chicken into a roasting tin and sprinkle with salt and pepper. Dot with butter and pour the stock around the bird. Roast in a moderately hot oven (400°F., 200°C., Gas Mark 6) for 1¼ hours. Remove the giblets, and serve the chicken with the thin pan gravy.

Pot roast chicken

IMPERIAL · METRIC	AMERICAN
3½-lb./1¾-kg. chicken	3½-lb. chicken
1½ oz./40 g. butter	3 tablespoons butter
2 sticks celery	2 stalks celery
6 small onions	6 small onions
2 medium carrots	2 medium carrots
1 small turnip	1 small turnip
½ pint/3 dl. stock	1¼ cups stock
salt and pepper	salt and pepper

Wipe the chicken inside and out. Melt the butter and brown the
chicken lightly on all sides. Add the sliced vegetables, stock, salt
and pepper. Cover and simmer for 1½ hours, basting occasionally
with the stock. This dish may be cooked on top of the cooker or
in a moderately hot oven (375°F., 190°C., Gas Mark 5). Sprinkle
with a little chopped parsley just before serving.

Royal chicken

IMPERIAL · METRIC	AMERICAN
8 chicken pieces	8 chicken pieces
4 oz./100 g. bacon	¼ lb. bacon slices
2 oz./50 g. butter	¼ cup butter
4 small onions	4 small onions
4 oz./100 g. mushrooms	1 cup sliced mushrooms
¼ pint/1½ dl. stock	⅔ cup stock
bay leaf, thyme and parsley	bay leaf, thyme and parsley
salt and pepper	salt and pepper
½ pint/3 dl. red wine	1¼ cups red wine
1 tablespoon flour	1 tablespoon all-purpose flour

Wipe the chicken joints. Cut the bacon into dice. Melt half the
butter and fry the onions until golden, then add the bacon and
chicken. Add the sliced mushrooms, stock, herbs, salt and pepper.
Cover and cook slowly until the chicken is tender. Take out
chicken and mushrooms and keep hot. Skim the fat from the
gravy, and stir in the wine. Melt the remaining butter and stir in
the flour. Add the chicken gravy and simmer until creamy and
smooth. Pour over the chicken and mushrooms and serve at once.

Grilled chicken and mushrooms

IMPERIAL·METRIC	AMERICAN
2½-lb./1¼-kg. chicken	2½-lb. chicken
1 small lemon	1 small lemon
1½ oz./40 g. butter	3 tablespoons butter
salt and pepper	salt and pepper
1 small onion	1 small onion
2 oz./50 g. mushrooms	½ cup sliced mushrooms
chopped parsley	chopped parsley

Cut the chicken in half lengthwise and skewer the halves as flat as possible. Rub over with the cut lemon. Melt the butter, brush all over the chicken, and sprinkle with salt and pepper. Put the halves, skin side down, in a grill pan with the rack removed and cook under a gentle heat with the pan 5 or 6 inches (13 or 15 cm.) below the heat, for 12–15 minutes, adding a little more butter once or twice. When cooked the skin should be crisp and golden. The juices, when the thigh is pierced, should be colourless. If not, cook a little longer. Meanwhile, fry the chopped onion in the remaining butter until soft, add the sliced mushrooms and cook for 3 minutes. Put the chicken on a serving dish, pour over the onion and mushrooms with the juices and sprinkle on parsley.

Chicken pie

IMPERIAL·METRIC	AMERICAN
1 lb./450 g. cooked chicken	2 cups chopped cooked chicken
1 lb./450 g. potatoes	1 lb. potatoes
½ pint/3 dl. chicken stock	1¼ cups chicken stock
½ pint/3 dl. single cream	1¼ cups half-and-half
salt and pepper	salt and pepper
1 tablespoon chopped parsley	1 tablespoon chopped parsley
12 oz./350 g. puff pastry	¾ lb. puff paste

Cut the chicken and peeled potatoes into small cubes. Make the chicken stock from the carcass and see that it is richly-flavoured and contains plenty of herbs. Put the chicken and potatoes into a pie dish and pour over the stock and cream. Season well with salt, pepper and parsley. Cover with the pastry and bake in a hot oven (425°F., 220°C., Gas Mark 7) for 45 minutes.

Brimstone chicken

IMPERIAL · METRIC	AMERICAN
2 cold cooked chicken legs	2 cold cooked chicken legs
1 teaspoon made mustard	1 teaspoon prepared mustard
1 teaspoon curry powder	1 teaspoon curry powder
1 oz./25 g. butter	2 tablespoons butter
2 teaspoons Worcestershire sauce	2 teaspoons Worcestershire sauce
2 teaspoons tomato ketchup	2 teaspoons tomato catsup
2 teaspoons cider vinegar	2 teaspoons cider vinegar
1 teaspoon olive oil	1 teaspoon olive oil

Joint the chicken legs. Mix the mustard and curry powder into
half the butter. Make deep slashes into the flesh of the chicken
and fill each space with the mustard mixture. Put the chicken in
a fairly shallow fireproof dish. Mix together the sauce, ketchup,
vinegar and oil and pour over the chicken. Sprinkle with salt and
pepper. Dot with the remaining butter. Cover and bake in a hot
oven (425°F., 220°C., Gas Mark 7) for 10–15 minutes. This dish
may be served with fresh pineapple.

Chicken liver pâté

IMPERIAL · METRIC	AMERICAN
3 oz./75 g. butter	6 tablespoons butter
1 small clove garlic	1 small clove garlic
4 unsmoked streaky bacon rashers	4 bacon slices
1 small onion, or 2 oz./50 g. mushrooms, chopped	1 small onion, or ½ cup chopped mushrooms
8 oz./225 g. chicken livers	½ lb. chicken livers
small pinch mixed spice	small pinch mixed spice
pinch celery salt	pinch celery salt
1 tablespoon cream	1 tablespoon cream
1 tablespoon sherry	1 tablespoon sherry

Melt 2 oz. (50 g., ¼ cup) of the butter in a pan. Add the chopped
garlic, chopped bacon and onion or mushrooms. Cook until soft.
Add the chopped livers, seasonings and cook gently for about 6
minutes. Allow to cool, add the cream and sherry. Pass twice
through the mincer, or liquidise. Turn into a serving dish,
smooth surface and cover with remaining butter, melted. Chill.

13

Chicken, ham and egg pie

IMPERIAL · METRIC	AMERICAN
8 oz./225 g. shortcrust pastry	basic pie dough made with 2 cups all-purpose flour etc.
2 oz./50 g. butter	¼ cup butter
½ teaspoon thyme	½ teaspoon thyme
2 oz./50 g. mushrooms	½ cup chopped mushrooms
1 medium onion	1 medium onion
salt and pepper	salt and pepper
4 oz./100 g. cooked chicken	½ cup chopped cooked chicken
4 oz./100 g. ham	½ cup chopped ham
1 hard-boiled egg	1 hard-cooked egg
little milk to glaze	little milk to glaze

Divide the pastry in half. Line an 8-inch (20-cm.) tart plate with half the pastry. Heat the butter in a pan, add the thyme, chopped mushrooms and onion, and season with salt and pepper. Simmer for 2 minutes. Stir in the chopped chicken, ham and egg. Turn into the pastry-lined plate and leave to cool. Moisten the edges of the pastry with water, and cover with remaining pastry. Flute the edges. Brush with milk and slit the top. Bake in a moderately hot oven (375°F., 190°C., Gas Mark 5) for 40 minutes.

Cider chicken bake

IMPERIAL · METRIC	AMERICAN
4 chicken pieces	4 chicken pieces
2 oz./50 g. butter	¼ cup butter
1 small onion	1 small onion
2 oz./50 g. mushrooms	½ cup chopped mushrooms
pinch mixed herbs	pinch mixed herbs
salt and pepper	salt and pepper
1 oz./25 g. flour	¼ cup all-purpose flour
¼ pint/1½ dl. dry cider	⅔ cup dry cider
¼ pint/1½ dl. chicken stock	⅔ cup chicken stock
2 oz./50 g. Cheddar cheese	½ cup grated Cheddar cheese
4 tablespoons single cream	⅓ cup coffee cream

Fry or grill the chicken pieces gently with a little of the butter until cooked and golden. Remove and keep hot. Fry the chopped onion and mushrooms in the remaining butter. Add the herbs and seasoning. Add the flour and cook gently, stirring well. Gradually add the cider and stock, and allow to thicken. Remove from the heat and stir in the grated cheese, and finally the cream. Pour over the chicken and serve.

Country chicken broth

IMPERIAL·METRIC	AMERICAN
1 boiling fowl	1 stewing chicken
water	water
2 lb./1 kg. leeks	2 lb. leeks
1 lb./450 g. potatoes	1 lb. potatoes
salt and pepper	salt and pepper
1 bay leaf	1 bay leaf
sprig parsley	sprig parsley
sprig thyme	sprig thyme
1 oz./25 g. butter	2 tablespoons butter
1 oz./25 g. plain flour	$\frac{1}{4}$ cup all-purpose flour
2 tablespoons single cream	3 tablespoons half-and-half

Prepare the chicken and put it into a large pan. Cover with water and simmer for 1½ hours. Chop the leeks into neat pieces, but keep the potatoes whole. Remove the chicken from the pan, put the vegetables into the liquid and simmer for 20 minutes, or until the potatoes are cooked, but not mushy. Return the chicken to the pan to reheat. Serve the chicken and potatoes with a green vegetable for the first meal.

Cut any leftover chicken into small pieces and return to the pan. Leave the soup to get cold, then remove the fat from the top. For the soup, measure approximately 2 pints (generous litre, 5 cups) cooking liquid into a pan, add the herbs and adjust the seasoning if necessary. Bring to the boil, then simmer for a few minutes. Heat the butter and work in the flour. Blend in a little soup to make a smooth, thin sauce. Stir back into the soup. Bring to the boil, stirring constantly until the thickening mixture is cooked. Just before serving, stir in the cream and heat through, but do not boil.

Chicken with herb rice

IMPERIAL · METRIC	AMERICAN
1 boiling fowl	1 stewing chicken
1½ pints/scant litre stock	3¾ cups stock
1 onion stuck with 4–5 cloves	1 onion stuck with 4–5 cloves
1 bay leaf	1 bay leaf
sprig thyme	sprig thyme
sprig parsley	sprig parsley
sprig rosemary	sprig rosemary
salt and pepper	salt and pepper
6 oz./175 g. long-grain rice	scant 1 cup long-grain rice

Put the chicken in a saucepan, add the stock to come
three-quarters of the way up the bird, the onion, herbs and
seasoning. (The breast can be covered with greaseproof paper to
keep it white, or the chicken can be rubbed all over with lemon
before cooking to keep the skin white.) Put a tight-fitting lid on
the pan, bring to the boil and simmer for 1½–2 hours – it must
not do more than simmer. Add the rice about 30 minutes before
the end of the cooking, adding more stock if necessary. Serve the
bird surrounded by the rice which should be a little moist.

Chicken in the pot

IMPERIAL · METRIC	AMERICAN
4 bacon rashers	4 bacon slices
12 small onions	12 small onions
1 oz./25 g. butter	2 tablespoons butter
3-lb./1½-kg. chicken	3-lb. chicken
1 lb./450 g. potatoes	1 lb. potatoes
4 oz./100 g. mushrooms	1 cup mushrooms
½ teaspoon salt	½ teaspoon salt
¼ teaspoon pepper	¼ teaspoon pepper
¼ pint/1½ dl. chicken stock	⅔ cup chicken stock
1 teaspoon meat extract	½ teaspoon gravy coloring

Cut bacon into strips, and peel the onions. Plunge the bacon and
onions into boiling water, and cook for 5 minutes. Drain well,
then brown lightly in the melted butter. Remove from the butter
and put into a casserole. Brown the chicken on all sides in the

butter, and put into the casserole. Add the diced potatoes, whole cleaned mushrooms, salt, pepper, stock and meat extract. Cover and cook in a moderate oven (350°F., 180°C., Gas Mark 4) for 1½ hours.

Surrey chicken casserole

IMPERIAL·METRIC	AMERICAN
3½-lb./1¾-kg. chicken	3½-lb. chicken
1 tablespoon flour	1 tablespoon all-purpose flour
4 oz./100 g. fat bacon	¼ lb. bacon slices
8 oz./225 g. onions	½ lb. onions
1 lb./450 g. potatoes	1 lb. potatoes
1 teaspoon chopped fresh parsley	1 teaspoon chopped fresh parsley
1 teaspoon chopped fresh thyme	1 teaspoon chopped fresh thyme
salt and pepper	salt and pepper
8 oz./225 g. pork sausagemeat	1 cup sausagemeat
2 hard-boiled eggs	2 hard-cooked eggs

Cut the chicken into joints, or if preferred use this recipe for the equivalent weight of individual joints. Coat the chicken pieces with flour. Chop the bacon and put into a heavy pan. Heat gently until the fat runs. Remove the bacon and keep on one side. Fry the chicken joints in the bacon fat until golden, and drain them well. Slice the onions and potatoes. Put a layer of potatoes in a greased casserole and then a layer of onions. Sprinkle with herbs and seasoning. Put in a layer of sausagemeat, then potatoes, onions, chicken, sliced eggs, bacon, onion and finally potatoes. Use herbs and seasoning between each layer. Pour in ¾ pint (4 dl., scant 2 cups) water. Pour any remaining bacon fat on to the top layer. Cover with greased greaseproof paper and a lid. Cook in a moderate oven (350°F., 180°C., Gas Mark 4) for 1½ hours. Remove the lid and paper and return the dish to the oven for 15 minutes to brown the potatoes.

Duck with peas

IMPERIAL · METRIC	AMERICAN
½ oz./15 g. butter	1 tablespoon butter
4 bacon rashers	4 bacon slices
12 small onions	12 small onions
5-lb./2¼-kg. duck	5-lb. duck
1 tablespoon flour	1 tablespoon all-purpose flour
½ pint/3 dl. stock	1¼ cups stock
2 lb./1 kg. green peas (weight before shelling)	2 lb. green peas (weight before shelling)
4 lettuce leaves	4 lettuce leaves
1 bay leaf	1 bay leaf
sprig parsley	sprig parsley
sprig thyme	sprig thyme
½ teaspoon salt	½ teaspoon salt
¼ teaspoon pepper	¼ teaspoon pepper

Melt the butter and cook the chopped bacon until lightly browned. Add the whole onions, and brown well. Put the bacon and onions into a casserole. Brown duck in the remaining fat, then remove to the casserole. Mix the flour with the fat and cook until browned. Stir in the stock and cook for 5 minutes. Pour over the duck in the casserole, and add the shelled peas, lettuce leaves, herbs, salt and pepper. Cover and cook in a moderate oven (350°F., 180°C., Gas Mark 4) for 1 hour. Carve the duckling and arrange on serving plate; surround with the peas and strained sauce.

Roast duck with apple stuffing

IMPERIAL METRIC	AMERICAN
6 slices brown bread	6 slices brown bread
1 lb./450 g. cooking apples	1 lb. baking apples
1 medium onion	1 medium onion
1 teaspoon mixed herbs	1 teaspoon mixed herbs
2 tablespoons honey	3 tablespoons honey
1 tablespoon dry sherry	1 tablespoon dry sherry
5-lb./2¼-kg. duck	5-lb. duck
salt and pepper	salt and pepper

Remove the crusts from the bread and crumble into large pieces. Peel the apples and onion and chop finely. Combine with the bread. Add the other ingredients and mix well together. Use to stuff the duck. Rub the outside of the duck with salt and pepper and roast in a hot oven (425°F., 220°C., Gas Mark 7) for 15 minutes, and then reduce the heat to moderately hot (375°F., 190°C., Gas Mark 5), allowing 15 minutes to the lb. ($\frac{1}{2}$ kg.), plus 15 minutes over.

Duck with port

IMPERIAL · METRIC	AMERICAN
5-lb./2¼-kg. duck	5-lb. duck
salt and pepper	salt and pepper
2 thick slices white bread, crusts removed	2 thick slices white bread, crusts removed
milk	milk
1 heaped teaspoon sage	1 heaped teaspoon sage
1 tablespoon chopped onion	1 tablespoon chopped onion
little grated orange rind (optional)	little grated orange rind (optional)
2 medium onions	2 medium onions
4 fl. oz./1 dl. port	½ cup port
1 lemon	1 lemon

Wipe the duck inside and out and season with salt and pepper. Soak the bread in the milk, then squeeze out the liquid. Mix the crumbs with sage, 1 tablespoon chopped onion, salt and pepper and a little grated orange rind if liked. Stuff the duck with the stuffing mixture. Simmer the giblets in water to cover to make stock. Strain and add the onions, chopped finely, and simmer until onions are just soft, and there is about ½ pint (3 dl., 1¼ cups) liquid. Put the duck in a casserole with this liquid and cook in a moderate oven (325°F., 160°C., Gas Mark 3) for 2 hours, adding the port about 15 minutes before the cooking time finishes. Add the juice of the lemon when the casserole is removed from the oven. Serve the gravy separately, and garnish the duck with triangles of fried bread.

Duck in cider sauce

IMPERIAL · METRIC	AMERICAN
4-lb./1¾-kg. duck	4-lb. duck
3 oz./75 g. butter	6 tablespoons butter
2 oz./50 g. breadcrumbs	1 cup fresh soft bread crumbs
8 oz./225 g. cooking apples	½ lb. baking apples
grated rind of 1 orange	grated rind of 1 orange
¾ pint/4 dl. cider	scant 2 cups cider
juice of 1 orange	juice of 1 orange

Wipe the duck inside and out. Melt the butter in a frying pan and fry the breadcrumbs lightly. Add the chopped apples and grated orange rind and fry until cooked. Stuff the duck with this mixture. Prick the duck with a fork, and put on its side in a roasting tin. Cook in a moderate oven (325°F., 160°C., Gas Mark 3) for 30 minutes. Strain off the fat and turn so the backbone is uppermost. Pour over the cider and orange juice and cook for a further 30 minutes. Turn the duck so the breast is uppermost and cook for another 30 minutes. Serve the duck with its pan juices.

Any leftover duck is good served with a fresh orange salad.

Duckling pâté

IMPERIAL · METRIC	AMERICAN
4-lb./1¾-kg. duckling	4-lb. duckling
duck liver	duck liver
8 oz./225 g. lean pork	½ lb. lean pork
4 oz./100 g. streaky bacon	¼ lb. bacon slices
1 clove garlic	1 clove garlic
pinch ground mace	pinch ground mace
pinch ground nutmeg	pinch ground nutmeg
3 tablespoons dry white wine	scant ¼ cup dry white wine
1 tablespoon dry sherry	1 tablespoon dry sherry
salt and pepper	salt and pepper

Roast the duck lightly and then mince the duck meat with the liver and pork twice. Line a terrine or loaf tin with the streaky bacon (make this very thin by flattening it out with a wide-bladed knife). Mix this meat with all the other ingredients and pack into the terrine. Cover with a lid or foil and stand the dish in a roasting tin with 1 inch (2·5 cm.) of water. Cook in a moderate oven (325°F., 160°C., Gas Mark 3) for 1½ hours, or until the mixture shrinks from the sides of the dish. Cool under weights. Serve with toast and crisp lettuce.

Roast goose

IMPERIAL·METRIC	AMERICAN
10-lb./4½-kg. goose	10-lb. goose
4 oz./100 g. pork	¼ lb. pork
4 oz./100 g. veal	¼ lb. veal
1 large onion	1 large onion
½ oz./15 g. butter	1 tablespoon butter
2 slices bread, crusts removed	2 slices bread, crusts removed
6 tablespoons milk	½ cup milk
1 teaspoon parsley	1 teaspoon parsley
1 teaspoon thyme	1 teaspoon thyme
1 teaspoon sage	1 teaspoon sage
1 egg yolk	1 egg yolk
salt and pepper	salt and pepper
4 tablespoons red wine	⅓ cup red wine

Take the goose liver and chop it very finely with the pork, veal and onion. Brown the mixture in the butter. Soak the bread in the milk and then squeeze it until almost dry. Mix the bread with the meat mixture, chopped herbs, egg yolk, salt and pepper to taste, and just enough wine to bind the mixture. Stuff the goose and roast in a hot oven (450°F., 230°C., Gas Mark 8) for 15 minutes. Reduce the heat to moderately hot (400°F., 200°C., Gas Mark 6) and continue cooking, allowing 20 minutes per lb. (½ kg.) and 20 minutes over, and basting with the remaining wine.

Scots goose

IMPERIAL · METRIC	AMERICAN
2 tablespoons chopped onion	3 tablespoons chopped onion
1 oz./25 g. butter	2 tablespoons butter
2 oz./50 g. shredded suet	$\frac{1}{2}$ cup shredded suet
2 teaspoons chopped sage	2 teaspoons chopped sage
1 egg	1 egg
5 oz./150 g. fine oatmeal	scant 1 cup fine oatmeal
10-lb./4$\frac{1}{2}$-kg. goose	10-lb. goose

Soften the onion in the butter and mix with the suet, sage and egg. Simmer the oatmeal in a little water until soft and mix with the other ingredients. Stuff the bird and roast in a hot oven (450°F., 230°C., Gas Mark 8) for 15 minutes. Reduce the heat to moderately hot (400°F., 200°C., Gas Mark 6) and continue cooking, allowing 20 minutes per lb. ($\frac{1}{2}$ kg.) and 20 minutes over. Serve with red cabbage.

Honeyed turkey

IMPERIAL · METRIC	AMERICAN
12 large prunes	12 large prunes
1 medium onion	1 medium onion
1 lb./450 g. pork sausagemeat	2 cups pork sausagemeat
1 egg	1 egg
12 walnuts	12 walnuts
7 tablespoons honey	generous $\frac{1}{2}$ cup honey
6-lb./2$\frac{3}{4}$-kg. turkey	6-lb. turkey

Soak the prunes overnight, if necessary. Place the chopped onion, sausagemeat and egg in a bowl and mix thoroughly. Stone the prunes and fill them with the walnut pieces. Dip the filled prunes in half the honey and put in the sausagemeat mixture. Pack this stuffing into the bird. Wrap the turkey in double thickness of foil and place in a roasting tin in the middle of a preheated moderate oven (350°F., 180°C., Gas Mark 4). Roast for 3 hours. Halfway through the cooking, open the foil, baste the turkey in its own juices and pour over the remaining honey. Re-close the foil. For a very crisp skin open the foil for the last 20 minutes of cooking.

Goose pâté

IMPERIAL·METRIC	AMERICAN
4 oz./100 g. butter	½ cup butter
8 oz./225 g. cooked goose	1 cup ground cooked goose
1¼ tablespoons dry sherry	1¼ tablespoons dry sherry
pinch ground cloves	pinch ground cloves
pinch black pepper	pinch black pepper
½ teaspoon salt	½ teaspoon salt
½ teaspoon lemon juice	½ teaspoon lemon juice
3 drops Tabasco sauce	3 drops Tabasco sauce
3 oz./75 g. butter, melted	6 tablespoons butter, melted

Cream the butter well, and beat in the minced goose, the sherry, cloves, pepper, salt, lemon juice and Tabasco sauce. Pot, and pour melted butter over the top. Serve with toast.

Braised turkey and celery

IMPERIAL·METRIC	AMERICAN
3 oz./75 g. butter	6 tablespoons butter
4 turkey joints	4 turkey joints
2 bacon rashers	2 bacon slices
1 large onion	1 large onion
1 head celery	1 head celery
2 heads chicory	2 heads endive
1½ oz./40 g. plain flour	6 tablespoons all-purpose flour
1¼ pints/¾ litre stock	generous 3 cups stock
salt and pepper	salt and pepper
pinch mixed herbs	pinch mixed herbs

Melt the butter in a large frying pan. Fry the turkey joints until golden brown, then remove them to a casserole. Lightly fry the chopped bacon and vegetables for 5 minutes, and add to the casserole. Stir the flour into the remaining butter, and gradually add the stock, stirring until it boils. Cook for 2 minutes, season, add herbs and then pour into the casserole. Cover and cook in a moderate oven (350°F., 180°C., Gas Mark 4) for 2–2¼ hours.

Chicken or duck may be used in place of turkey.

Turkey roll

IMPERIAL · METRIC	AMERICAN
12 oz./350 g. cooked turkey	1½ cups ground cooked turkey
8 oz./225 g. cooked ham	1 cup chopped cooked ham
1 small onion	1 small onion
pinch mace	pinch mace
salt and pepper	salt and pepper
½ teaspoon fresh mixed herbs	½ teaspoon fresh mixed herbs
1 egg	1 egg
breadcrumbs	bread crumbs

Mince the turkey, ham and onion finely and mix with the mace, salt and pepper and herbs. Bind with the beaten egg. Put into a greased dish or tin, cover and steam for 1 hour. (The mixture may be cooked in a loaf tin, a large cocoa tin lined with paper or a stone marmalade jar.) While warm, turn the mixture out and roll in the breadcrumbs, then cool completely. Slice and serve with salad, or in sandwiches.

Game

Game makes some delicious rich autumn and winter meals, and goes perfectly with all the other autumn treats like mushrooms, red and white cabbage, celery, chestnuts and apples. Pheasant, pigeon, rabbit and hare are most frequently found and can be economical to use because the leftovers and the trimmings make good pies, pâtés and soups. They mix well together so that they can often be combined in second-day dishes, and can be extended with a little pork (or sausagemeat) or veal. There is no need to be frightened of preparing game for cooking, as your butcher will usually help.

Pheasant

In season from October 1st. to February 1st. The young birds are best for roasting, but the older ones are excellent for casseroles and other long-cooking dishes. Hen birds are smaller, but less dry and more tender with a good flavour. The young ones have soft feet and light feathers, while the older hen has hard feet and dark feathers. The cock bird has round spurs in the first year, short pointed ones in the second year, and sharp long ones when older. Pheasant tastes best if hung for seven days in a cool place (otherwise it can be as bland as chicken). A roast pheasant needs only about 45 minutes cooking in a moderately hot oven (400°F., 200°C., Gas Mark 6); it benefits from some extra fat in the form of bacon or butter, and a little red wine for basting. Traditionally it is served with a clear gravy, bread sauce and fried breadcrumbs, and it goes well with chestnuts, mushrooms or celery. A large pheasant will feed four people.

Pigeon
These little birds are in season all through the year, but are at their best in late summer and early autumn when they have stolen plenty of ripe corn. Do not use very hot fat in cooking pigeons as it toughens them and destroys their flavour. For roasting, cover them with fat bacon or they may be dry, but only roast young birds, and use the others for casseroles. Allow one pigeon for two people, or one each if you are catering for large appetites, or using only pigeon breasts, as in pies and puddings.

Rabbit
A good rabbit should feed six people and can be prepared in dozens of ways. Most people like plenty of seasoning and herbs with their rabbit, and it goes particularly well with onions and mushrooms. When a rabbit has been prepared and jointed, soak the joints in plenty of salted water for an hour or two, and dry well before using.

Hare
A hare is best eaten between early autumn and the end of February. A young hare has white pointed teeth and fresh-looking fur, while an older one will have cracked brown teeth and scruffy fur. A hare is very large and will feed ten people, so it can be used economically for a main dish, as well as for a casserole, pie, soup or pâté.

Game pie

IMPERIAL · METRIC	AMERICAN
1½ lb./¾ kg. uncooked hare	1½ lb. uncooked hare
8 oz./225 g. uncooked pheasant or rabbit	½ lb. uncooked pheasant or rabbit
4 oz./100 g. calves' or lambs' liver	¼ lb. calf or lamb liver
pepper and salt	pepper and salt
2 oz./50 g. butter or dripping	¼ cup butter or drippings
4 oz./100 g. mushrooms	1 cup sliced mushrooms
1 pint/6 dl. brown gravy	2½ cups brown gravy
1 bay leaf	1 bay leaf
12 oz./350 g. shortcrust pastry	basic pie dough made with 3 cups all-purpose flour etc.

Cut the flesh away from the bones of the hare and pheasant or rabbit; cut in neat pieces. Cut the liver in small pieces. Season well and brown lightly in the heated butter in a pan. Turn into a pie dish with the sliced mushrooms, gravy and bay leaf. Leave to cool, then cover with pastry and bake in a moderately hot oven (375°F., 190°C., Gas Mark 5) for 1½ hours. Serve hot or cold.

Pheasant in cider

IMPERIAL · METRIC	AMERICAN
1 old pheasant	1 old pheasant
1 lb./450 g. cooking apples	1 lb. baking apples
8 oz./225 g. onions	½ lb. onions
butter	butter
½ pint/3 dl. cider	1¼ cups cider
bunch mixed herbs	bunch mixed herbs
salt and pepper	salt and pepper

Clean and wipe the pheasant. Cut the peeled and cored apples in quarters and put into a casserole. Slice the onions and cook until soft in a little butter. Put the pheasant on to the apples and cover with the onions. Pour on the cider and add the herbs. Season with salt and pepper. Cover and cook in a moderate oven (325°F., 160°C., Gas Mark 3) for 2½ hours. Remove the herbs before serving.

Pheasant pâté

IMPERIAL · METRIC	AMERICAN
8 oz./225 g. calves' liver	½ lb. calf liver
4 oz./100 g. bacon	¼ lb. bacon slices
butter	butter
1 small onion	1 small onion
salt and pepper	salt and pepper
1 cooked pheasant	1 cooked pheasant
cloves	cloves
ground allspice	ground allspice

Cook the liver and bacon lightly in a little butter, and put through the mincer with the onion. Season with salt and pepper. Remove the meat in neat pieces from the pheasant and season lightly with cloves and allspice. Put a layer of liver mixture into a loaf tin or terrine, and add a layer of pheasant. Continue in layers finishing with a layer of liver mixture. Cover and put in a roasting tin of water. Cook in a moderate oven (350°F., 180°C., Gas Mark 4) for 1½ hours. Cool under heavy weights. Use a sharp knife for slicing the pâté.

Pheasant in milk

IMPERIAL · METRIC	AMERICAN
1 pheasant	1 pheasant
flour	flour
salt and pepper	salt and pepper
½ pint/3 dl. milk	1¼ cups milk
½ pint/3 dl. stock	1¼ cups stock

The pheasant should be trussed as for roasting. Season the flour with salt and pepper and dust the pheasant with it. Put the milk in a roasting tin or casserole, and put in the pheasant. Pour over the stock. Do not cover. Cook in a moderately hot oven (400°F., 200°C., Gas Mark 6) for 50 minutes, basting frequently with the liquid in the pan. Put the pheasant on a serving dish. Stir together all the pan juices and reheat gently to serve as gravy with the pheasant.

Pheasant stuffed with mushrooms

IMPERIAL · METRIC	AMERICAN
3 oz./75 g. butter	6 tablespoons butter
8 oz./225 g. mushrooms	2 cups sliced mushrooms
salt and pepper	salt and pepper
1 pheasant	1 pheasant
3 tablespoons flour	4 tablespoons all-purpose flour
¾ pint/4 dl. stock	scant 2 cups stock
4 tablespoons dry sherry	⅓ cup dry sherry

Melt half the butter in a frying pan and use to cook the sliced mushrooms gently for 10 minutes. Season lightly with salt and pepper, and cool. Stuff the bird with three-quarters of the mushrooms. Brown the pheasant in the remaining butter and put it into a casserole. Mix the flour with the pan juices, and gradually work in the stock and sherry. Season well and pour over the bird. Cover tightly and cook in a moderate oven (325°F., 160°C., Gas Mark 3) for 1½ hours. (Allow about 30 minutes longer if the bird is an old one.) Just before serving, add the remaining mushrooms.

This dish is very good served with plenty of watercress.

Lincoln pheasant

IMPERIAL · METRIC	AMERICAN
1 young pheasant	1 young pheasant
1 carrot	1 carrot
1 onion	1 onion
4 oz./100 g. dripping	½ cup drippings
salt and pepper	salt and pepper
2 tablespoons flour	3 tablespoons all-purpose flour
1½ pints/scant litre water or stock	3¾ cups water or stock
4 tomatoes	4 tomatoes
8 oz./225 g. mushrooms	2 cups mushrooms
1 tablespoon chopped parsley	1 tablespoon chopped parsley

Cut the pheasant into serving pieces. Chop the carrot and onion finely. Melt the dripping and fry the vegetables for 5 minutes, stirring well. Add the pheasant pieces, season with salt and pepper and fry for 5 minutes. Add the flour and stir well for

3 minutes, and then gradually add the water or stock and stir until it boils. Peel the tomatoes and cut them in quarters. Use the mushrooms whole if they are small, but otherwise cut them in quarters. Add to the pan together with the parsley and simmer for 30 minutes. Put the pheasant pieces on a hot dish and pour over the gravy.

Pigeon pâté

IMPERIAL·METRIC	AMERICAN
3 pigeons	3 pigeons
8 fl. oz./2½ dl. red wine	1 cup red wine
4 fl. oz./1¼ dl. vinegar	½ cup vinegar
1 bay leaf	1 bay leaf
1 small teaspoon thyme	1 small teaspoon thyme
grating of nutmeg	grating of nutmeg
salt and pepper	salt and pepper
4 onions	4 onions
8 oz./225 g. sausagemeat	1 cup sausagemeat
1 slice bread	1 slice bread
little milk	little milk

Joint the pigeons. Mix together the wine, vinegar, bay leaf, thyme, nutmeg, salt and pepper and finely chopped onions, and pour this over the birds. Leave to soak in a cool place for 3 days. Remove the flesh from the birds, and mince twice. Mix with the sausagemeat. Remove the crusts from the bread, and soak in enough milk to moisten the bread. Beat this into the meat mixture. Press the mixture into a terrine, loaf tin, or ovenproof dish and cover with a lid or foil. Stand the dish in a roasting tin of water and cook in a moderate oven (350°F., 180°C., Gas Mark 4) for 1½ hours. Cool completely under weights. Leave for 24 hours before serving.

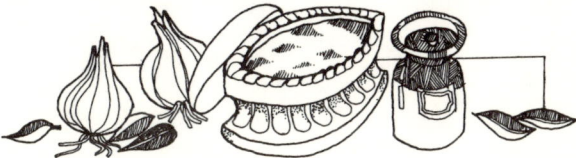

Pigeons with cabbage

IMPERIAL · METRIC	AMERICAN
1 cabbage	1 cabbage
8 fat bacon rashers	8 fat bacon slices
salt and pepper	salt and pepper
sprig thyme	sprig thyme
sprig parsley	sprig parsley
2 pigeons	2 pigeons
fat	fat
1 bay leaf	1 bay leaf

Plunge the cabbage into boiling water for 10 minutes. Drain
and put into cold water. Leave for 10 minutes, drain well and
press out the water. Chop the cabbage and line a greased
casserole with it and half the bacon cut into squares. Season
with salt and pepper and put in the thyme and parsley. Brown
the pigeons all over in a little hot fat and put in the casserole. Add
the bay leaf and top with the remaining bacon rashers. Cover
and cook in a moderate oven (350°F., 180°C., Gas Mark 4) for
1½ hours. Cut the birds in half and serve on the bed of cabbage.
If it is more convenient, the birds may be allowed to simmer on
top of the cooker for 2 hours.

Pigeons in cider

IMPERIAL · METRIC	AMERICAN
2 pigeons	2 pigeons
1 oz./25 g. butter	2 tablespoons butter
1 small apple	1 small apple
1 small onion	1 small onion
1 oz./25 g. plain flour	¼ cup all-purpose flour
¾ pint/4 dl. stock	scant 2 cups stock
¼ pint/1½ dl. cider	⅔ cup cider
salt and pepper	salt and pepper
1 bay leaf	1 bay leaf
sprig thyme	sprig thyme
sprig parsley	sprig parsley

Clean the pigeons and brown them on all sides in hot butter.
Split the birds in half. Slice the apple and onion and soften the

slices in the fat remaining in the pan. Sprinkle on the flour, and cook until golden. Add the stock and cider and bring to the boil, stirring. Season with salt and pepper and add the pigeons and herbs. Cover tightly. Simmer on top of the cooker, or cook in a moderate oven (325°F., 160°C., Gas Mark 3) for 2 hours. Serve the pigeons in the gravy.

For a special occasion meal, garnish with some apple rings fried in butter, and bacon rolls.

Pigeon casserole

IMPERIAL · METRIC	AMERICAN
2 pigeons	2 pigeons
8 oz./225 g. chuck steak	½ lb. chuck steak
2 bacon rashers	2 bacon slices
2 oz./50 g. butter	¼ cup butter
½ pint/3 dl. stock	1¼ cups stock
2 oz./50 g. button mushrooms	½ cup button mushrooms
salt and pepper	salt and pepper
1 tablespoon redcurrant jelly	1 tablespoon redcurrant jelly
1 tablespoon lemon juice	1 tablespoon lemon juice
1 tablespoon cornflour	1 tablespoon cornstarch

Cut the pigeons in halves, the steak in cubes and the bacon in small pieces. Melt the butter and cook the pigeons, steak and bacon until just coloured. Put into a casserole with the stock, sliced mushrooms, salt and pepper. Cover and cook in a moderate oven (325°F., 160°C., Gas Mark 3) for 2 hours. Stir in the redcurrant jelly, lemon juice and cornflour blended with a little water, and continue cooking for a further 30 minutes.

Pigeon pie

IMPERIAL·METRIC	AMERICAN
4 pigeons	4 pigeons
8 oz./225 g. chuck steak	½ lb. chuck steak
salt and pepper	salt and pepper
mace	mace
2 hard-boiled eggs	2 hard-cooked eggs
4 oz./100 g. button mushrooms	1 cup mushrooms
butter	butter
8 oz./225 g. shortcrust pastry	basic pie dough made with 2 cups all-purpose flour etc.

Some countrywomen make their pies with whole or jointed birds, but others prefer to use the breasts only. When this is the case, the remains of the birds should be simmered in a little water to produce a rich gravy.

With a sharp knife, remove the breasts from the pigeons and put them into a pie dish with the steak cut into small pieces. Season well with salt, pepper and mace. Just cover with water and put on a lid. Cook in a moderate oven (350°F., 180°C., Gas Mark 4) for 1 hour. Remove from the oven and add the hard-boiled eggs cut in quarters. Toss the mushrooms in a little butter for 2 minutes, and add to the meat. Cool. Cover with a pastry lid, brush with a little beaten egg and bake in a hot oven (425°F., 220°C., Gas Mark 7) for 40 minutes. Cover the pastry with greaseproof paper if it becomes too brown. Serve with extra gravy from the pigeon carcasses.

Pigeon pudding

IMPERIAL·METRIC	AMERICAN
3 pigeons	3 pigeons
8 oz./225 g. shin beef	½ lb. heel of round
4 oz./125 g. ox kidney	¼ lb. beef kidney
8 oz./225 g. self-raising flour	2 cups all-purpose flour sifted with 2 teaspoons baking powder
4 oz./125 g. shredded suet	scant 1 cup shredded suet
salt and pepper	salt and pepper
mace	mace

Remove the breasts from the pigeons and simmer the carcasses in water to make a rich stock. Cut the beef and kidney into small pieces. To make the suet pastry, mix the flour, suet, a pinch of salt and cold water to give a firm dough. Roll out and line a basin with two-thirds of the pastry. Put in the pigeon breasts mixed with the beef and kidney and season well with salt, pepper and mace. Pour in the stock from the bones and trimmings just to cover the meat. Cover with the remaining pastry. Put on greaseproof paper and foil and cook in a pan of boiling water for 3 hours.

Fried pigeons

IMPERIAL·METRIC	AMERICAN
3 oz./75 g. butter	6 tablespoons butter
2 pigeons, plucked and drawn	2 pigeons, plucked and drawn
salt and pepper	salt and pepper
4 slices buttered toast	4 slices buttered toast

Melt the butter in a large frying pan. Wash, dry, and cut the pigeons in halves. Season and fry gently in the butter for 25 minutes, turning during cooking. Serve on hot buttered toast, and pour the butter and pigeon juices over the top. Serve with a green salad.

Rabbit brawn

IMPERIAL·METRIC	AMERICAN
2 pig's feet	2 pig's feet
1 rabbit, jointed	1 rabbit, jointed
salt and pepper	salt and pepper
nutmeg	nutmeg

Cover the pig's feet with water and simmer for 1½ hours. While the pig's feet are cooking, soak the rabbit joints. After 1½ hours, add the joints to the saucepan and simmer for 2 hours, until tender. Take the meat from the bones and cut into neat pieces. Pack into a bowl and season with salt, pepper and nutmeg. Leave overnight in the refrigerator before turning out. Serve with salad or in sandwiches.

Potted rabbit

IMPERIAL · METRIC	AMERICAN
1 rabbit, jointed	1 rabbit, jointed
10 oz./275 g. butter	1¼ cups butter
1 lump sugar	1 lump sugar
1 onion thickly stuck with cloves	1 onion thickly stuck with cloves
12 whole allspice	12 whole allspice
6 peppercorns	6 peppercorns
nutmeg	nutmeg
2 teaspoons Worcestershire sauce	2 teaspoons Worcestershire sauce

Put the rabbit into a casserole with a tight-fitting lid. Add 2 oz. (50 g., ¼ cup) butter, the sugar, onion stuck with cloves, allspice, peppercorns and a good sprinkling of nutmeg. Cook in a cool oven (300°F., 150°C., Gas Mark 2) for 3 hours. Cool the meat and take out the bones. Put through a mincer twice, with the juices from the casserole. Beat in the remaining butter and the sauce and put into small pots. Cool and cover with melted butter.

Rabbit pudding

IMPERIAL · METRIC	AMERICAN
1 rabbit, jointed	1 rabbit, jointed
8 oz./225 g. self-raising flour	2 cups all-purpose flour sifted with 2 teaspoons baking powder
4 oz./125 g. shredded suet	scant 1 cup shredded suet
salt and pepper	salt and pepper
2 large onions	2 large onions
4 oz./100 g. mushrooms	1 cup mushrooms
4 oz./100 g. fat bacon	¼ lb. fat bacon
sage	sage

Soak the rabbit joints in cold salted water for 2 hours and dry well. To make the suet pastry, stir the flour and suet together with a pinch of salt and bind with cold water. Line a pudding basin with two-thirds of the pastry. Put in layers of boned rabbit, chopped onions, mushrooms and bacon, a few sage leaves, salt and pepper. Sprinkle a little flour on each layer. Fill the basin two-thirds full with water, cover with pastry and tie on greaseproof paper and foil. Steam for 3 hours.

Rabbit pie

IMPERIAL·METRIC	AMERICAN
1 rabbit, jointed	1 rabbit, jointed
8 oz./225 g. stewing steak	½ lb. beef stew meat
4 oz./100 g. pork sausagemeat	½ cup pork sausagemeat
salt and pepper	salt and pepper
nutmeg	nutmeg
chopped parsley	chopped parsley
8 oz./225 g. shortcrust pastry	basic pie dough made with 2 cups all-purpose flour etc.

Soak the rabbit joints in cold salted water for 2 hours and dry thoroughly. Cut the steak into cubes. Form the sausagemeat into small round balls. Put layers of rabbit, steak and sausagemeat balls into a pie dish, sprinkling each layer with salt and pepper, a grating of nutmeg and chopped parsley. Cover with water or chicken stock if available. Put on a pastry lid and bake in a hot oven (450°F., 230°C., Gas Mark 8) for 20 minutes, then reduce the heat to moderate (350°F., 180°C., Gas Mark 4) and bake for a further 1¼ hours.

Rabbit in cider

IMPERIAL·METRIC	AMERICAN
1 rabbit	1 rabbit
1 tablespoon lemon juice	1 tablespoon lemon juice
1 oz./25 g. bacon fat	2 tablespoons bacon drippings
4 large onions	4 large onions
1 bay leaf	1 bay leaf
sprig thyme	sprig thyme
2 bacon rashers	2 bacon slices
8 oz./225 g. tomatoes	½ lb. tomatoes
¼ pint/1½ dl. dry cider	⅔ cup cider

Joint the rabbit and soak in water with lemon juice for 1 hour, then dry well. Fry the joints in bacon fat, and add the sliced onions. Cook until the onions are soft, and add the bay leaf, thyme, chopped bacon and peeled, sliced tomatoes. Simmer for 10 minutes, then pour on the cider. Cover and cook in the oven (325°F., 160°C., Gas Mark 3) for 1¾ hours. Season and serve.

Jugged hare

IMPERIAL · METRIC	AMERICAN
1 hare	1 hare
1 carrot	1 carrot
1 onion	1 onion
1 blade mace	1 blade mace
parsley, thyme and bay leaf	parsley, thyme and bay leaf
4 cloves	4 cloves
salt and pepper	salt and pepper
4 pints/2¼ litres water	5 pints water
seasoned flour	seasoned flour
2 oz./50 g. butter	¼ cup butter
2 tablespoons oil	3 tablespoons oil
1 tablespoon cornflour	1 tablespoon cornstarch
½ pint/3 dl. port	1¼ cups port
forcemeat balls (see next recipe)	forcemeat balls (see next recipe)

Soak the head, heart and liver of the hare for 1 hour in cold, salted water. Put into a pan with the carrot, onion, mace, herbs, cloves, salt and pepper and water. Simmer for 3 hours, skimming frequently. Coat the pieces of hare lightly in seasoned flour and brown in a mixture of butter and oil. Put into a casserole. Strain the stock and mix with the cornflour blended with a little water. Simmer until reduced to 3 pints (1½ litres, 7½ cups), then pour over the hare. Cover and cook in a moderate oven (325°F., 160°C., Gas Mark 3) for 4 hours. Add the port to the liquid and continue cooking until of a coating consistency. Add the forcemeat balls 10 minutes before serving.

Forcemeat balls

IMPERIAL · METRIC	AMERICAN
2 oz./50 g. suet	scant $\frac{1}{2}$ cup shredded suet
4 oz./100 g. fresh white breadcrumbs	2 cups fresh soft bread crumbs
2 teaspoons chopped parsley	2 teaspoons chopped parsley
1 teaspoon chopped thyme	1 teaspoon chopped thyme
grated rind of $\frac{1}{2}$ lemon	grated rind of $\frac{1}{2}$ lemon
salt and pepper	salt and pepper
1 egg	1 egg

Grate the suet and mix all the ingredients together, binding with the egg. Form into small balls and fry until golden, before adding to the jugged hare.

Cambridge hare in beer

IMPERIAL · METRIC	AMERICAN
1 hare	1 hare
2 large onions	2 large onions
8 oz./225 g. carrots	$\frac{1}{2}$ lb. carrots
3 oz./75 g. dripping	6 tablespoons drippings
1$\frac{1}{2}$ oz./40 g. plain flour	6 tablespoons all-purpose flour
salt and pepper	salt and pepper
$\frac{1}{2}$ pint/3 dl. brown ale or stout	1$\frac{1}{4}$ cups brown ale
$\frac{1}{2}$ pint/3 dl. stock	1$\frac{1}{4}$ cups stock

Cut the hare into joints. Cut the onions into thin slices, and the carrots more thickly. Melt the dripping and soften the onions, but do not let them colour. Drain the onions and put in a casserole. Season the flour with salt and pepper and coat the hare joints with it. Cook the hare until golden in the dripping. Put the hare on top of the onions and add the carrots. Work the remaining flour into the dripping and cook for 2 minutes. Gradually add the ale or stout, and the stock, stirring; simmer until smooth. Pour over the hare and put on a lid. Cook in a moderate oven (350°F., 180°C., Gas Mark 4) for 2$\frac{1}{2}$ hours.

   This dish is very good served with potatoes baked in their jackets.

Hare mould

IMPERIAL · METRIC	AMERICAN
8 oz./225 g. jugged hare (see page 36)	½ lb. jugged hare (see page 36)
forcemeat balls	forcemeat balls
gravy	gravy
2 tablespoons redcurrant jelly	3 tablespoons redcurrant jelly
½ oz./15 g. gelatine	2 envelopes gelatin

Cut the meat into neat pieces and the cooked forcemeat balls into quarters. Warm the gravy with the redcurrant jelly and add the gelatine dissolved in a little hot water. When cold, but not set, stir in the meat and forcemeat and pour into a well-seasoned mould to set.

If a full recipe of jugged hare is rather large for a family, it is useful to prepare this secondary dish at the same time. It is delicious served with a winter salad of celery and watercress.

Hare pâté

IMPERIAL · METRIC	AMERICAN
1½ lb./¾ kg. uncooked hare	1½ lb. uncooked hare
4 oz./100 g. fat bacon	¼ lb. fat bacon
3 tablespoons brandy	4 tablespoons brandy
12 oz./350 g. minced pork and veal	1½ cups ground pork and veal
salt and pepper	salt and pepper
nutmeg	nutmeg
1 egg	1 egg

A mixture of game and rabbit can also be used for this recipe.

Cut the hare into small pieces and the bacon into dice and mix together in a dish with the brandy. Leave for 1 hour, then put through a mincer with the pork and veal. Add the seasonings, add the egg and mix well. Press the mixture into a buttered container, cover with greased paper and a lid and put the dish in a roasting tin of water. Bake in a moderately hot oven (400°F., 200°C., Gas Mark 6) for 1 hour. Leave under weights until cold, and do not cut for 24 hours.

Hare pie

IMPERIAL · METRIC	AMERICAN
3 joints hare	3 joints hare
1 teaspoon chopped fresh herbs	1 teaspoon chopped fresh herbs
salt and pepper	salt and pepper
3 tablespoons cider	4 tablespoons cider
8 oz./225 g. plain flour	2 cups all-purpose flour
pinch salt	pinch salt
2 oz./50 g. lard	$\frac{1}{4}$ cup lard
4 tablespoons milk and water	$\frac{1}{3}$ cup milk and water
stock	stock
1 egg, beaten	1 egg, beaten

This is a useful way of making a second dish from a hare which may be rather large. The stock can be made from the bones and trimmings of the hare simmered in water.

Strip the flesh from the hare and chop or mince it finely. Season with the herbs, salt and pepper and leave to stand overnight in the cider. Sieve the flour and salt into a warm bowl. Bring the lard, milk and water to the boil and pour into the middle of the flour, stirring until the mixture is cool enough to handle. Knead until smooth and put into a bowl. Put the bowl to stand in warm water for 15 minutes, covered with a tea towel wrung out in hot water, so that the dough is just warm. Roll out three-quarters of the pastry and line a loose-bottomed cake tin. Mix the hare meat well and stir in 1 tablespoon of stock. Put into the pastry case, packing it firmly, to within 1 inch (2.5 cm.) of the top. Brush the top edge of the pastry with a little beaten egg and top with the remaining pastry. Brush with beaten egg containing a pinch of salt. Make a small hole in the centre of the lid. Bake in a moderately hot oven (400°F., 200°C., Gas Mark 6) for 20 minutes, then reduce the heat to moderate (350°F., 180°C., Gas Mark 4) and bake for a further 1 hour. Cover the top with a piece of thick paper to prevent burning if it seems to be browning too quickly. Cool the pie in the tin, and when it is lukewarm, pour in a little more stock which has jellied almost to setting point. Leave in the tin until cold.

It is best to make the stock the night before when the meat is stripped from the bones. It should be cooked until really concentrated and left in a cold place to jellify.

Bacon and ham

Bacon is popular for almost every meal, and there is no waste when it is cooked. Even the bacon rinds can be crisply fried and crushed for seasoning soups or stews, while small pieces of leftover bacon can be used to add flavour to dozens of dishes. Never add extra cooking oil or fat to bacon for cooking as it will spoil the flavour. Cook it in the fat which runs out when a pan is heated with bacon in it, and drain off any excess fat, which can be used for cooking other foods.

When cooking bacon joints, always weigh the joint before soaking, so that cooking time can be calculated. Allow 20 minutes per lb. ($\frac{1}{2}$ kg.) for small joints; over 10 lb. ($4\frac{1}{2}$ kg.) weight, 15 minutes per lb. ($\frac{1}{2}$ kg.) will be enough. Some of today's bacon does not need to be soaked, but if you have any doubt, soak in cold water for 2–3 hours before preparation. A potato in the cooking water will help to take up the salt. For a sweeter flavour, put 1 tablespoon of Demerara sugar and a bay leaf in the cooking water (country cooks used to use a wisp of hay as well). There are three good ways of cooking bacon joints:

Boiling
Cuts to choose Whole gammon, corner gammon, middle gammon, collar, forehock, streaky in the piece.

Place the joint in a pan and cover with cold water. Bring slowly to the boil, lower the heat so that the joint is just simmering, and simmer for the entire cooking time. If the joint is allowed to boil it will cause the lean to break up. If the joint is to be served hot, remove from the pan and strip off the skin. If serving cold, dust skinned surfaces with brown breadcrumbs. Allow to become firm in a cold place before carving. The bacon water left over from cooking is good for making soups.

Baking
Cuts to choose Middle and corner gammon, collar, forehock.

For the initial cooking, place the joint in cold water, bring to the boil and reduce the heat. Simmer gently for 45 minutes less than the calculated cooking time. Remove the joint from the pan and strip off the skin. Score the fat into diamonds and cook for the remaining 45 minutes of the cooking time in a moderate oven (350°F., 180°C., Gas Mark 4). Serve hot.

Roasting
Cuts to choose Whole gammon, middle gammon, corner gammon, collar, forehock, gammon slipper, gammon hock.

For the initial cooking, place the joint in a pan and cover with cold water. Bring to the boil, reduce the heat and simmer for half the calculated cooking time. Remove from the pan and strip off the skin. Enclose the joint in aluminium foil, or a soft dough made with flour and water and rolled out to a $\frac{1}{4}$ inch ($\frac{1}{2}$ cm.) thick. Place in a roasting tin and cook in a moderate oven (350°F., 180°C., Gas Mark 4) for the remainder of the calculated cooking time. Remove the foil or paste from the joint and sprinkle the fat surface with browned breadcrumbs. If the joint is to be served cold, the foil may be removed when the joint is cold. This enables any jelly to set round it. Sprinkle fat with crumbs.

Preparing a large gammon
Soak the joint in cold water for 2–3 hours, to remove the excess salt. Place in a large saucepan of fresh cold water and bring to the boil very slowly. Simmer for 20–25 minutes to each lb. ($\frac{1}{2}$ kg.). Remove from the pan, strip off the skin, and sprinkle the fat with browned breadcrumbs.

If you intend to serve the gammon for a party, allow it to cool a little, strip off the skin, score the fat in large squares, making deep cuts and stick a clove in each square. Sprinkle the joint with brown sugar and place in the oven (400°F., 200°C., Gas Mark 6) for 20 minutes, basting with cider or beer.

It is very important that bacon or ham should only simmer.

Simmering times for large, whole gammons and hams
10 lb. ($4\frac{1}{2}$ kg.) – 3   hours   14 lb. ($6\frac{1}{4}$ kg.) – $3\frac{3}{4}$ hours
11 lb. (5   kg.) – $3\frac{1}{4}$ hours   15 lb. ($6\frac{3}{4}$ kg.) – $3\frac{3}{4}$ hours
12 lb. ($5\frac{1}{2}$ kg.) – $3\frac{1}{2}$ hours   20 lb. (9   kg.) – $4\frac{1}{2}$ hours
13 lb. (6   kg.) – $3\frac{1}{2}$ hours

If you want your whole gammon or ham to serve a lot of people, leave it to cool in the water in which it was cooked. This has the effect of 'setting' the joint. It also helps retain the flavour and makes it easier to carve the gammon in thin, appetising slices. Skin before it cools completely, score and cover with golden rusk or browned breadcrumbs. Try the following glazes for a special finish.

Treacle glaze

The rind should be removed while it is still warm, and the joint put on a rack in a roasting tin before the glaze is used. Mix 2 tablespoons plain flour and 2 tablespoons Demerara sugar, stir in 2 tablespoons golden syrup, and mix to a smooth paste with 3 tablespoons warm liquid from boiling the bacon. Spread the paste over the gammon, place in a hot oven (425°F., 220°C., Gas Mark 7) and bake for 20–30 minutes, until the glaze is crisp and well browned.

Honey glaze

Spread 2 tablespoons clear honey over the gammon, and sprinkle with 1 tablespoon fine breadcrumbs. Mix $\frac{1}{4}$ pint ($1\frac{1}{2}$ dl., $\frac{2}{3}$ cup) pineapple juice and $\frac{1}{4}$ pint ($1\frac{1}{2}$ dl., $\frac{2}{3}$ cup) vinegar, and pour over the gammon. Place in hot oven (425°F., 220°C., Gas Mark 7) and bake for 20–30 minutes, until golden brown, basting occasionally.

Clove and sugar glaze

Score the fat surface of the gammon in a criss-cross pattern, then stud with cloves. Mix 1 teaspoon powdered cloves with 2 tablespoons soft brown sugar. Mix to a smooth paste with a little ginger ale. Spread on the gammon, and bake in hot oven (425°F., 220°C., Gas Mark 7) for 20–30 minutes, until crisp.

Redcurrant glaze

Melt 2 tablespoons redcurrant jelly and add 2 tablespoons cider. Spoon over the gammon in the roasting tin and sprinkle all over with Demerara sugar. Bake in hot oven (425°F., 220°C., Gas Mark 7) for 20–30 minutes until crisp, basting from time to time.

Mustard glaze

Mix 2 teaspoons mustard, 2 tablespoons wine vinegar and 2 tablespoons liquor from boiling the bacon. Pour over the gammon in the roasting tin. Mix together 2 tablespoons fine breadcrumbs and 1 tablespoon Demerara sugar, and sprinkle over the gammon. Bake in a hot oven (425°F., 220°C., Gas Mark 7) for 20–30 minutes, until crisp.

Bacon spread

IMPERIAL · METRIC	AMERICAN
4 oz./100 g. cooked bacon	½ cup cooked ground ham
2 teaspoons grated onion	2 teaspoons grated onion
1 tablespoon chopped parsley	1 tablespoon chopped parsley
pepper	pepper
2 oz./50 g. butter	¼ cup butter

Mince the bacon. Mix in the remaining ingredients and beat well until the mixture is smooth. Pack into a dish and if liked melt a little extra butter to pour over the top. Chill, then use for sandwiches or spreading on toast.

Potted bacon

IMPERIAL · METRIC	AMERICAN
2 lb./1 kg. lean bacon	4 cups ground ham
8 oz./225 g. fat bacon	1 cup ground bacon slices
¼ teaspoon black pepper	¼ teaspoon black pepper
¼ teaspoon nutmeg	¼ teaspoon nutmeg
pinch cayenne pepper	pinch cayenne pepper
1 hard-boiled egg	1 hard-cooked egg
little clarified butter	little clarified butter

Mince the lean and fat bacon twice. Mash and season highly. Turn into a greased ovenproof dish. Cover with foil and bake in a moderate oven (350°F., 180°C., Gas Mark 4) for about 30 minutes. Drain any excess fat off the top and spoon the mixture into eight individual dishes. Press down very firmly, garnish with egg slices and brush with butter. Chill slightly and serve with a small salad and hot toast.

Bacon and potato pie

IMPERIAL · METRIC	AMERICAN
12 oz./350 g. cooked bacon	1½ cups cooked ground ham
1 onion	1 onion
1 oz./25 g. butter	2 tablespoons butter
2 tablespoons tomato sauce	3 tablespoons tomato sauce
1 teaspoon made mustard	1 teaspoon prepared mustard
2 tablespoons milk	3 tablespoons milk
salt and pepper	salt and pepper
1 lb./450 g. cooked mashed potato	2 cups cooked mashed potato

Mince the bacon and chop the onion. Lightly cook the onion in the butter. Stir in the bacon, tomato sauce, mustard and milk. Season with salt and pepper if necessary. Allow to heat through, then spoon the hot bacon mixture into a buttered pie dish. Cover with the mashed potato, roughed up with a fork. Dot with butter and bake in a moderately hot oven (375°F., 190°C., Gas Mark 5) for 30 minutes, until golden.

Bacon galantine

IMPERIAL · METRIC	AMERICAN
8 oz./225 g. bacon	1 cup ground ham
4 oz./100 g. stewing steak	½ cup ground beef
4 oz./100 g. fresh white breadcrumbs	2 cups fresh soft bread crumbs
1 egg	1 egg
½ teaspoon ground nutmeg	½ teaspoon ground nutmeg
pinch mixed spice	pinch mixed spice
1 teaspoon Worcestershire sauce	1 teaspoon Worcestershire sauce
salt and pepper	salt and pepper
little stock	little stock
Glaze	*Glaze*
4 tablespoons stock	⅓ cup stock
1 teaspoon meat extract	1 teaspoon bouillon or consommé
1 teaspoon gelatine	1 teaspoon gelatin

Mince the bacon (which may be raw or cooked) and the stewing steak. Mix with the breadcrumbs, beaten egg, spices, sauce, salt and pepper. Add a little stock if necessary, but keep the mixture firm. Shape into a rectangle and wrap in greased greaseproof paper. Tie, quite loosely, in a cloth. Steam for 1½ hours. Lift out the roll, take out of the paper and cloth and leave to cool. When the galantine is cold, put on to a serving dish. Put the stock and meat extract into a small pan with the gelatine and dissolve over a low heat. When the gelatine has melted, allow the glaze to cool and just before it sets, brush over the galantine.

Bacon soup with dumplings

IMPERIAL · METRIC	AMERICAN
12-oz./350-g. collar bacon joint	¾-lb. piece smoked ham butt
2 pints/generous litre water	5 cups water
1 bay leaf	1 bay leaf
4 carrots	4 carrots
2 onions	2 onions
1 parsnip	1 parsnip
½ small white cabbage	½ small white cabbage
salt and pepper	salt and pepper
1 tablespoon tomato chutney	1 tablespoon tomato chutney
4 oz./100 g. self-raising flour	1 cup all-purpose flour sifted with 1 teaspoon baking powder
4 oz./100 g. pork sausagemeat	½ cup pork sausagemeat
1 oz./25 g. suet	3 tablespoons shredded suet
chopped parsley	chopped parsley

Place the bacon in the cold water and add the bay leaf, chopped carrots, sliced onions and chopped parsnip. Bring to the boil, cover and simmer gently for 40 minutes. Remove the bacon joint and cut it into small cubes. Return to the pan, and add the finely shredded cabbage, seasoning and tomato chutney. Meanwhile, mix the flour into the sausagemeat; season and mix with the suet. Mix to a stiff dough with a little water. Divide into eight or ten balls and place on top of the boiling soup. Cover and simmer gently for a further 15 minutes. Serve hot, garnished with chopped parsley.

This makes a substantial main course dish.

Bacon floddies

IMPERIAL · METRIC	AMERICAN
1 large potato	1 large potato
1 medium onion	1 medium onion
1 egg	1 egg
1 oz./25 g. self-raising flour	¼ cup all-purpose flour sifted with ¼ teaspoon baking powder
3 oz./75 g. bacon	scant ½ cup chopped bacon
salt and pepper	salt and pepper
lard for frying	lard for frying

Grate the potato and onion into a basin. Add the beaten egg, flour, chopped bacon, salt and pepper. Fry spoonfuls in hot lard until golden on both sides.

A pinch of chopped fresh herbs improves the flavour of these little bacon pancakes, which are very good with eggs at breakfast.

Bacon roly-poly

IMPERIAL · METRIC	AMERICAN
10 oz./275 g. cooked bacon	1¼ cups cooked ground ham
1 small onion	1 small onion
¼ teaspoon mixed herbs	¼ teaspoon mixed herbs
6 oz./175 g. self-raising flour	1½ cups all-purpose flour sifted with 1½ teaspoons baking powder
pinch salt	pinch salt
3 oz./75 g. shredded suet	generous ½ cup shredded suet

Mince the bacon and onion and mix with the herbs. Put the flour and salt into a bowl and mix in the suet. Add enough water to give a soft, but not sticky dough. Knead lightly on a floured board until smooth and roll to an oblong approximately 12 inches (30 cm.) by 8 inches (20 cm.). Put the minced bacon mixture on to the dough to within ½ inch (1 cm.) of the edges, and roll up like a Swiss roll. Wrap securely in a piece of greased foil, or tie in a pudding cloth. Put into a large saucepan one-third full of boiling water. Cover and boil steadily for 1 hour, topping up with boiling water if necessary. Serve with gravy or hot tomato sauce.

Bacon hotpot

IMPERIAL · METRIC	AMERICAN
3-lb./1½-kg. collar bacon joint	3-lb. piece smoked ham butt
1½ oz./40 g. dripping	3 tablespoons drippings
12 button onions	12 button onions
12 small carrots	12 small carrots
4 leeks	4 leeks
stock	stock
1 bay leaf	1 bay leaf
sprig parsley	sprig parsley
sprig thyme	sprig thyme

Put the bacon in cold water, bring to the boil and simmer for
45 minutes. Skin the joint and score the fat into squares.
Melt the fat in a flameproof casserole and fry the onions,
carrots and chopped leeks until lightly browned. Add enough
stock to cover. Put in the bacon and the herbs. Cover and bake
in a moderate oven (350°F., 180°C., Gas Mark 4) for 40
minutes. Remove the lid and continue cooking in a hot oven
(425°F., 220°C., Gas Mark 7) for a further 15 minutes.

Wiltshire bake

IMPERIAL · METRIC	AMERICAN
12 oz./350 g. bacon rashers	¾ lb. bacon slices
1 lb./450 g. cooking apples	1 lb. baking apples
sugar	sugar
¾ pint/4 dl. cheese sauce	scant 2 cups cheese sauce
1 tablespoon browned breadcrumbs	1 tablespoon dry bread crumbs
2 oz./50 g. Cheddar cheese	½ cup grated Cheddar cheese

Roll the bacon rashers, thread on skewers and grill until golden
on all sides. Cook the peeled and sliced apples in a little water
until just tender. Strain off any surplus liquid. Place the apple
slices in the bottom of a shallow ovenproof dish. Sprinkle the top
with sugar and pop under a hot grill to melt the sugar. Place the
rolled bacon from the skewers on top of the sugar, coat with hot
cheese sauce, top with breadcrumbs and grated cheese. Brown
under the hot grill and serve immediately.

Poacher's roll

IMPERIAL · METRIC	AMERICAN
12 oz./350 g. puff pastry	¾ lb. puff paste
6 oz./175 g. streaky bacon rashers	9–10 bacon slices
1 lb./450 g. pork sausagemeat	2 cups pork sausagemeat
2 oz./50 g. button mushrooms	½ cup chopped mushrooms
1 small onion	1 small onion
1 tablespoon chopped fresh mixed herbs	1 tablespoon chopped fresh mixed herbs
1 teaspoon made mustard	1 teaspoon prepared mustard
salt and pepper	salt and pepper
beaten egg to glaze	beaten egg to glaze

Roll out the pastry to an oblong about 13 inches (32·5 cm.) by 10 inches (26 cm.). Chop the bacon and mix with the sausagemeat, chopped mushrooms and onion, herbs, mustard and seasoning. Form into a sausage shape and put in the centre of the pastry. Brush the pastry edges with water and roll up. Seal the pastry at both ends to enclose the filling completely. Turn the roll over so that the join is underneath and put on a wetted baking sheet. Decorate with pastry trimmings, and cut three slashes in the top. Brush with the egg beaten with a pinch of salt. Bake in a hot oven (425°F., 220°C., Gas Mark 7) for 20 minutes, and then reduce the heat to moderately hot (375°F., 190°C., Gas Mark 5) and bake for a further 40 minutes. Serve hot or cold.

Bacon and apple roll

IMPERIAL · METRIC	AMERICAN
12 oz./350 g. cooked bacon, minced	1½ cups ground cooked ham
1 large cooking apple	1 large baking apple
1 small onion	1 small onion
2 tablespoons stock or water	3 tablespoons stock or water
8 oz./225 g. puff pastry	½ lb. puff paste
beaten egg to glaze	beaten egg to glaze

Mix together the minced bacon, peeled and chopped apple, chopped onion and stock. Roll the pastry into an oblong on a floured board, and spread the bacon mixture over it. Damp the edges of pastry and form into a roll. Place on a baking sheet with the join underneath. Brush the roll with a little beaten egg, and cut slits along the surface to allow the steam to escape. Decorate with leaves cut from the pastry trimmings, if liked. Bake in a hot oven (425°F., 220°C., Gas Mark 7) until the pastry is just beginning to brown, about 20 minutes. Reduce the heat to moderately hot (375°F., 190°C., Gas Mark 5) and continue cooking for a further 40 minutes. Serve hot or cold.

Stuffed roast bacon

IMPERIAL · METRIC	AMERICAN
3-lb./1½-kg. rolled bacon joint	3-lb. piece smoked rolled shoulder butt
2 oz./50 g. butter	¼ cup butter
4 oz./100 g. fresh white breadcrumbs	2 cups fresh soft bread crumbs
2 tablespoons chopped parsley	3 tablespoons chopped parsley
2 teaspoons chopped fresh thyme	2 teaspoons chopped fresh thyme
grated rind of 1 lemon	grated rind of 1 lemon
1 small egg	1 small egg
pepper	pepper

Bring the joint to the boil in cold water. Reduce the heat and simmer for 20 minutes. Melt the butter and stir in the breadcrumbs, herbs, lemon rind, egg and pepper. Drain the bacon well and take off the string and the rind. Put the stuffing in the centre of the joint and roll it again, tying it firmly with string. Score the fat in a criss-cross pattern, put in a roasting tin and bake in a moderate oven (350°F., 180°C., Gas Mark 4) for 1 hour.

This is good served with baked tomatoes and jacket potatoes.

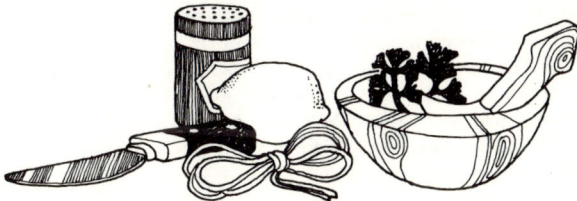

Roast bacon

IMPERIAL·METRIC	AMERICAN
4-lb./2-kg. boned and rolled forehock	4-lb. piece smoked rolled shoulder butt
Glaze	*Glaze*
3 tablespoons marmalade	4 tablespoons marmalade
1 teaspoon dry mustard	1 teaspoon dry mustard
1 tablespoon Demerara sugar	1 tablespoon brown sugar
2 teaspoons wine vinegar	2 teaspoons wine vinegar
pepper	pepper

Wrap the joint in foil and calculate the cooking time at 30 minutes to the lb. (½ kg.). Place the joint in a roasting tin and cook in a hot oven (425°F., 220°C., Gas Mark 7) for the calculated time. Remove the foil and take the rind off the joint. Mix the ingredients for the glaze together and brush half of it over the meat. Return the joint to the oven and cook for a further 30 minutes uncovered, spooning over the remaining glaze during cooking. Serve hot or cold.

Bacon and potato casserole

IMPERIAL·METRIC	AMERICAN
1½ lb./¾ kg. potatoes	1½ lb. potatoes
2 large onions	2 large onions
salt and pepper	salt and pepper
1 egg	1 egg
½ pint/3 dl. milk	1¼ cups milk
1 oz./25 g. butter	2 tablespoons butter
1 lb./450 g. collar bacon rashers	1 lb. Canadian bacon slices
1 teaspoon bottled brown sauce	1 teaspoon bottled brown sauce

Peel the potatoes and cut in slices. Peel and slice the onions thinly. Grease a casserole, and put in alternate layers of potatoes and onions, seasoning with salt and pepper, and finishing with potatoes. Beat together the egg and milk and pour over the potatoes and onions. Dot with butter, and cover with slices of bacon brushed with sauce. Cover and bake in a moderate oven (350°F., 180°C., Gas Mark 4) for 1 hour. Remove the cover for 10 minutes to brown the bacon.

Bacon in cider

IMPERIAL · METRIC	AMERICAN
2½-lb./1¼-kg. bacon joint	2½-lb. piece smoked ham butt
½ pint/3 dl. cider or pale ale	1¼ cups cider or light beer
1 small onion	1 small onion
1 carrot	1 carrot
1 bay leaf	1 bay leaf
sprig thyme	sprig thyme
sprig parsley	sprig parsley
peppercorns	peppercorns
toasted breadcrumbs (optional)	dry bread crumbs (optional)

Bring the bacon to the boil in cold water. Drain and place the
joint in the cider or ale and enough water to cover. Add the
onion, carrot, herbs and peppercorns. Bring back to the boil,
reduce the heat and simmer the joint gently allowing 20
minutes per lb. (½ kg.) and 20 minutes over. Drain the joint,
remove the string and rind. Coat with toasted breadcrumbs if
serving cold.

Baked bacon chops

IMPERIAL · METRIC	AMERICAN
4 bacon chops	4 thick smoked ham slices
1 onion	1 onion
2 sticks celery	2 stalks celery
1 oz./25 g. butter	2 tablespoons butter
8 oz./225 g. tomatoes, peeled	½ lb. tomatoes, peeled
4 tablespoons dry cider	⅓ cup dry cider
pepper	pepper
1 tablespoon chopped parsley	1 tablespoon chopped parsley

Remove the rind from the chops and place them in a large
shallow ovenproof dish. Chop the onion and celery and fry
gently in the butter until soft. Add the quartered tomatoes and
cider and a sprinkling of pepper. Spoon over the chops, cover
with a lid and cook in a moderately hot oven (375°F., 190°C.,
Gas Mark 5) for 35 minutes. Sprinkle with parsley and serve
with mashed potatoes.

Braised bacon forehock

IMPERIAL · METRIC	AMERICAN
2½-lb./1¼-kg. boned bacon forehock	2½-lb. piece smoked ham butt or picnic ham
2 onions	2 onions
½ cucumber	½ cucumber
4 potatoes	4 potatoes
1 lb./450 g. tomatoes	1 lb. tomatoes
½ pint/3 dl. meat stock	1¼ cups meat stock
1 bay leaf	1 bay leaf
1 clove	1 clove
salt and pepper	salt and pepper

Soak the bacon for 2 hours. Slice the onions and cucumber and chop the potatoes. Peel and quarter the tomatoes. Place the drained joint in a casserole, add the potatoes, onions, stock, bay leaf, clove and seasoning. Cover and bake in a moderate oven (350°F., 180°C., Gas Mark 4) for 1½ hours. Add the tomatoes and cucumber and cook for a further 30 minutes. Remove the skin from the bacon before serving.

Bacon and liver sausage

IMPERIAL · METRIC	AMERICAN
8 oz./225 g. fat bacon	1 cup ground fat bacon slices
1 lb./450 g. liver	2 cups ground liver
6 oz./175 g. breadcrumbs	3 cups bread crumbs
2 teaspoons chopped parsley	2 teaspoons chopped parsley
2 teaspoons chopped sage	2 teaspoons chopped sage
2 teaspoons finely chopped onion	2 teaspoons finely chopped onion
salt and pepper	salt and pepper
1 egg	1 egg

Mince the bacon and liver. Mix with the other ingredients and bind with the egg. Roll in a floured cloth and boil gently for 2 hours in salted, boiling water. Leave in the water to become cold; leave in the cloth until firm, pressing the sausage under a weight.

Bacon and liver loaf

IMPERIAL · METRIC	AMERICAN
1½ lb./¾ kg. minced lean bacon	3 cups ground ham
8 oz./225 g. liver, minced	1 cup ground liver
4 oz./100 g. breadcrumbs	2 cups bread crumbs
1 egg	1 egg
salt and pepper	salt and pepper
2 teaspoons brown sugar	2 teaspoons brown sugar
1 teaspoon ground cloves	1 teaspoon ground cloves
6 tablespoons milk	scant ⅔ cup milk
4 thin streaky bacon rashers	4 bacon slices

Place the bacon and liver in a basin. Mix the breadcrumbs
with the egg, salt and pepper, sugar and cloves. Stir in the milk
and leave to soak for 5 minutes. Stir the breadcrumb mixture
into the meat. When blended, pack into a greased 2-lb. (1-kg.)
loaf tin lined with the thin streaky rashers, from which the rind
has been removed. Bake in a moderate oven (325°F., 160°C.,
Gas Mark 3) for 1½ hours. Cool under a heavy weight. Serve
with a salad, or in sandwiches.

Honeyed bacon

IMPERIAL · METRIC	AMERICAN
6 oz./175 g. brown sugar	¾ cup brown sugar
½ teaspoon dry mustard	½ teaspoon dry mustard
8 tablespoons honey	9 tablespoons honey
3-lb./1½-kg. bacon joint	3-lb. piece smoked ham butt
¼ pint/1½ dl. orange juice	⅔ cup orange juice

Mix the sugar, mustard and 2 tablespoons of the honey together.
Spread half this mixture over the bacon. Place in a shallow
roasting tin and bake in a moderate oven (350°F., 180°C., Gas
Mark 4) for 1 hour. Heat the orange juice and the rest of the
honey in a small pan and use to baste the bacon. Increase the
oven temperature to moderately hot (400°F., 200°C., Gas Mark
6), pour the remainder of the sugar and honey mixture over the
joint and bake for a further 30 minutes, when the bacon will be a
sticky, golden brown.

Eggs

What would a country housewife do without eggs? They come in handy for every meal, add nourishment to even the quickest snack, and are the basis of so many delicious cakes and puddings. To get the best out of eggs, you need to treat them with respect, store them carefully and cook them with loving care. Keep them pointed end down in a cool place (it isn't necessary to keep them in the refrigerator), and make sure they are not near any strong-smelling foods such as onions or fish which may flavour them. Simply cooked eggs are always delicious, but simple methods are sometimes slap-dash, so it is worth practising for perfect results.

Boiled eggs

If the water boils too fast, the egg whites will coagulate too quickly and become hard; excessive bubbling of the water makes the eggs collide and sometimes crack, so take it gently. The easiest way to boil eggs is to put them into a pan and cover completely with cold water. Bring to boiling point, reduce the heat to simmering and start timing. Allow 3 minutes for large and $2\frac{1}{4}$ minutes for small *soft-boiled* eggs. For a *hard white and soft yolk*, allow $4\frac{1}{2}$ minutes (large) or 3 minutes (small). *Hard-boiled* eggs need 8 minutes (large) or 6 minutes (small), and should be plunged straight into cold water when they have finished cooking. People who prefer soft-boiled eggs might like to try *coddling* them. To do this, carefully put the eggs into a pan of boiling water to cover them completely, put the lid on the pan, and take the pan from the heat. Time from this minute, allowing 8–9 minutes for large eggs and $6\frac{1}{2}$ minutes for small ones.

Poached eggs

Poaching means that the cooking liquid, or the water, must be barely simmering, never bubbling in the pan. This method is ideally suited to the cooking of eggs which, when perfectly poached, should be shapely and the white covering a lightly set yolk. Choose a wide, shallow pan such as a frying pan. Add the water to a depth of about 1½ inches (3·5 cm.) which will cover the eggs. Bring the water to the boil, then reduce the heat until the merest simmering bubbles show on the base of the pan. Break each egg into a cup and slip it into the water from just above its surface. Simmer for 2–3 minutes without moving them. Lift the eggs on a perforated spoon, starting with the egg placed first in the pan, 'blot' on a clean folded cloth or tissue and serve immediately.

Salt and vinegar are unnecessary to successful poaching. Salt will raise the boiling point of the water, making it slightly hotter at simmering point without causing a bubbling movement, but the salt flavours. The acidity of the vinegar hastens coagulation or 'setting' of the egg, preventing the white from breaking away, but vinegar also flavours. A special poaching pan with water heated under a hollowed metal cover does not provide the traditional poached egg, as eggs are not in contact with the liquid. A truer description of this method of cooking eggs would be steamed eggs.

Fried eggs

Use butter, lard or bacon fat. Butter colours the whites golden, and flavours. Lard retains egg whiteness and flavours slightly. Bacon fat must be clean, and it colours golden brown and flavours. Heat the butter until beginning to bubble; heat lard or bacon fat for ½ minute after melting. Test by dropping a little egg white into the fat which should cloud and set immediately without sizzling. Adjust the heat to maintain the fat at this temperature. Break 1 egg at a time into a saucer or cup, slide the egg into the fat and fry 2–3 minutes. Lift the egg on a slice starting with egg first into the pan, 'blot' on absorbent paper and serve. All fried eggs are best served immediately and not kept hot for more than 2–3 minutes. Fat may be flipped over the yolk to make a glossy film, or the eggs may be turned to 'set' both sides. The heat may be increased to brown and crisp the whites, if liked.

Eggs are cooked for 2 minutes for a soft yolk, up to 6 minutes for a firm yolk.

Scrambled eggs

These are useful for all sorts of dishes but they need careful cooking. Scrambled eggs should be soft and creamy, and if they are overcooked they become dry and granulated. If too much liquid is added, they become watery. It is best to add no liquid until the eggs are cooked and taken from the heat, when a little cream or top of the milk may be stirred in.

Use 1 oz. (25 g., 2 tablespoons) butter, salt and pepper to 4 eggs, and be sure to use a thick pan so that the eggs cook evenly. Cook over a gentle heat, as a fierce heat makes the eggs tough and rubbery. Melt the butter in the pan and add the eggs, beaten with seasoning. Stir all the time and never leave the eggs. Remove from the heat before all the eggs are fully set, as they will continue cooking in their own heat. Stir in 1 tablespoon of cream as soon as the eggs come off the heat. Additional flavouring such as chopped herbs, grated cheese, chopped ham or shellfish can be stirred into the beaten eggs before being cooked. If bacon or mushrooms are added, they should be chopped and cooked lightly in the butter before the eggs are added.

Pancakes

Thin, lightly browned pancakes are traditionally served on just one day of the year, rolled and sprinkled with lemon juice and sugar, but they are worth making all the year round. They are good with a savoury creamy filling (try creamed chicken, kidneys or smoked haddock), but most people prefer them with jam, fresh summer fruit, or fruit purée and a sprinkling of castor sugar.

The egg acts as a raising agent in the basic batter and nothing else is needed, so use plain flour and see that it is dry and free from lumps. Grandmother always left her batter to stand. Today's cooks know this isn't necessary so leave it or not, whichever is easier. Use a fairly heavy frying pan about 7 inches (18 cm.) across. Grease it lightly with butter or lard, only just enough to stop the pancakes sticking. It is best, of course, to cook the pancakes and eat them at once, but they can be kept in a covered dish for a few hours, then reheated in a moderate oven (350°F., 180°C., Gas Mark 4).

Basic pancakes

IMPERIAL · METRIC	AMERICAN
4 oz./100 g. plain flour	1 cup all-purpose flour
pinch salt	pinch salt
2 eggs	2 eggs
½ pint/3 dl. milk	1¼ cups milk
butter or lard for cooking	butter or lard for cooking

Sieve the flour and salt into a basin. Make a well in the centre, add the eggs and a little of the milk. Stir, drawing in the flour from the sides, and beat well until the mixture is smooth. Add the remainder of the milk gradually, stirring and beating thoroughly. Transfer the batter to a jug, so that just the right amount may be poured into the pan. Too much batter makes the pancake thick and stodgy.

Melt a small piece of butter or lard in the frying pan, just enough to cover the base, pour off any excess fat and use for the next pancake. When the pan is hot, pour in sufficient batter from the jug to cover the bottom of the pan thinly. When the underside is sufficiently brown, toss or turn the pancake over and cook the other side. Turn out on to a warmed plate, and keep hot. Repeat this with the remainder of the batter.

Omelettes

There is no mystery about making an omelette, but just a few simple rules. The frying pan must be thick, quite flat, clean and absolutely dry. The ingredients are only 2 large eggs, some pepper and salt, and ½ oz. (15 g., 1 tablespoon) butter for cooking the omelette.

Break the eggs into a basin. Add the seasoning and beat with a metal fork until the eggs are lightly mixed. An old dinner fork is ideal for this. Now put the pan on the heat with the butter in it. Slowly get it very hot but not so hot that the butter browns. Without drawing the pan off the heat, pour the egg mixture into the hot fat. It will cover the pan and start cooking at once. Use the fork to keep drawing some of the mixture to the middle from the sides of the pan. In 1½-2 minutes the omelette will still be soft but no longer runny. Draw the pan off the heat and using the fork, fold the omelette away from you, but only half over. Now grasp the pan by the handle and tilt it forward over a hot plate. The omelette will slip forward on to the plate, neatly folded.

The nicest omelettes are made one at a time and eaten at once, but omelettes for a family can be made as one, and divided into four. The method is identical, but you will need 8 eggs and a 10-inch (26-cm.) pan instead of a 7-inch (18-cm.) one.

You can eat your omelette plain, or you can add flavourings, such as herbs and cheese, to the mixed eggs, or you can put a mixture in after the omelette has been cooked.

Don't make an omelette wait for its filling, but see that the filling is ready when the omelette is cooked so that you can serve it at once. Have a hot dish and hot plates ready. Nothing is nastier than an omelette which has cooled on the plate. Don't overcook the omelette. The centre should be just a little runny when the filling is put in, because the heat of the filling will finish cooking the omelette. Here are three recipes for slightly more filling omelettes for supper.

Friar's omelette

IMPERIAL·METRIC	AMERICAN
2 slices white bread	2 slices white bread
2 oz./50 g. butter	¼ cup butter
2 tomatoes	2 tomatoes
6 eggs	6 eggs
salt and pepper	salt and pepper
¼–½ teaspoon mixed herbs	¼–½ teaspoon mixed herbs

Remove the crusts and cut the bread into small cubes. Heat the butter in a large omelette pan and fry the bread in it until lightly browned all over. Peel and chop the tomatoes and add to the pan. Beat the eggs well together with the seasoning and herbs. Pour the eggs into the pan and keep the mixture moving from the edges toward the centre until beginning to set in the middle. Fold the omelette over and tip on to a serving dish. Serve hot or cold with salads.

Murphy's omelette

IMPERIAL · METRIC	AMERICAN
1 oz./25 g. butter	2 tablespoons butter
8 oz./225 g. cold cooked potatoes	1 cup cold cooked potatoes
4 eggs	4 eggs
salt and black pepper	salt and black pepper
1 tablespoon water	1 tablespoon water
2 oz./50 g. cheese, grated	½ cup grated cheese

Melt the butter in an omelette pan, add the potatoes and cook until beginning to brown, adding a little more butter if necessary. Beat the eggs well with the seasoning and water. Pour into the pan and cook over a good heat until beginning to set. Sprinkle in the cheese and brown the surface under a hot grill. Serve in wedges, with rolls and butter and a winter salad.

Supper omelette

IMPERIAL · METRIC	AMERICAN
1½ oz./40 g. butter	3 tablespoons butter
1 small onion	1 small onion
1 tablespoon cooked potato	1 tablespoon cooked potato
1 tablespoon cooked peas	1 tablespoon cooked peas
1 tablespoon diced corned beef	1 tablespoon diced corned beef
or cooked meat	or cooked meat
3 eggs	3 eggs
1½ tablespoons water	2 tablespoons water
salt and pepper	salt and pepper

Melt the butter in a 7-inch (18-cm.) omelette pan. Fry the chopped onion lightly. Add the potato, peas and meat, and cook for 2–3 minutes, until thoroughly hot. Lightly beat the eggs with the water and seasoning, and pour on to the mixture in the pan. Cook until just set and serve flat instead of folded.

Egg yolks

If you can, use them immediately, but they can be kept for 2–3 days if put whole into a screw-topped jar, covered with cold water and put in the refrigerator. Egg yolks can be frozen if lightly beaten with a pinch of sugar or salt (according to possible end use) and put into small containers. An egg yolk will add richness to pastry, scones and batters. Add an extra yolk or two to scrambled eggs, or use them to thicken sauces and soups (don't boil the mixture when an egg yolk has been added).

Add an egg yolk to butter cream for cakes, or to milk drinks for extra nourishment. If you have plenty of egg yolks, use them for mayonnaise or for baked custards. If egg yolks are poached and mashed, they are excellent for sandwich fillings.

Egg whites

These will keep for several days in a covered bowl in the refrigerator, or they can be lightly stirred together and frozen in usable quantities. Add egg whites to soufflés or mousses, or whisk them into just-setting jelly. Use them for meringues, or for meringue toppings to puddings. Whip egg whites into double cream to make it go further, and into fruit-and-cream whips to lighten them.

To whisk egg whites successfully, add a small pinch of salt (too much will make them watery). The bowl must be absolutely clean and dry with no trace of grease or egg yolk, and the utensils should be cold. A flat or rotary whisk gives greater volume than an electric mixer. If eggs are separated the day before use, the whites will hold more air when whisked.

Breakfast, lunch and supper dishes

Poached egg and kippers

IMPERIAL · METRIC	AMERICAN
4 kippers	4 kippers
4 eggs	4 eggs
1 oz./25 g. butter	2 tablespoons butter

Put the kippers into a tall jug. Pour in boiling water to cover them and tuck foil over the top. Leave for 5 minutes. Heat water to a depth of 1½ inches (3·5 cm.) in a wide, shallow pan to simmering point. Slide in the eggs, one at a time, from a saucer and poach gently for 3½–4 minutes. Lift out the kippers, drain and top with butter. Lift the eggs, blot dry on kitchen paper and place on kippers. Serve with brown bread and butter.

Haddock with eggs

IMPERIAL · METRIC	AMERICAN
12 oz.–1 lb./350–450 g. smoked haddock fillets	¾–1 lb. smoked haddock fillets
½ pint/3 dl. milk	1¼ cups milk
¾ oz./20 g. flour	3 tablespoons all-purpose flour
pepper	pepper
½ teaspoon made mustard	½ teaspoon prepared mustard
2 oz./50 g. butter	¼ cup butter
4 eggs	4 eggs
4 tablespoons double cream	⅓ cup whipping cream

Wash and cut up the fish. Dry and put into a saucepan with the milk. Cover and cook gently for 7–10 minutes. Strain off the milk and leave to cool. Flake the fish. Pour the cool milk back into the saucepan, whisk in the flour, pepper and mustard. Stir until thickened and cooked. Mix in the fish, place in a serving dish and keep hot. Heat the butter and fry the eggs in it, drain and put on the fish. Spoon the cream over each egg and flash under a hot grill to melt the cream.

Baked eggs and tomato

IMPERIAL · METRIC	AMERICAN
2 large tomatoes	2 large tomatoes
½ oz./15 g. butter	1 tablespoon butter
salt and pepper	salt and pepper
little sugar	little sugar
4 eggs	4 eggs

Skin and slice the tomatoes. Butter four small individual ovenproof dishes. Put some tomato slices in each and sprinkle with seasoning and sugar. Put near the top of a moderately hot oven (375°F., 190°C., Gas Mark 5) for 4 minutes. Break an egg into each dish, top with butter and cover with buttered paper. Bake for 7–8 minutes.

Boiled eggs and ham

IMPERIAL·METRIC	AMERICAN
4 eggs	4 eggs
½ oz./15 g. butter	1 tablespoon butter
4 thick slices cooked ham	4 thick slices cooked ham

Put the eggs into a saucepan and cover with cold water. Bring to simmering point and cook for 2–2½ minutes. Put the eggs into cold water for ½ minute, shell them and serve, topped with butter, on the ham.

Eggs in cream

IMPERIAL·METRIC	AMERICAN
½ pint/2¼ dl. single cream	generous ¾ cup half-and-half
8 eggs	8 eggs
salt and black pepper	salt and black pepper
8 slices toast	8 slices toast

Gently heat the cream in a large pan and break in the eggs, one at a time. Cover and cook the eggs slowly until the whites are firm. Season and serve immediately on toast.

Egg fritters

IMPERIAL·METRIC	AMERICAN
12 oz./350 g. potatoes	¾ lb. potatoes
1 onion	1 onion
1 oz./25 g. self-raising flour	¼ cup all-purpose flour sifted with ¼ teaspoon baking powder
salt and pepper	salt and pepper
pinch nutmeg	pinch nutmeg
2 eggs	2 eggs
fat for frying	oil for frying

Peel the potatoes and onion. Grate them coarsely into a bowl and drain off the liquid. Beat in the flour, seasonings and eggs. Heat deep or shallow fat and fry tablespoonsful of the batter on both sides until crisp and browned. Drain on absorbent paper and serve hot with bacon, sausages, tomatoes or mushrooms.

Egg savoury batter

IMPERIAL·METRIC	AMERICAN
1 lb./450 g. onions	1 lb. onions
2 oz./50 g. butter	¼ cup butter
4 oz./100 g. lean bacon rashers (or skinless sausages)	¼ lb. Canadian bacon slices (or sausage links)
8 eggs	8 eggs
salt and pepper	salt and pepper

Peel and chop the onions. Melt the butter in a frying pan and fry the onions until soft and lightly browned. Spread them in a shallow baking dish. Remove the rinds and chop the bacon (or sausages) and fry quickly in the same pan. Drain and mix with the onions. Beat the eggs well with the seasoning and pour into the dish. Bake in the top of a moderately hot oven (400°F., 200°C., Gas Mark 6) for 15 minutes. Serve, cut in squares, with baked tomatoes and fried potatoes.

Egg and leek potato cake

IMPERIAL·METRIC	AMERICAN
1 lb./450 g. leeks	1 lb. leeks
1 lb./450 g. cooked mashed potato	2 cups cooked mashed potato
salt and pepper	salt and pepper
6 eggs	6 eggs
1 oz./25 g. butter	2 tablespoons butter
2 oz./50 g. cheese, grated	½ cup grated cheese
fat or oil for frying	oil for frying

Trim and slice the leeks, wash and cook in salted water until tender, then drain well. Mix the potato with the seasoning, and 1 egg, beaten. Heat the butter in a frying pan; spread the potato mixture in it and cook for about 5 minutes over a moderate heat. Cover with the leeks and cook a little longer. Beat another egg with seasoning, pour over the leeks and sprinkle with cheese. Put under a heated grill, reduced to a moderate heat, and turn the pan to brown the cheese evenly. Meanwhile, heat the fat and fry the remaining eggs quickly. Drain on absorbent paper and arrange on top of the leeks. Serve hot, with buttered carrots or peas.

Potato egg bake

IMPERIAL · METRIC	AMERICAN
2 lb./1 kg. potatoes	2 lb. potatoes
1 large onion	1 large onion
4 bacon rashers	4 bacon slices
salt and pepper	salt and pepper
¼ pint/1½ dl. milk	⅔ cup milk
1 oz./25 g. butter	2 tablespoons butter
8 eggs	8 eggs

Peel the potatoes and cut into small cubes. Thinly slice the onion and chop the bacon. Butter a deep ovenproof dish. Place a layer of potato cubes in the bottom of the dish, and season with salt and pepper. Cover with half the sliced onion and chopped bacon. Repeat these two layers again, seasoning the potatoes. Finally cover with a layer of potatoes. Pour over the milk and dot the top with butter. Cover tightly and bake in a moderately hot oven (400°F., 200°C., Gas Mark 6) for 1 hour, removing the cover after 45 minutes. The potatoes should be cooked and the milk absorbed. Remove from the oven and make eight hollows in the potatoes with a spoon. Break an egg into each hollow. Return to the oven and bake for a further 6–7 minutes. The eggs should be set when removed from the oven. Serve at once.

Egg and bacon turnovers

IMPERIAL · METRIC	AMERICAN
6 eggs	6 eggs
4 oz./100 g. bacon rashers	¼ lb. bacon slices
1 tablespoon breadcrumbs	1 tablespoon bread crumbs
salt and pepper	salt and pepper
1 egg, beaten	1 egg, beaten
6 oz./175 g. shortcrust pastry	basic pie dough made with 1½ cups all-purpose flour etc.

Hard boil the eggs, shell and chop them. Chop the bacon and mix with the eggs, breadcrumbs, seasoning and beaten egg. Divide the pastry into four and roll out each piece to a large circle. Dampen the pastry edges and pile the egg mixture to one side of each circle, fold pastry over, seal and flute the edges

together. Place on a baking sheet and bake near the top of a
moderately hot oven (400°F., 200°C., Gas Mark 6) for 15–20
minutes. Serve hot or cold.

Egg and bacon pie

IMPERIAL·METRIC	AMERICAN
8 oz./225 g. shortcrust pastry	basic pie dough made with 2 cups all-purpose flour etc.
4 oz./100 g. streaky bacon rashers	¼ lb. bacon slices
6 eggs	6 eggs
pepper	pepper

Roll out two-thirds of the pastry to line a 7-inch (18-cm.) pie
plate. Remove the rinds, chop the bacon and spread over the
pastry base. Break 5 eggs on to the bacon and sprinkle with
pepper. Beat the remaining egg and use to dampen the pastry
edge. Roll out the rest of the pastry to make a lid and place
carefully on top of the pie. Seal the edges well together, make a
slit in the top and brush with the remaining egg. Bake in a
moderately hot oven (400°F., 200°C., Gas Mark 6) for 30
minutes. Serve hot with vegetables, or cold with salads.

Buck rarebit

IMPERIAL·METRIC	AMERICAN
6 eggs	6 eggs
8 oz./225 g. cheese, grated	2 cups grated cheese
1 teaspoon Worcestershire sauce	1 teaspoon Worcestershire sauce
pepper	pepper
4 slices bread	4 slices bread

Beat two of the eggs well together. Mix in the cheese,
Worcestershire sauce and pepper to taste. Toast the bread lightly
both sides. Spread the cheese mixture on to each slice and put
under a heated grill until the cheese melts and browns.
Meanwhile, poach the remaining eggs and serve one on each
toasted cheese slice. Serve hot.

Egg and sausage roll

IMPERIAL·METRIC	AMERICAN
8 oz./225 g. pork sausagemeat	1 cup pork sausagemeat
6 hard-boiled eggs	6 hard-cooked eggs
salt and pepper	salt and pepper
1 small onion	1 small onion
¼ teaspoon mixed herbs	¼ teaspoon mixed herbs
7 oz./200 g. puff pastry	7 oz. puff paste
1 egg, beaten	1 egg, beaten

Mix the sausagemeat with the chopped, hard-boiled eggs, salt and pepper, grated onion and herbs. Roll out the pastry to an oblong about 14 inches (36 cm.) by 12 inches (30 cm.) and brush the long side with beaten egg. Pile the egg filling evenly along the pastry and fold the pastry over the filling to seal on the damp side. Put the roll on a baking sheet with pastry join underneath. Make several slits through the top, brush with egg and bake near the top of a hot oven (425°F., 220°C., Gas Mark 7) for 15 minutes. Reduce the heat to moderately hot (400°F., 200°C., Gas Mark 6) and bake for 15–20 minutes. Serve hot or cold.

Egg and sausage tart

IMPERIAL·METRIC	AMERICAN
4 oz./100 g. shortcrust pastry	basic pie dough made with 1 cup all-purpose flour etc.
8 oz./225 g. sausagemeat	1 cup sausagemeat
8 eggs	8 eggs
salt and pepper	salt and pepper
1½ oz./40 g. cheese, grated	generous ¼ cup grated cheese

Roll out the pastry to cover the base of a tin approximately 7 inches (18 cm.) square. Bake blind in a moderately hot oven (400°F., 200°C., Gas Mark 6) for 15 minutes. Shape the sausagemeat into rolls to form a border; press firmly on to the pastry edges. Break the eggs inside the sausage and sprinkle with seasoning. Cover with cheese and bake in a hot oven (425°F., 220°C., Gas Mark 7) for 25 minutes. Serve hot with vegetables.

To serve cold, bake in a moderately hot oven (400°F., 200°C., Gas Mark 6) for 30 minutes.

Egg and kidney flan

IMPERIAL · METRIC	AMERICAN
6 oz./175 g. shortcrust pastry	basic pie dough made with 1½ cups all-purpose flour etc.
1 small onion	1 small onion
½ oz./15 g. butter	1 tablespoon butter
2 lamb's kidneys	2 lamb kidneys
1 tablespoon plain flour	1 tablespoon all-purpose flour
salt and pepper	salt and pepper
¼ pint/1½ dl. stock or water	⅔ cup stock or water
6 eggs	6 eggs
chopped parsley	chopped parsley

Line an 8-inch (20-cm.) flan ring or sandwich tin with the pastry. Bake blind in a hot oven (425°F., 220°C., Gas Mark 7) for 20 minutes. Meanwhile, chop the onion finely and cook gently in the butter. Skin and core the kidney and cut up. Add to the cooked onion. Cook for 2 minutes, then add the flour and cook for another 2 minutes, stirring all the time. Add the seasoning and stock. Simmer for 15 minutes, stirring occasionally. Scramble the eggs as in the basic recipe (see page 56) and place around the edges of the flan; spoon the kidney mixture in the centre. Sprinkle the eggs with chopped parsley and serve.

Egg saucers

IMPERIAL · METRIC	AMERICAN
4 thin slices bread	4 thin slices bread
1½ oz./40 g. butter	3 tablespoons butter
4 eggs	4 eggs
salt and pepper	salt and pepper

Use old saucers to make this dish.

Remove the crusts from the bread. Melt the butter and dip the bread slices in it. Line four saucers with the bread and bake in a moderately hot oven (375°F., 190°C., Gas Mark 5) for 5 minutes. Break an egg into each bread-lined saucer, season and return to the oven until the eggs are set – about 8 minutes.

Scotch eggs

IMPERIAL · METRIC	AMERICAN
6 hard-boiled eggs	6 hard-cooked eggs
little flour	little all-purpose flour
1 lb./450 g. pork sausagemeat	2 cups pork sausagemeat
1 egg	1 egg
4 teaspoons cold water	4 teaspoons cold water
1½ oz./40 g. fresh breadcrumbs	scant 1 cup fresh soft bread crumbs
fat for deep frying	oil for deep frying

Dust the eggs with flour. Divide the sausagemeat into six even portions. Wrap each hard-boiled egg completely in a portion of sausagemeat. Beat the egg with water. Dip the sausagemeat in the egg mixture, then coat with breadcrumbs. Fry in hot fat for 8–10 minutes, then drain on absorbent paper. Serve with salad.

Pickled eggs

IMPERIAL · METRIC	AMERICAN
6 eggs	6 eggs
1 pint/6 dl. white vinegar	2½ cups white vinegar
½ oz./15 g. pickling spice	2 tablespoons pickling spice

Hard boil the eggs, remove the shells and put the eggs into a wide-neck jar. Put the vinegar and spice into a saucepan and boil for 10 minutes. Strain and pour into the jar while the vinegar is hot. (The eggs should be covered by ½-inch (1-cm.) depth of vinegar.) Cover the jar with an acid-resistant lid.

Pickled eggs are ready to use after 14 days, but will keep for up to 6 months.

Puddings and cakes

Burnt cream

IMPERIAL·METRIC	AMERICAN
1 pint/6 dl. single cream	2½ cups half-and-half
1 vanilla pod	1 vanilla bean
strip of orange rind	strip of orange rind
5 egg yolks	5 egg yolks
4 oz./100 g. castor sugar	½ cup granulated sugar

Put the cream into the top of a double saucepan, or into a bowl placed over a pan of hot water. Put in the vanilla pod and orange rind and heat slowly. Beat the egg yolks with 1 tablespoon of the sugar. Pour strained hot cream on to the eggs and stir. Return to the saucepan and cook gently, stirring all the time until the mixture has thickened. Pour into a heatproof bowl and leave until cold. Sprinkle over the remaining sugar to cover the top completely. Put under a very hot grill to caramelise the sugar. Serve chilled.

This is very good served with fresh raspberries and thick cream.

Whisky flummery

IMPERIAL·METRIC	AMERICAN
4 egg yolks	4 egg yolks
3 oz./75 g. castor sugar	6 tablespoons granulated sugar
3 tablespoons whisky	scant ¼ cup whisky
⅓ pint/2¼ dl. double cream	generous ¾ cup heavy cream

If a whisky liqueur is used instead of whisky, this will be even more delicious.

Put the egg yolks and sugar into a double saucepan, or into a basin placed over a pan of simmering water. Beat them well until thick and foamy. Add the whisky and continue beating until the mixture stands in peaks. Remove from the heat. Whip the cream lightly and fold it into the egg mixture. Pour into four bowls and chill. Serve with small sweet biscuits.

Foam whip

IMPERIAL·METRIC	AMERICAN
4 egg whites	4 egg whites
4 tablespoons icing sugar	5 tablespoons confectioners' sugar
4 tablespoons strawberry jam	5 tablespoons strawberry jam
2 tablespoons redcurrant jelly	3 tablespoons redcurrant jelly

Put the egg whites into a bowl and whip until foamy. Gradually add the other ingredients, continuing to whip until the mixture is very thick. Spoon into four bowls and chill before serving, with cream.

Dundee creams

IMPERIAL·METRIC	AMERICAN
4 eggs	4 eggs
1 oz./25 g. castor sugar	2 tablespoons granulated sugar
6 tablespoons brandy	½ cup brandy
1 pint/6 dl. milk	2½ cups milk
1 oz./25 g. candied peel	3 tablespoons candied peel
3 tablespoons marmalade	4 tablespoons marmalade

Whip the eggs with the sugar and brandy. Warm the milk, without boiling, and stir into the egg mixture. Strain into a 1-pint (½-litre) baking dish and stir in the thinly sliced peel. Cover with foil and put the dish in a roasting tin of hot water. Bake in a moderate oven (325°F., 160°C., Gas Mark 3) for 1 hour. Leave until cold, then spread the top with marmalade and serve with thick cream.

Wine cream

IMPERIAL·METRIC	AMERICAN
3 eggs	3 eggs
1 tablespoon redcurrant jelly	1 tablespoon redcurrant jelly
6 tablespoons red wine	½ cup red wine
¼ pint/1½ dl. double cream	⅔ cup heavy cream

Separate the eggs and put the yolks into a basin with the redcurrant jelly and wine. Place the basin over a saucepan of hot water and stir until thick and creamy. Remove from the heat. Whip the cream and beat the egg whites to stiff peaks. Fold the cream into the wine mixture and then fold in the egg whites. Spoon into four bowls and chill.

Strawberry snow

IMPERIAL · METRIC	AMERICAN
4 egg whites	4 egg whites
8 oz./225 g. castor sugar	1 cup granulated sugar
¼ pint/1½ dl. double cream	⅔ cup heavy cream
8 oz./225 g. strawberries	1½ cups strawberries

Whisk the whites stiffly, sprinkle in 2 tablespoonsful sugar and whisk again. Add half the sugar in this way, then fold in the remainder. Butter the inside of a 1½–2-pint (about 1-litre) basin and coat with castor sugar. Fill with the meringue and stand the basin in a roasting tin filled to a depth of 1½ inches (3·5 cm.) with hot water. Bake in a moderate oven (350°F., 180°C., Gas Mark 4) for 1 hour. The meringue will be coloured on top, well risen and firm to the touch. Remove from the roasting tin, leave for 10 minutes, then turn the basin upside down over a serving dish. Lift off when cool. Whip the cream until thick and halve or slice the strawberries. Cover the meringue with the cream and decorate with the strawberries.

Summer kisses

IMPERIAL · METRIC	AMERICAN
3 egg whites	3 egg whites
4 oz./100 g. castor sugar	½ cup granulated sugar
4 oz./100 g. chopped mixed nuts	1 cup chopped mixed nuts
1 oz./25 g. chopped mixed peel	3 tablespoons chopped mixed peel

Put the egg whites into a bowl and whip until foamy. Put the bowl over hot water and gradually whip the sugar into the eggs to make a stiff froth. Remove from the heat and fold in the nuts and peel. Grease a baking sheet. With two teaspoons, make small egg shapes of the mixture on the sheet. Bake in a cool oven (300°F., 150°C., Gas Mark 2) for 20 minutes.

Bakewell tart

IMPERIAL · METRIC	AMERICAN
6 oz./175 g. puff pastry	6 oz. puff paste
4 tablespoons strawberry jam	5 tablespoons strawberry jam
4 oz./100 g. butter	½ cup butter
6 oz./175 g. castor sugar	¾ cup granulated sugar
5 egg yolks	5 egg yolks
few drops almond essence	few drops almond extract
3 egg whites	3 egg whites

Line a 7-inch (18-cm.) pie plate with the pastry and spread with the jam. Melt the butter and sugar together. Remove from the heat and stir in the egg yolks and almond essence. Whip the egg whites until stiff and fold them into the mixture. Put into the pastry case and bake in a hot oven (425°F., 220°C. Gas Mark 7) for 15 minutes, then reduce the heat to moderate (350°F., 180°C., Gas Mark 4) and bake for a further 25 minutes.

Lemon curd

IMPERIAL · METRIC	AMERICAN
3 oz./75 g. unsalted butter	6 tablespoons sweet butter
3 lemons	3 lemons
8 oz./225 g. granulated sugar	1 cup granulated sugar
3 eggs	3 eggs

Put the butter, finely grated rind and juice of the lemons with the sugar into a double boiler, or bowl placed over a pan of hot water. Stir occasionally until the sugar has dissolved and the butter has melted. Whisk the eggs lightly in another bowl, strain the lemon mixture into them and stir constantly over water until the mixture is like a creamy custard – this takes about 15 minutes. Pour into warmed jars and seal.

Lemon curd will keep for about 3 months in a cool place.

Lemon dream pudding

IMPERIAL · METRIC	AMERICAN
1 oz./25 g. butter	2 tablespoons butter
2 oz./50 g. sugar	¼ cup sugar
2 tablespoons plain flour	3 tablespoons all-purpose flour
juice and grated rind of 1 lemon	juice and grated rind of 1 lemon
2 eggs	2 eggs
8 fl. oz./2½ dl. milk	1 cup milk

Cream the butter and sugar and work in the flour. Add the lemon juice, rind and the lightly beaten egg yolks. Stir in the milk and finally fold in the stiffly beaten egg whites. Turn into a buttered baking dish and put this in a roasting tin of hot water. Bake in a moderate oven (350°F., 180°C., Gas Mark 4) for 30 minutes.

Orange almond cake

IMPERIAL · METRIC	AMERICAN
2 oz./50 g. fine breadcrumbs	1 cup fresh soft bread crumbs
grated rind of 1 orange	grated rind of 1 orange
juice of 3 oranges	juice of 3 oranges
4 oz./100 g. ground almonds	1 cup ground almonds
4 eggs	4 eggs
4 oz./100 g. castor sugar	½ cup granulated sugar
pinch salt	pinch salt
fine breadcrumbs or semolina	fine soft bread crumbs or semolina flour
icing sugar or whipped cream	confectioners' sugar or whipped cream

Mix the breadcrumbs, orange rind and juice and ground almonds. Beat the egg yolks, sugar and salt until creamy and add to the crumb mixture. Beat the egg whites stiffly and fold into the cake mixture. Grease a 7-inch (18-cm.) cake tin and coat it with a sprinkling of fine breadcrumbs or semolina. Put in the mixture and bake in a moderate oven (325°F., 160°C., Gas Mark 3) for 50 minutes. Allow to cool, turn out very carefully and put in a cool place to become firm. Serve dusted with sifted icing sugar, or top with whipped cream.

Chocolate cream sponge

IMPERIAL · METRIC	AMERICAN
4 eggs	4 eggs
4 oz./100 g. castor sugar	½ cup granulated sugar
2½ oz./65 g. plain flour	½ cup plus 2 tablespoons all-purpose flour
1½ oz./40 g. cocoa powder	generous ¼ cup unsweetened cocoa
3 drops vanilla essence	3 drops vanilla extract
Filling and topping	*Filling and topping*
2 oz./50 g. butter	¼ cup butter
6 oz./175 g. icing sugar	1½ cups confectioners' sugar
½ oz./15 g. cocoa powder mixed with 1 tablespoon boiling water	2 tablespoons unsweetened cocoa mixed with 1 tablespoon boiling water
1 egg yolk	1 egg yolk
3 drops vanilla essence	3 drops vanilla extract
1½ tablespoons apricot jam	2 tablespoons apricot jam
½ oz./15 g. walnuts, finely chopped	2 tablespoons finely chopped walnuts

Grease two 7-inch (18-cm.) sandwich tins, cover the bases with paper and coat the insides with an equal mixture of flour and sugar.

Separate the egg whites and whisk them stiffly. Whisk in the egg yolks one at a time. Sprinkle in the sugar 1 tablespoon at a time and whisk well. The mixture should be thick and creamy. Sift the flour and cocoa powder into the bowl, fold into the egg mixture with the vanilla essence, using a metal spoon and a cutting movement. Spread the mixture in the prepared tins and bake in a moderate oven (350°F., 180°C., Gas Mark 4) for 25 minutes – sponges should be springy to touch in the centre. Turn on to a wire rack to cool.

To make the filling, soften the butter and work in half the sugar. Mix the cooled cocoa mixture with the egg yolk and essence and beat into the butter mixture with the rest of the sugar. Continue beating until smooth. Spread one sponge with some of the butter cream and the other with jam. Sandwich the covered sides together and coat the sides and top with the remaining butter cream. Decorate with chopped walnuts.

Cheese

There are over a dozen varieties of English cheeses – Caerphilly, Cheddar, Red, White and Blue Cheshire, Derby, Lancashire, Leicester, Dorset Blue or Blue Vinny, Double Gloucester, White and Blue Stilton, White and Blue Wensleydale. A sage variety of some of the cheeses is also made.

Caerphilly Originally a Welsh cheese, but now mostly produced in Somerset and adjoining counties. Caerphilly used to be made of partially skimmed milk but today is manufactured from full cream milk. Easily recognisable by its flat shape and thin flour-dusted rind, it has always been a favourite of the Welsh miners who used to take wedge-shaped hunks of it to eat at work. Maturing quickly, within a fortnight or so after having been made, it has a mild, bland flavour and is whiter in colour than most cheeses, whilst its texture is firm and close. As with most cheeses it is at its best when freshly bought, and is often eaten in its county of origin with celery and bread and butter at teatime.

Cheddar The most famous of all cheeses. It is made in many parts of the world besides the village of Cheddar and other places in England. One of the reasons for its world-wide popularity is that being a firm-bodied cheese it travels and keeps well. English Cheddar is a creamy colour, and when ripe is smooth, and adheres to the surface of a knife. As a food it is very versatile and goes well with a sweet biscuit for a mid-morning snack, in sandwiches for lunch, or grated in an omelette for supper. It is a large cheese and in this country is normally made up to 70 lb. (32 kg.) in weight. Though in America, cheeses have been made up to 3000 lb. (1364 kg.) in weight for exhibitions, it is not a good idea for selling purposes, as beyond a certain point in size the cheese does not ripen well. A good Cheddar should be firm-bodied with a close, uniform texture and have a nutty flavour, neither too sweet nor too acid. A well made cheese should be ready to eat in 3–6 months but would keep in perfect order for considerably longer.

Cheshire Unlike Caerphilly and Cheddar, a high percentage of Cheshire cheese is made in its own county. Somebody once called it the most patriotic of English cheeses, as there are red, white and blue varieties. The red colouring is due to the addition of a pure vegetable dye during the manufacturing process. This dye is called annatto, and is extracted from the berries of a tropical plant. Whilst adding nothing to the flavour, the warm colour produced makes the cheese appear more attractive to some people. Mrs. Beeton referred to Cheshire cheese as being 'known all over Europe for its rich quality and fine piquant flavour.' It is at its best when eaten with a salad, and if sprinkled with onion salt is tasty in sandwiches.

Blue Cheshire occurs occasionally when, during the later stages of ripening, a certain type of mould finds its way into the cheese. When this happens the cheese will sell for a much higher price, and so can be a profitable accident. It has a much richer, stronger flavour than either the white or coloured types; though not suitable for cooking it is a worthy addition to any cheese board, whilst the other two varieties may be used to replace Cheddar in almost any recipe.

Derby This is another cheese popular in mining communities. Flat in shape, it is about three times the size of a Caerphilly and weighs about 30 lb. (13½ kg.). It is white in colour, mild in flavour and takes about two months to mature. As it is still fairly difficult to obtain a regular supply, Derby is not well known outside its own district, but production of it is increasing.

Sage Derby is also made in small quantities. Chopped sage is mixed with the cheese curd during the manufacturing process and imparts a distinctive, herby flavour to the cheese.

Lancashire There are three types of Lancashire cheese; the most common is eaten when quite young, and has a mild, slightly acid flavour, in keeping with the increasing demand for a mild cheese. For those whose palate demands a stronger cheese, a slower maturing variety is made which is rich and mellow. The third, and rarest, variety is sage Lancashire. Originally made only for Christmas, it is now in demand all year round.

Falling between the categories of hard-pressed and soft cheeses, Lancashire is typified by a loose and crumbly texture, a characteristic which makes it particularly suitable for cooking purposes. Modern Lancastrians refer to it as 'tastie', which is no doubt, a corruption of its ancient nickname 'Leigh toaster'.

Double Gloucester The county of Gloucester has given its name to two cheeses, Single and Double Gloucester, of which only the latter is made at present. Usually slightly coloured, when fully mature, about four months after being made, it has a full, mellow flavour. It is close and smooth in texture, somewhat akin to Cheddar. Single Gloucester is not well known outside its home county and little, if any, is made at the moment. Half the size of Double Gloucester, its appearance is quite different as it has an open texture and is soft-bodied with a mild flavour. Like Lancashire it is renowned for its toasting qualities and ripens quickly in two months.

Leicester This cheese is large and round and has a rich orange colour. Though lacking a strong flavour, it is a succulent cheese and its colour reflects a richness and warmth which makes it most appealing to the eye. This cheese should be treated carefully when stored, as its loose and flaky texture makes it liable to crack and dry out easily; this is particularly noticeable once cut.

Stilton Blue Stilton, the most difficult to make, has a tremendous market at Christmas time but it is available the rest of the year and tastes just as good. Being only a small cheese, about 14 lb. (6 kg.) in weight, it used to be the recognised Christmas gift for those who could afford it. It has never been a cheap cheese as it is expensive to make, due to the enormous amount of care that is needed to bring it to perfection, and quite rightly it has been referred to as the King of Cheeses. It first became well known in the 1800s when it was sold to coach and carriage traffic at the Bell Inn in the village of Stilton. A prime Stilton is creamy white in colour with plenty of blue veins in evidence. The texture should be open and flaky, and the body soft and slightly moist. The flavour is rich, mellow and strong. The best Stiltons are made in the late spring and summer.

White Stilton is made the year round, having a similar texture and body to the blue variety, but its flavour, though still rich, is milk-mild and finds great favour in the industrial cities of the North.

Wensleydale The recipe for Wensleydale was brought to the Yorkshire Dales by Cistercian Monks in early Norman times. When the monasteries were pillaged during the reign of Henry VIII the monks fled, but the recipe remained with the local farmers' wives, who continued to make the cheese from sheeps' milk until the 17th century when they gradually changed to cows' milk. In spite of the saying 'Apple pie without Wensleydale cheese is like a kiss without a squeeze!' it was not until the 1930s that Wensleydale cheese became well known outside its county.

White Wensleydale, which is the most common, has a velvety texture and when mature, after a month or so, is creamy enough to spread. Blue Wensleydale is difficult to obtain.

Dorset Blue or Blue Vinny This rare cheese is made from skim milk and only in Dorset; it takes many months to mature. A perfect cheese has a tough, wrinkled rind, grey in colour. When the cheese is cut, it will be found that single blue veins run through the hard creamy white body. Its strong, pungent taste is intensified by the dry, crumbly texture.

Buying and storing cheese

Buy only about a week's supply at a time. Cheese does deteriorate after it has been cut but this depends on the place and method of storage. The best way to keep cheese is to protect it from draughts and too free circulation of air. This prevents the cheese from drying out. Keep cheese wrapped in a polythene bag, aluminium foil or good quality greaseproof paper and store it in a cool place. Cheese kept in a refrigerator should be taken out at least an hour before use to regain normal temperature and its full flavour.

Cheese for cooking

There are many delicious cheese dishes and you will probably find that Cheddar or Cheshire are the best and cheapest cheeses to use for cooking. The food value of cheese is not altered by cooking, but be careful not to overcook it. It requires only slow cooking and gentle heat to melt the cheese and impart its full natural flavour to other ingredients.

Cheese scraps
Don't waste the odd pieces of cheese. Grate them finely and put into a screw-top jar and keep in the refrigerator. You can use the grated cheese to add to sauces, and to sprinkle on all sorts of dishes before grilling them to a golden brown. If you have a large quantity of grated cheese store it in 2-oz. (50-g.) bags in the freezer, or mix it with breadcrumbs and freeze ready for topping savoury dishes.

Large pieces of cheese, perhaps left over from a party, can be tightly wrapped and frozen, and will keep for two or three months. The cheese may be a little crumbly when thawed, so cut it just before it is fully thawed if you want a nice clean slice. Leftover strong cheese, including Stilton, can be potted for later use.

Potted cheese
Grate leftover cheese and pound it to a paste. Add one-third the weight of the cheese in butter, with a dash of port or dry sherry, pepper and a pinch of grated nutmeg. Cream together until well blended and press into small pots. Cover tightly and store in the refrigerator. Serve with toast or biscuits.

Ale and egg rarebit

IMPERIAL · METRIC	AMERICAN
6 oz./175 g. Cheddar cheese	1½ cups grated Cheddar cheese
1 teaspoon dry mustard	1 teaspoon dry mustard
pepper	pepper
2 tablespoons brown ale	3 tablespoons dark beer
4 poached eggs	4 poached eggs
4 slices buttered toast	4 slices buttered toast

Grate the cheese and put in a saucepan with the mustard, a good shake of pepper and the ale. Heat gently until the cheese has melted, stirring occasionally. Put the eggs on the toast, pour over the cheese mixture and brown under the grill. Serve immediately.

Country cheese soup

IMPERIAL · METRIC	AMERICAN
8 oz./225 g. cauliflower	½ lb. cauliflower
1 onion	1 onion
2 carrots	2 carrots
2 potatoes	2 potatoes
2 sticks celery	2 stalks celery
4 oz./100 g. butter	½ cup butter
1½ pints/scant litre chicken stock	3¾ cups chicken stock
salt and pepper	salt and pepper
4 lean bacon rashers	4 Canadian bacon slices
4 small slices white bread	4 small slices white bread
4 oz./100 g. Cheddar cheese	¼ lb. Cheddar cheese

Divide the cauliflower into florets and dice the remaining vegetables. Melt half the butter in a large pan and gently fry all the vegetables for 5 minutes. Add the stock, bring to the boil and simmer for 20 minutes. Season to taste. Melt remaining butter in a frying pan and gently fry the chopped bacon for 4–5 minutes. Drain well and add to the soup. Remove the crusts from the bread and fry in the pan until crisp and golden. Drain. Place the soup in an ovenproof tureen or casserole and arrange the bread to float on top. Cover the bread with sliced cheese and place under a moderate grill until the cheese melts and browns slightly. Serve immediately.

Boiled cheese

IMPERIAL · METRIC	AMERICAN
4 oz./100 g. mild cheese	¼ lb. mild cheese
1 oz./25 g. butter	2 tablespoons butter
2 tablespoons double cream	3 tablespoons whipping cream
1 egg	1 egg

Cut the cheese in thin slices and put into a saucepan with the butter and cream. Stir until the mixture comes to the boil and is smooth. Beat the egg lightly and stir it in quickly. Pour into a shallow ovenproof dish and brown under the grill. Serve with fingers of dry toast.

Old English herb cheese

IMPERIAL · METRIC	AMERICAN
1 tablespoon minced fresh herbs	1 tablespoon ground fresh herbs
4 oz./100 g. Cheddar cheese, grated	1 cup grated Cheddar cheese
3 tablespoons dry sherry	scant ¼ cup dry sherry
salt and pepper	salt and pepper
½ oz./15 g. butter	1 tablespoon butter
2 tablespoons cream	3 tablespoons cream

Use as many kinds of herbs as possible and mince them very
finely.

   Put all the ingredients into a double saucepan, or into a bowl
over a saucepan of hot water. Stir over a gentle heat until creamy
and pale green. Put into small pots and chill before using as a
spread on toast or biscuits.

Cauliflower cheese puff

IMPERIAL · METRIC	AMERICAN
1 medium cauliflower	1 medium cauliflower
2 oz./50 g. butter	¼ cup butter
2 heaped tablespoons grated Cheddar cheese	3–4 tablespoons grated Cheddar cheese
2 eggs	2 eggs
little milk	little milk
1 oz./25 g. onion, finely chopped	¼ cup chopped onion
salt and pepper	salt and pepper

Break the cauliflower into florets and cook in salted water until
just tender. Drain well. Cream the butter and work in the grated
cheese. Separate the eggs, and work in the egg yolks singly, and
then enough milk to give a soft creamy texture. Fold the
cauliflower and onion into the egg mixture and season well with
salt and pepper. Beat the egg whites until stiff and fold them into
the mixture. Put into a greased ovenproof dish and bake in a
moderately hot oven (400°F., 200°C., Gas Mark 6) for 40 minutes
until risen and golden brown. Serve at once.

Marrow cheese

IMPERIAL · METRIC	AMERICAN
1 small vegetable marrow	1 small summer squash
2 oz./50 g. butter	¼ cup butter
4 oz./100 g. fresh white breadcrumbs	2 cups fresh soft bread crumbs
salt and pepper	salt and pepper
3 oz./75 g. cheese, grated	¾ cup grated cheese

Peel the marrow and scoop out the seeds. Cut the marrow into thick rings. Grease a large, flat ovenproof dish with a little of the butter and put in a layer of breadcrumbs. Add the marrow slices, and sprinkle well with salt and pepper. Cut half the butter into flakes and put on top. Sprinkle on the grated cheese and the remaining breadcrumbs; top with the remaining butter cut in flakes. Bake in a moderate oven (350°F., 180°C., Gas Mark 4) for 45 minutes.

Cheese puff balls

IMPERIAL · METRIC	AMERICAN
1 egg	1 egg
4 oz./100 g. Cheddar cheese, finely grated	1 cup finely grated Cheddar cheese
pinch cayenne pepper	pinch cayenne pepper
½ teaspoon salt	½ teaspoon salt
fat for deep frying	oil for deep frying

Separate the egg. Mix the cheese, pepper and salt, and stir in the beaten egg yolk. Fold in the stiffly beaten egg white and shape lightly with the hands into small balls. Fry a few at a time in hot, deep fat (350°F., 180°C., approximately) to a golden brown, taking 3–4 minutes. Drain on absorbent paper and serve as a snack, or with a salad.

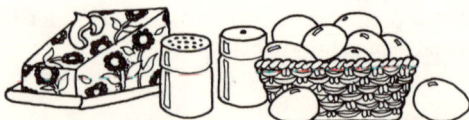

Cheese bread and butter pudding

IMPERIAL · METRIC	AMERICAN
6 thin slices bread and butter	6 thin slices bread and butter
2 eggs	2 eggs
salt and pepper	salt and pepper
¼ teaspoon made mustard	¼ teaspoon prepared mustard
½ teaspoon Worcestershire sauce	½ teaspoon Worcestershire sauce
1 pint/6 dl. milk	2½ cups milk
4 oz./100 g. cheese, grated	1 cup grated cheese
1 oz./25 g. breadcrumbs	½ cup fresh soft bread crumbs

Cut the bread and butter slices into quarters and put them in a greased pie dish. Beat the eggs with the salt, pepper, mustard and Worcestershire sauce and add the milk and three-quarters of the cheese. Pour over the bread and leave to soak for 15 minutes. Sprinkle on the rest of the cheese and sprinkle with the breadcrumbs. Bake in a moderate oven (350°F., 180°C., Gas Mark 4) for 45 minutes.

Cheese puff

IMPERIAL · METRIC	AMERICAN
6 slices day-old bread	6 slices day-old bread
12 oz./350 g. cheese, grated	3 cups grated cheese
2 eggs	2 eggs
½ pint/3 dl. milk	1¼ cups milk
½ teaspoon salt	½ teaspoon salt
dash pepper and paprika	dash pepper and paprika

Arrange the slices of bread in alternate layers with the cheese in a greased 1½-pint (scant 1-litre) baking dish. Beat the eggs lightly, add the milk and seasonings and pour over the bread. Cover and keep in the refrigerator, or a cool place for at least 30 minutes. Place in a roasting tin of hot water and bake in a moderate oven (350°F., 180°C., Gas Mark 4) until set, about 45 minutes. If thoroughly chilled before baking, the puff will rise up like a soufflé.

Cheese mould

IMPERIAL · METRIC	AMERICAN
1 pint/6 dl. milk	2½ cups milk
2 oz./50 g. butter	¼ cup butter
4 oz./100 g. fresh white breadcrumbs	2 cups fresh soft bread crumbs
2 eggs	2 eggs
4 oz./100 g. cheese, grated	1 cup grated cheese
salt and pepper	salt and pepper

Heat the milk and butter until lukewarm, pour on to the breadcrumbs and leave covered for 30 minutes. Separate the eggs and beat the yolks. Add the yolks to the breadcrumbs with the cheese, salt and pepper. Beat the egg whites until they are stiff and fold into the cheese mixture. Turn into a greased ovenproof dish and bake in a moderate oven (350°F., 180°C., Gas Mark 4) for 1 hour. Leave until cold, then turn out and serve with salad.

Cheese and apple pie

IMPERIAL · METRIC	AMERICAN
8 oz./225 g. shortcrust pastry	basic pie dough made with 2 cups all-purpose flour etc.
1 lb./450 g. cooking apples	1 lb. baking apples
1 oz./25 g. plain flour	¼ cup all-purpose flour
5 oz./150 g. sugar	⅔ cup sugar
pinch salt	pinch salt
1 teaspoon ground cinnamon	1 teaspoon ground cinnamon
½ teaspoon ground nutmeg	½ teaspoon ground nutmeg
4 oz./100 g. Cheddar cheese, diced	generous ½ cup diced Cheddar cheese
1 oz./25 g. butter	2 tablespoons butter

Roll out the pastry and line a 9-inch (23-cm.) pie plate. (Reserve the trimmings to make a lattice decoration.) Peel, core and slice the apples thinly. Mix with the flour, sugar, salt, spices and cheese. Put into the pastry case, and dot with pieces of butter. Cover with a pastry lattice and bake in a moderately hot oven (400°F., 200°C., Gas Mark 6) for 35 minutes.

Little cheese tarts

IMPERIAL · METRIC	AMERICAN
8 oz./225 g. shortcrust pastry	basic pie dough made with 2 cups all-purpose flour etc.
1 oz./25 g. butter	2 tablespoons butter
¾ oz./20 g. plain flour	3 tablespoons all-purpose flour
⅓ pint/2¼ dl. milk	generous ¾ cup milk
2 eggs	2 eggs
1 egg yolk	1 egg yolk
salt and cayenne pepper	salt and cayenne pepper
2 oz./50 g. cheese, grated	½ cup grated cheese

Line tartlet tins with the pastry. Melt the butter and work in the flour. Mix in the milk and stir over a low heat until thick and creamy. Cool and stir in the beaten eggs and egg yolk, salt and cayenne pepper and cheese. Mix thoroughly and put into the pastry cases, filling about two-thirds full. Bake in a moderately hot oven (400°F., 200°C., Gas Mark 6) for 20 minutes. Serve hot.

Cheese and ham tart

IMPERIAL · METRIC	AMERICAN
8 oz./225 g. shortcrust pastry	basic pie dough made with 2 cups all-purpose flour etc.
2 oz./50 g. soft white breadcrumbs	1 cup fresh soft bread crumbs
4 oz./100 g. cooked ham	½ cup finely chopped cooked ham
8 oz./225 g. cheese	2 cups grated cheese
3 eggs	3 eggs
½ teaspoon made mustard	½ teaspoon prepared mustard
1 carton natural yogurt	1 carton unflavored yogurt

Line an 8-inch (20-cm.) flan ring or sponge tin with the pastry. Bake blind in a moderately hot oven (400°F., 200°C., Gas Mark 6) for 15 minutes. Mix together the breadcrumbs, minced or finely chopped ham, grated cheese, lightly beaten eggs, mustard and yogurt. Pour into the pastry case and bake in a moderate oven (350°F., 180°C., Gas Mark 4) for 35 minutes, until golden. Serve hot or cold.

Cheese potato cakes

IMPERIAL · METRIC	AMERICAN
8 oz./225 g. cooked potatoes	1 cup cooked potatoes
1 oz./25 g. butter	2 tablespoons butter
2 oz./50 g. plain flour	½ cup all-purpose flour
2 oz./50 g. cheese, grated	½ cup grated cheese
1 egg	1 egg

Use Cheddar or Double Gloucester cheese in this recipe for the best results.

Mash the potatoes with the butter and work in the flour and grated cheese. Beat the egg and use to bind the mixture. Roll out ½ inch (1 cm.) thick. Bake in a moderate oven (325°F., 160°C., Gas Mark 3) for 20 minutes. Alternatively, cook the potato cakes in a greased frying pan or on a griddle, turning once. Serve hot with butter.

Queen's biscuits

IMPERIAL · METRIC	AMERICAN
4 oz./100 g. plain flour	1 cup all-purpose flour
4 oz./100 g. cheese, grated	1 cup grated cheese
4 oz./100 g. butter	½ cup butter
salt and pepper	salt and pepper

Mix the flour and cheese and rub in the butter to make a stiff paste. Season. Chill for 30 minutes. Roll out thinly and cut into shapes. Prick with a fork. Put on to a baking sheet and bake in a moderate oven (350°F., 180°C., Gas Mark 4) for 15 minutes. Cool on a wire rack and store in an airtight tin.

Cheese crisps

IMPERIAL · METRIC	AMERICAN
4 oz./100 g. puff pastry	¼ lb. puff paste
little beaten egg	little beaten egg
1 oz./25 g. salted nuts, chopped	¼ cup chopped salted nuts
1½ oz./40 g. cheese, finely grated	scant ½ cup finely grated cheese

Roll out the pastry thinly to an oblong strip about 8 inches (20 cm.) wide. Brush with beaten egg and sprinkle the mixed chopped nuts and grated cheese over half, lengthwise. Fold over the uncovered strip of pastry and press lightly together. Cut into ½-inch (1-cm.) wide strips, twist several times and place on an ungreased baking sheet. Bake in a hot oven (450°F., 230°C., Gas Mark 8) for 10–15 minutes, until golden brown. Serve hot or cold.

Cheese and walnut crisps

IMPERIAL·METRIC	AMERICAN
6 oz./175 g. plain flour	1½ cups all-purpose flour
pinch salt	pinch salt
2 oz./50 g. butter	¼ cup butter
2 oz./50 g. lard or cooking fat	¼ cup lard or shortening
cold water to mix	cold water to mix
4 oz./100 g. Cheddar cheese, grated	1 cup grated Cheddar cheese
little beaten egg	little beaten egg
2 oz./50 g. walnuts, chopped	½ cup chopped walnuts

Sieve the flour and salt into a mixing basin. Mix together the butter and lard, divide into four, and rub one quarter into the flour. Mix to a soft dough with ice cold water. Knead lightly, and roll out to an oblong strip. Flake on another quarter of fat over two-thirds of the strip and sprinkle a third of the cheese on top. Fold the strip in three putting the lower third of the strip on top of the middle third and bringing down the top third. Seal the open edges with the rolling pin and give one half turn to the right. Repeat twice with the remaining fat and cheese. Use the refrigerator as necessary to rest the pastry in between each rolling and folding. Roll and fold the pastry once more and rest it for at least 20 minutes in the refrigerator before use.

Roll out the pastry to ¼ inch (½ cm.) thickness, brush with beaten egg and sprinkle with chopped walnuts. Cut into 2½-inch (6-cm.) squares and then in half to make triangles. Place on a baking sheet and bake in a hot oven (425°F., 220°C., Gas Mark 6–7) for 15–20 minutes. Serve hot or cold.

Cheese muffins

IMPERIAL · METRIC	AMERICAN
3 tablespoons sugar	4 tablespoons sugar
½ teaspoon salt	½ teaspoon salt
1 tablespoon baking powder	1 tablespoon baking powder
12 oz./350 g. plain flour	3 cups all-purpose flour
3 oz./75 g. cheese, grated	¾ cup grated cheese
1 egg	1 egg
½ pint/3 dl. milk	1¼ cups milk
3 tablespoons melted butter	4 tablespoons melted butter

Sift together the sugar, salt, baking powder and flour and stir in the cheese. Beat the egg until thick and pale, and add the milk and melted butter. Stir the milk mixture into the flour mixture just enough to dampen the ingredients (the batter should have a rough appearance). Put into buttered tartlet tins filling about two-thirds full. Bake in a hot oven (425°F., 220°C., Gas Mark 7) for 20 minutes. Serve hot.

Cheese shortcake

IMPERIAL · METRIC	AMERICAN
6 oz./175 g. plain flour	1½ cups all-purpose flour
¼ teaspoon salt	¼ teaspoon salt
¼ teaspoon dry mustard	¼ teaspoon dry mustard
½ teaspoon celery seed	½ teaspoon celery seed
2 oz./50 g. butter	¼ cup butter
3 oz./75 g. cheese, grated	¾ cup grated cheese
1 egg	1 egg
3 tablespoons milk	4 tablespoons milk
sea salt	coarse salt

Sieve the flour with the salt and mustard and add the celery seed. Rub in the butter and add the cheese, well beaten egg and milk to make a stiff paste. Roll out ½ inch (1 cm.) thick and cut into rounds or fingers. Sprinkle lightly with sea salt and put on a greased baking sheet. Bake in a moderately hot oven (400°F., 200°C., Gas Mark 6) for 15 minutes. Serve hot or cold.

Cheese wholemeal biscuits

IMPERIAL·METRIC	AMERICAN
2 oz./50 g. wholemeal flour	$\frac{1}{2}$ cup wholewheat flour
pinch salt	pinch salt
cayenne pepper	cayenne pepper
$\frac{1}{2}$ oz./15 g. butter	1 tablespoon butter
4 oz./100 g. Cheddar cheese, finely grated	1 cup finely grated Cheddar cheese
1 tablespoon cold water	1 tablespoon cold water

Mix the flour and seasonings in a bowl and rub in the butter. Add the grated cheese and bind with cold water. Knead the dough firmly and roll out to $\frac{1}{8}$ inch ($\frac{1}{4}$ cm.) thick. Prick with a fork and cut into small, fancy shapes. Place on a lightly greased baking sheet and bake at the top of a hot oven (450°F., 230°C., Gas Mark 8) for 6–8 minutes, until golden brown.

Cheese pastry

IMPERIAL·METRIC	AMERICAN
3 oz./75 g. plain flour	$\frac{3}{4}$ cup all-purpose flour
pinch salt	pinch salt
cayenne pepper	cayenne pepper
1 oz./25 g. butter	2 tablespoons butter
2 oz./50 g. Cheddar cheese, finely grated	$\frac{1}{2}$ cup finely grated Cheddar cheese
$\frac{1}{2}$ egg yolk	$\frac{1}{2}$ egg yolk
2 teaspoons cold water	2 teaspoons cold water

Sieve the flour, salt and cayenne pepper. Rub in the butter, mix in grated Cheddar cheese and bind with beaten yolk and cold water. Knead lightly, cut into shapes and bake in a moderately hot oven (400°F., 200°C., Gas Mark 6) for 10–12 minutes.

Use as a base for all kinds of savoury snacks.

Caraway twists

IMPERIAL · METRIC	AMERICAN
1 oz./25 g. fresh yeast	1 cake compressed yeast
2 tablespoons sugar	3 tablespoons sugar
$\frac{1}{2}$ pint/3 dl. lukewarm water	1$\frac{1}{4}$ cups lukewarm water
2$\frac{1}{4}$ teaspoons salt	2$\frac{1}{4}$ teaspoons salt
1 lb./450 g. self-raising flour	4 cups all-purpose flour sifted with 4 teaspoons baking powder
2 eggs	2 eggs
8 oz./225 g. Cheddar cheese, grated	2 cups grated Cheddar cheese
$\frac{1}{2}$ oz./15 g. caraway seeds	2 tablespoons caraway seeds
6 oz./175 g. quick-cooking porridge oats	1$\frac{1}{2}$ cups quick-cooking rolled oats
melted butter	melted butter

Cream the yeast with a little of the sugar, and gradually add the remaining sugar and the water. Beat in the sifted salt and half the flour. Add the eggs, cheese and caraway seeds and continue beating. Stir in the remaining flour and the oats, beating well to make a soft dough. Turn the dough on to a lightly floured board, cover with the bowl and leave to rest for 10 minutes. Knead thoroughly to make a smooth elastic dough, using the palms of the hands and not fingers, to ensure greater pressure. Place the dough in a clean bowl, cover with a damp cloth and leave in a warm place to rise for 1$\frac{1}{2}$ hours. Knead lightly and form into strips about 9 inches (23 cm.) long by $\frac{1}{2}$ inch (1 cm.) wide and tie each strip into a knot. Place on greased baking sheets and leave to prove for about 40 minutes, until double in bulk. Brush the tops lightly with melted butter and bake in a moderately hot oven (375°F., 190°C., Gas Mark 5) for 35–40 minutes.

Yogurt, cottage cheese and soured cream

In the old days, country people made use of plenty of sour milk and cream in a wide range of recipes, not only because they hated to waste anything, but also because they enjoyed the tangy flavour. Often their baked goods in particular were actually improved by the addition of sour milk or cream. Today we have hygienically produced yogurt, cottage cheese and soured cream which are delicious in themselves, but they are also marvellous recipe ingredients.

Ideas for using yogurt
Try using natural yogurt to give added richness and a full, creamy flavour to fish, meat and vegetable dishes.

Add it to minced beef. Stir in yogurt when the dish is prepared, and allow it to heat through.

Make a delicious pan gravy for liver or kidneys. You'll probably prefer it browned and seasoned with a little Worcestershire sauce.

Baked fish is creamier and has extra flavour if cooked in yogurt. Yogurt also makes a wonderful sauce for grilled or steamed fish.

Heat up leftovers (particularly chicken and veal) in a tablespoon or two of stock and when well heated add the yogurt and warm through.

Yogurt is good with vegetables, especially young carrots, spinach, broccoli and baby turnips. Cook them in a saucepan with a little stock, or in a casserole with a little butter, and add the yogurt just before serving.

For a quick sauce, flavour yogurt with herbs – chives, parsley or rosemary for fish – capers or gherkins for a savoury touch.

For a quick potato salad, cook potatoes and allow to cool. Season well with salt and pepper. Add finely chopped onion to taste and mix with a carton of natural yogurt. Or use soured cream instead and add 2 teaspoons chopped capers.

Creamed shrimps

IMPERIAL·METRIC	AMERICAN
4 oz./100 g. shrimps	⅔ cup shrimp
2 oz./50 g. butter	¼ cup butter
salt and freshly ground pepper	salt and freshly ground pepper
1 teaspoon lemon juice	1 teaspoon lemon juice
2 egg yolks	2 egg yolks
2 tablespoons soured cream	3 tablespoons sour cream

Prawns may be used instead of shrimps, and frozen fish can be used if it is thawed first. Potted shrimps may also be substituted for the fish and butter.

Stir the shrimps into the melted butter and cook for 1 minute. Season with salt, pepper and lemon juice. Beat the egg yolks lightly with the cream and pour over the shrimps. Stir gently over a low heat until the mixture thickens, but do not let it boil. Spoon on to slices of buttered wholemeal toast.

Cottage cheese and smoked haddock

IMPERIAL·METRIC	AMERICAN
2 oz./50 g. button mushrooms	½ cup sliced mushrooms
1 oz./25 g. butter	2 tablespoons butter
3 eggs	3 eggs
¼ pint/1½ dl. milk	⅔ cup milk
3 oz./75 g. soft white breadcrumbs	1½ cups fresh soft bread crumbs
8 oz./225 g. cooked smoked haddock, flaked	1 cup cooked flaked smoked haddock
12 oz./350 g. cottage cheese	1½ cups cottage cheese
salt and freshly ground pepper	salt and freshly ground pepper

Lightly fry the sliced mushrooms in the butter, and put a few slices to one side for garnish. Beat the eggs with the milk and pour on to the breadcrumbs. Leave for 10 minutes, then add all other ingredients, mix well, season to taste and put in buttered 2-pint (1-litre) casserole dish, about 7 inches (18 cm.) in diameter and 2½ inches (6 cm.) in depth. Top with the reserved sliced mushrooms. Place in a roasting tin of warm water and bake in a moderate oven (350°F., 180°C., Gas Mark 4) for 45–50 minutes, until set. Serve hot.

Yogurt and cucumber soup

IMPERIAL · METRIC	AMERICAN
1 large cucumber	1 large cucumber
salt and freshly ground pepper	salt and freshly ground pepper
2 5-fl. oz./1½-dl. cartons natural yogurt	1¼ cups unflavored yogurt
chopped chives	chopped chives
chopped parsley	chopped parsley
¼ pint/1½ dl. milk	⅔ cup milk

Wipe the cucumber and grate it into a bowl. Sprinkle lightly with salt and set aside for a few minutes. Mix in the yogurt, chives, parsley and pepper. Check the seasoning. Add enough milk to give the preferred consistency. Chill and serve, garnished with a slice of cucumber, in glasses.

Savoury bacon tart

IMPERIAL · METRIC	AMERICAN
6 oz./175 g. shortcrust pastry	basic pie dough made with 1½ cups all-purpose flour etc.
4–6 bacon rashers	4–6 bacon slices
2 small onions	2 small onions
1 oz./25 g. butter (see method)	2 tablespoons butter (see method)
½ teaspoon mixed herbs	½ teaspoon mixed herbs
8 oz./225 g. cottage cheese	1 cup cottage cheese
1 egg	1 egg
1 teaspoon salt	1 teaspoon salt
½ teaspoon pepper	½ teaspoon pepper

Line a greased 9-inch (23-cm.) flan ring with the pastry. Bake blind in a moderately hot oven (400°F., 200°C., Gas Mark 6) for 15 minutes. Fry the bacon rashers until crisp, and cut into small pieces. Peel and slice the onions and cook gently in the bacon fat (adding the butter if necessary) until soft but not brown. Allow to cool a little and place in the pastry case with the bacon. Sprinkle with the mixed herbs. Mix together the sieved cottage cheese and beaten egg; season with the salt and pepper and pour over the bacon and onions. Bake in a moderate oven (350°F., 180°C., Gas Mark 4) for 40 minutes.

Picnic pasties

IMPERIAL · METRIC	AMERICAN
Pastry	*Pastry*
4 oz./100 g. butter	½ cup butter
8 oz./225 g. plain flour	2 cups all-purpose flour
1 teaspoon salt	1 teaspoon salt
1 egg, lightly beaten	1 egg, lightly beaten
4 oz./100 g. cottage cheese	½ cup cottage cheese
water to mix	water to mix
beaten egg to glaze	beaten egg to glaze
Filling	*Filling*
12 oz./350 g. cooked cold meat or chicken, minced	1½ cups ground cooked meat or chicken
little well seasoned white sauce	little well seasoned white sauce

Rub the butter into the flour and salt, until it is the consistency of breadcrumbs. Add the egg and cottage cheese and mix well together. Gradually add the water, mixing to a firm dough. Roll out the pastry and cut into six 6-inch (15-cm.) squares. Mix together the minced meat or chicken and sauce and spoon a little into the centre of each square. Moisten the edges and fold the pastry squares over, cornerwise, to form triangles. Seal the edges and place on a baking sheet. Prick the tops with a fork, brush lightly with beaten egg and bake in a moderately hot oven (400°F., 200°C., Gas Mark 6) for 15 minutes.

Cottage cheese and bacon pudding

IMPERIAL · METRIC	AMERICAN
½ oz./15 g. butter	1 tablespoon butter
1 onion	1 onion
6 oz./175 g. streaky bacon	9 bacon slices
2 tablespoons chopped parsley	3 tablespoons chopped parsley
2 oz./50 g. fresh white breadcrumbs	1 cup fresh soft bread crumbs
12 oz./350 g. cottage cheese	1½ cups cottage cheese
½ pint/3 dl. milk	1¼ cups milk
2 eggs	2 eggs
salt and freshly ground black pepper	salt and freshly ground black pepper

Heat the butter in a pan and cook the chopped onion and bacon gently for 3–4 minutes. Place in a basin and add the parsley, breadcrumbs and cottage cheese. Beat the milk with the egg yolks and seasoning and stir into the cheese mixture. Leave to stand for 15 minutes. Whisk the egg whites until just stiff and fold into mixture. Turn into greased 1½-pint (1-litre) ovenproof dish and cook in a hot oven (425°F., 220°C., Gas Mark 7) for 25–30 minutes, until the pudding has risen and is browned. Serve very hot.

Apple and blackberry ice cake

IMPERIAL·METRIC	AMERICAN
3 5-fl. oz./1½-dl. cartons natural yogurt	scant 2 cups unflavored yogurt
grated rind of 1 orange	grated rind of 1 orange
7 oz./200 g. slightly sweetened apple purée	scant 1 cup slightly sweetened applesauce
6 teaspoons gelatine	6 teaspoons gelatin
6 tablespoons water	½ cup water
3 egg whites	3 egg whites
3 oz./75 g. slightly sweetened blackberry pulp	scant ½ cup slightly sweetened blackberry purée
2 5-fl. oz./1½-dl. cartons whipping cream	1¼ cups whipping cream

Mix together the two cartons of yogurt, the orange rind and apple purée. Dissolve 4 teaspoons of the gelatine in 4 tablespoons of the warm water. Cool and add to the pulp mixture. Stir well. Beat two of the egg whites stiffly and fold into the apple mixture. Divide between two 6-inch (15-cm.) cake tins and freeze. Repeat this process using the blackberry pulp and the remaining third quantities of ingredients, except the cream. Pour the blackberry mixture into one 6-inch (15-cm.) cake tin and freeze. Whip the cream until stiff and sandwich the ices together with the cream to make a tiered cake. Decorate and serve immediately.

Orange blossom

IMPERIAL · METRIC	AMERICAN
2 eggs	2 eggs
2 oz./50 g. castor sugar	¼ cup granulated sugar
grated rind and juice of 1 orange	grated rind and juice of 1 orange
8 oz./225 g. cottage cheese	1 cup cottage cheese
¼ pint/1½ dl. double cream	⅔ cup heavy cream

Separate the eggs. Blend the egg yolks, sugar, rind and juice in a bowl over a pan of simmering water. Stir until the mixture just coats the spoon. Remove from the heat and cool. Blend the sieved cottage cheese, whipped cream and cooled egg yolk mixture. Lastly, fold in whisked egg whites. Pour into small glasses. Chill and decorate each one with cream and a curl of orange rind.

As easy variations, sprinkle the tops with tiny ratafia biscuits, or pile the mixture into a crisp, baked pastry case and sprinkle with browned almonds.

Yogurt scones

IMPERIAL · METRIC	AMERICAN
8 oz./225 g. plain flour	2 cups all-purpose flour
½ teaspoon salt	½ teaspoon salt
1½ teaspoons baking powder	1½ teaspoons baking powder
1 oz./25 g. butter	2 tablespoons butter
5-fl. oz./1½-dl. carton natural yogurt	⅔ cup unflavored yogurt

Sift together the flour, salt and baking powder. Rub in the butter and stir in the yogurt to make a soft dough. Knead lightly until smooth. Roll out ½ inch (1 cm.) thick and cut into 2¼-inch (5·5-cm.) rounds. Put on a greased baking sheet and bake in a moderately hot oven (400°F., 200°C., Gas Mark 6) for 12 minutes.

These scones are excellent sandwiched together with home-made jam and whipped cream.

Wholemeal flour can be used for the scones. They are very good split and spread with butter to serve with salads.

Raspberry fool

IMPERIAL · METRIC	AMERICAN
1½ lb./¾ kg. raspberries	5 cups raspberries
sugar (optional)	sugar (optional)
½ pint/3 dl. double cream	1¼ cups heavy cream
5-fl. oz./1½-dl. carton natural yogurt	⅔ cup unflavored yogurt
rind of 1 orange	rind of 1 orange

Put a few raspberries aside for decoration and sieve the rest. Sweeten with sugar if necessary. Whip half the cream until just stiff and beat in the yogurt. Fold the raspberry pulp and grated orange rind into the cream and yogurt mixture. Put into a bowl and chill. Whip the remaining cream and use to decorate the top. Decorate with the reserved raspberries.

Walnut teabread

IMPERIAL · METRIC	AMERICAN
8 oz./225 g. cottage cheese	1 cup cottage cheese
6 oz./175 g. soft brown sugar	¾ cup brown sugar
3 eggs	3 eggs
2 oz./50 g. walnuts, chopped	½ cup chopped walnuts
grated rind of 2 oranges	grated rind of 2 oranges
8 oz./225 g. self-raising flour	2 cups all-purpose flour sifted with 2 teaspoons baking powder
1 teaspoon baking powder	1 teaspoon baking powder

Sieve the cottage cheese, then cream the cheese and sugar together. Beat in the eggs and stir in the walnuts and orange rind. Sift together the flour and baking powder and fold into the mixture. Line a 2-lb. (1-kg.) loaf tin with greaseproof paper and brush with oil. Put in the mixture and bake in a moderate oven (350°F., 180°C., Gas Mark 4) for 45 minutes. Leave in the tin for 5 minutes, then turn out and cool on a wire rack. Serve sliced with butter.

This teabread is particularly good served with marmalade or honey.

Gingerbread

IMPERIAL · METRIC	AMERICAN
4 oz./100 g. butter	½ cup butter
2 oz./50 g. soft brown sugar	¼ cup brown sugar
2 oz./50 g. black treacle	3 tablespoons molasses
6 oz./175 g. golden syrup	½ cup maple or corn syrup
5-fl. oz./1½-dl. carton natural yogurt	⅔ cup unflavored yogurt
2 eggs	2 eggs
8 oz./225 g. plain flour	2 cups all-purpose flour
1 teaspoon mixed spice	1 teaspoon mixed spice
3 teaspoons ground ginger	3 teaspoons ground ginger
½ teaspoon bicarbonate of soda	½ teaspoon baking soda

Warm the butter, sugar, treacle and syrup together gently, until
the butter has melted and the sugar has dissolved. Cool and then
stir in the yogurt and beaten eggs. Sift the flour, spice, ginger
and soda into a bowl. Add the liquid mixture and blend well.
Pour into a greased and lined 7-inch (18-cm.) square tin and
bake in a cool oven (300°F., 150°C., Gas Mark 2) for 1½ hours.
Leave in an airtight tin for at least 24 hours before serving.

If liked, 3 oz. (75 g., ⅓ cup) chopped preserved ginger and a
few chopped almonds may be added to the mixture.

Sauces

Herb sauce for vegetables

IMPERIAL · METRIC	AMERICAN
1 teaspoon chopped fresh parsley	1 teaspoon chopped fresh parsley
1 teaspoon chopped fresh chives	1 teaspoon chopped fresh chives
½ teaspoon chopped fresh thyme	½ teaspoon chopped fresh thyme
salt and pepper	salt and pepper
5-fl. oz./1½-dl. carton soured cream	⅔ cup sour cream

Stir the herbs and seasoning into the soured cream and heat very
gently until warm. Serve over new potatoes, broccoli, cauliflower,
carrots or broad beans.

Cucumber sauce for fish

IMPERIAL · METRIC	AMERICAN
½ small cucumber	½ small cucumber
5-fl. oz./1½-dl. carton soured cream	⅔ cup sour cream
salt and black pepper	salt and black pepper
1 teaspoon lemon juice	1 teaspoon lemon juice
1 teaspoon finely grated onion	1 teaspoon finely grated onion
1 teaspoon chopped fresh fennel or dill	1 teaspoon chopped fresh fennel or dill

Peel the cucumber, remove the seeds and cut the flesh into very small dice. Fold into the soured cream and season with salt and pepper, lemon juice, onion and herbs.

This is very good with cold salmon and mackerel.

Egg sauce for chicken

IMPERIAL · METRIC	AMERICAN
5-fl. oz./1½-dl. carton soured cream	⅔ cup sour cream
1 egg yolk	1 egg yolk
salt and pepper	salt and pepper
½ teaspoon made mustard	½ teaspoon prepared mustard

Warm the soured cream very gently with the beaten egg yolk, salt and pepper, and mustard. Serve with fried or grilled chicken, or with veal.

Caper sauce

IMPERIAL · METRIC	AMERICAN
1 tablespoon lemon juice	1 tablespoon lemon juice
¼ pint/1½ dl. natural yogurt	⅔ cup unflavored yogurt
salt and pepper	salt and pepper
2 teaspoons finely chopped capers	2 teaspoons finely chopped capers

Blend together the lemon juice and yogurt. Add the seasonings to taste. Mix in the chopped capers.

This sauce is delicious with chicken and cold lamb.

Lemon sauce for chicken

IMPERIAL · METRIC	AMERICAN
½ pint/3 dl. soured cream	1¼ cups sour cream
¼ pint/1½ dl. strong chicken stock	⅔ cup strong chicken stock
2 teaspoons lemon juice	2 teaspoons lemon juice
4 egg yolks	4 egg yolks
salt and pepper	salt and pepper
2 tablespoons dry sherry	3 tablespoons dry sherry

This sauce is particularly good with boiled chicken. The stock from the chicken should be reduced until it is really concentrated before using for the sauce.

Mix the soured cream, stock, lemon juice and beaten egg yolks. Heat very gently (a double saucepan is best) and do not allow to boil. Season with salt and pepper. When the sauce is thick and creamy, add the sherry. Cut the chicken into neat pieces and pour over the sauce.

Mustard dressing

IMPERIAL · METRIC	AMERICAN
1 tablespoon flour	1 tablespoon all-purpose flour
1 tablespoon castor sugar	1 tablespoon granulated sugar
1 teaspoon dry mustard	1 teaspoon dry mustard
pinch garlic salt	pinch garlic salt
6 tablespoons cold water	½ cup cold water
2 tablespoons wine vinegar	3 tablespoons wine vinegar
1 egg, lightly beaten	1 egg, lightly beaten
2 tablespoons olive or salad oil	3 tablespoons olive or salad oil
1 tablespoon soured cream	1 tablespoon sour cream

Mix together the flour, sugar, mustard and garlic salt, and blend together smoothly with the water. Cook over a low heat until the mixture thickens. Simmer for a further minute, stirring all the time. Remove from the heat and gradually add the vinegar and lightly beaten egg. Continue beating, and gradually add the oil. Allow to cool and lightly fold in the sour cream.

This dressing is good with potato or cabbage salads.

Yogurt salad dressing 1

IMPERIAL · METRIC	AMERICAN
juice of ½ lemon	juice of ½ lemon
¼ pint/1½ dl. natural yogurt	⅔ cup unflavored yogurt
salt and pepper	salt and pepper
1 tablespoon finely chopped parsley	1 tablespoon finely chopped parsley

Blend together the lemon juice and yogurt. Add seasoning to taste and sprinkle in the chopped parsley. Serve on salads.

Yogurt salad dressing 2

IMPERIAL · METRIC	AMERICAN
3 tablespoons natural yogurt	4 tablespoons unflavored yogurt
1½ tablespoons salad oil	2 tablespoons salad oil
¼ teaspoon salt	¼ teaspoon salt
pepper	pepper
2 teaspoons chopped chives	2 teaspoons chopped chives
2 tablespoons finely chopped parsley	3 tablespoons finely chopped parsley

Blend together the yogurt and salad oil. Add the salt and pepper and sprinkle in the chopped chives and parsley. Serve on salads.

Sweet yogurt dressing

IMPERIAL · METRIC	AMERICAN
2 tablespoons honey	3 tablespoon honey
1 teaspoon lemon juice	1 teaspoon lemon juice
½ pint/3 dl. natural yogurt	1¼ cups unflavored yogurt
1 teaspoon finely grated lemon rind	1 teaspoon finely grated lemon rind
1 tablespoon pineapple juice	1 tablespoon pineapple juice

Mix together the honey and lemon juice until completely blended. Beat the yogurt lightly and gradually add the honey, lemon juice and remaining ingredients. Chill before serving on fruit salads.

Cheesecakes

Tavistock cheesecake

IMPERIAL·METRIC	AMERICAN
6 oz./175 g. digestive biscuits	2¼ cups graham cracker crumbs
2 oz./50 g. dry white breadcrumbs	½ cup dry white bread crumbs
4 oz./100 g. butter	½ cup butter
1 lb. 2 oz./500 g. cream cheese	2¼ cups cream cheese
2 oz./50 g. sugar	¼ cup sugar
3 eggs	3 eggs
¼ teaspoon vanilla essence	¼ teaspoon vanilla extract
3 tablespoons lemon curd (see page 72)	4 tablespoons lemon curd (see page 72)
2 teaspoons lemon juice	2 teaspoons lemon juice

Crush the biscuits and mix with the breadcrumbs. Melt the butter and stir in the crumbs. Press into a 9-inch (23-cm.) buttered sponge tin. Beat the cream cheese, sugar, eggs and vanilla essence together until light and creamy. Pour into the biscuit crust and bake in a moderate oven (325°F., 160°C., Gas Mark 3) for 40 minutes. Cool the cheesecake. Mix the lemon curd and lemon juice and pour onto the centre of the cheesecake. Serve with thick cream.

Almond cheesecake

IMPERIAL·METRIC	AMERICAN
2 oz./50 g. butter	¼ cup butter
2 oz./50 g. sugar	¼ cup sugar
grated rind of 1 lemon	grated rind of 1 lemon
3 egg yolks	3 egg yolks
1 lb./450 g. cottage cheese	2 cups cottage cheese
2 oz./50 g. ground almonds	½ cup ground almonds
1 oz./25 g. sultanas	3 tablespoons seedless white raisins
2 oz./50 g. soft breadcrumbs	1 cup fresh soft bread crumbs
pinch salt	pinch salt

Cream the butter, sugar and lemon rind. Work in the egg yolks.
Sieve the cottage cheese and add to the butter mixture with
the remaining ingredients. Put into a buttered 8-inch (20-cm.)
tin and bake in a moderately hot oven (400°F., 200°C., Gas
Mark 6) for 40 minutes. Leave to cool in the oven. Sprinkle with
a little castor sugar before serving.

Summer fruit cheesecake

IMPERIAL·METRIC	AMERICAN
3 eggs	3 eggs
4 oz./100 g. castor sugar	$\frac{1}{2}$ cup granulated sugar
juice and grated rind of 1 lemon	juice and grated rind of 1 lemon
$\frac{1}{4}$ pint/1$\frac{1}{2}$ dl. soured cream	$\frac{2}{3}$ cup sour cream
12 oz./350 g. cottage cheese	1$\frac{1}{2}$ cups cottage cheese
$\frac{1}{2}$ oz./15 g. gelatine	2 envelopes gelatin
2 tablespoons water	3 tablespoons water
3 oz./75 g. butter	6 tablespoons butter
6 oz./175 g. digestive biscuits	2$\frac{1}{4}$ cups graham cracker crumbs
1 oz./25 g. soft brown sugar	2 tablespoons brown sugar
8 oz./225 g. strawberries or raspberries	about 2 cups strawberries or raspberries

Whisk together the egg yolks and sugar in a basin placed over a
pan of hot water, until thick and creamy. Remove from the heat
and stir in the lemon juice and rind, soured cream, sieved cottage
cheese and gelatine dissolved in the water. Whisk the egg whites
until just stiff and fold into mixture. Turn into an 8-inch (20-cm.)
greased cake tin. Leave in a refrigerator or cool place to set.
Melt the butter in a pan, remove from the heat and stir in the
crushed biscuits and brown sugar. Mix well and sprinkle evenly
over the set cheesecake, pressing down lightly. Return the
cheesecake to the refrigerator until firm. Invert the cheesecake
on to a serving plate and decorate the top with fresh strawberries
or raspberries.

Taunton strawberry cheesecake

IMPERIAL · METRIC	AMERICAN
8 digestive biscuits	1 cup graham cracker crumbs
1½ oz./40 g. granulated sugar	3 tablespoons granulated sugar
2 oz./50 g. butter	¼ cup butter
Filling	*Filling*
½ oz./15 g. gelatine	2 envelopes gelatin
¼ pint/1½ dl. cider	⅔ cup cider
¼ pint/1½ dl. double cream	⅔ cup whipping cream
¼ pint/1½ dl. single cream	⅔ cup half-and-half
8 oz./225 g. cottage cheese	1 cup cottage cheese
1 tablespoon clear honey	1 tablespoon clear honey
4 oz./100 g. strawberries	about 1 cup strawberries
Topping	*Topping*
8 oz./225 g. strawberries	about 2 cups strawberries
castor sugar to taste (optional)	granulated sugar to taste (optional)
¼ pint/1½ dl. cider	⅔ cup cider
1½ teaspoons arrowroot	1½ teaspoons arrowroot flour

Mix together the crushed biscuits and sugar. Add the melted butter and mix well. Turn into a 7-inch (18-cm.) loose-bottomed cake tin and press down well. Leave in a cool place while preparing the filling.

Dissolve the gelatine in 3 tablespoonsful of the cider, in a basin over a pan of hot water. When the gelatine has melted, gradually stir in the remaining cider, and allow to cool, but not set. Mix together the double and single creams, and whisk until fairly thick but not stiff. Add the sieved cottage cheese, honey and chopped strawberries. Gradually stir in cider mixture, mixing well between each addition. Pour the mixture into the prepared tin and leave until set.

Meanwhile, prepare the topping. Place the halved strawberries in a bowl, sprinkle with castor sugar, if liked, and add the cider. Cover and leave for about 2 hours. When the cheesecake has set, loosen by running a warm knife around the inside of the tin, then remove the cheesecake from the tin. Place on a serving plate. Drain the strawberries well, reserving the cider. Arrange the strawberries on top of the cheesecake. Blend the arrowroot with 2 tablespoons of the cider, and heat

the remaining cider in a saucepan. Pour the cider on to the
blended arrowroot, stirring well. Return to the saucepan, bring
to the boil, stirring, and cook for 1 minute. Allow to cool
slightly, then carefully spoon over the strawberries. Leave in a
cool place for the glaze to set.

Chilled lemon cheesecake

IMPERIAL · METRIC	AMERICAN
2 eggs	2 eggs
pinch salt	pinch salt
3 oz./75 g. sugar	6 tablespoons sugar
3 tablespoons orange juice	scant ¼ cup orange juice
3 tablespoons lemon juice	scant ¼ cup lemon juice
1 tablespoon gelatine softened in 2 tablespoons cold water	1 tablespoon gelatin softened in 3 tablespoons cold water
12 oz./350 g. cottage cheese	1½ cups cottage cheese
¼ pint/1½ dl. double cream	⅔ cup whipping cream
1 teaspoon butter	1 teaspoon butter
4 tablespoons finely crushed digestive biscuit crumbs	5 tablespoons finely crushed graham cracker crumbs

Beat the egg yolks, salt and 2 oz. (50 g., ¼ cup) of the sugar.
Stir in the fruit juices. Stir over boiling water until the mixture
begins to thicken and just coats the spoon. Add the softened
gelatine and stir until dissolved. Cool and stir in the sieved
cottage cheese. Blend in the whipped cream. Whisk the egg
whites with the remaining sugar and fold into the mixture.
Butter an 8-inch (20-cm.) sandwich tin and sprinkle liberally
with the crumbs. Pour in the cottage cheese mixture and chill
until firm. Turn out to serve. If liked, more crumbs can be
sprinkled over the cake before serving. It can also be topped with
sliced strawberries or crushed raspberries or other fruit.

Baked country cheesecake

IMPERIAL · METRIC	AMERICAN
6 oz./175 g. shortcrust pastry	basic pie dough made with 1½ cups all-purpose flour etc.
1¼ lb./550 g. cottage cheese	2½ cups cottage cheese
5 oz./150 g. castor sugar	⅔ cup granulated sugar
2 oz./50 g. plain flour	½ cup all-purpose flour
3 eggs	3 eggs
1 oz./25 g. butter	2 tablespoons butter
grated rind of 1 lemon	grated rind of 1 lemon
1 teaspoon icing sugar	1 teaspoon confectioners' sugar

Roll out the pastry and use to line a 7-inch (18-cm.) square, shallow cake tin. Cream together the sieved cottage cheese and sugar. Add the flour, beaten eggs, melted butter and grated lemon rind. Mix thoroughly, pour into the pastry case and bake in the oven (375°F., 190°C., Gas Mark 5) for about 1 hour, until firm to the touch. Sift top with icing sugar.

Chocolate cheesecake

IMPERIAL · METRIC	AMERICAN
4 eggs	4 eggs
1 lb./450 g. cottage cheese	2 cups cottage cheese
6 oz./175 g. castor sugar	¾ cup granulated sugar
½ pint/3 dl. soured cream	1¼ cups sour cream
2 tablespoons cocoa powder	3 tablespoons unsweetened cocoa
2 tablespoons strong black coffee	3 tablespoons strong black coffee
3 oz./75 g. cornflour	¾ cup cornstarch
1 oz./25 g. blanched almonds	¼ cup chopped blanched almonds
6 oz./175 g. shortcrust pastry	basic pie dough made with 1½ cups all-purpose flour etc.

Beat the eggs. Rub the cottage cheese through a sieve and stir in the sugar, cream, cocoa powder, coffee, cornflour and chopped almonds. Beat all together until smooth and well blended. Line bottom of an 8-inch (20-cm.) cake tin with pastry. Grease the sides of tin and sprinkle lightly with flour. Spoon in the cheesecake mixture and bake in a moderate oven (350°F., 180°C., Gas Mark 4) for 1½ hours. Turn out, serve with whipped cream.

Milk and cream

Few of us can do without a regular supply of milk, particularly for making puddings and nourishing drinks. Soups are improved with milk, and dozens of savoury recipes need the addition of milk-based sauces.

Untreated, pasteurised and *homogenised* milks can be used for all these, and so can *ultra-heat-treated* (long-keeping) milk, so it is worth keeping one or two extra pints in hand. *Sterilised* milk is rich and creamy, but has a slight caramel flavour, so its use is more limited. *Channel Islands* milk has a rich taste and high cream content, and should be used when creamy milk is particularly required for a recipe.

Cream also has many variations and the correct cream should be chosen for a recipe. *Single* cream is for pouring on to cereals, fruit and puddings, but it is also delicious in sauces and can be used for cooked dishes which do not require whipped cream. *Whipping* cream is ideal for piping and decorating and for cake and pastry fillings, and is lower in butterfat content than double cream. *Double* cream can be used for whipping and will float on coffee or soup. If a double cream is described as *thick*, it will not whip but is spoonable. *Extended life double cream* will whip lightly and is spoonable, and is useful for keeping up to 3 weeks under refrigeration. *Sterilised* creams are not suitable for savoury dishes. *Ultra-heat-treated* cream is single cream with a long storage life, which is suitable for pouring. *Clotted* cream is for spooning and spreading and is good with puddings, scones, cakes and fruit.

Cream should always be kept cool, clean and covered, and away from bright light and strong sunshine. Strongly-flavoured foods may taint cream if stored nearby. In order to whip cream, the bowl, whisk and cream should be really cold. Whip the cream quickly at first until the cream becomes matt, and then continue slowly until it stands in smooth peaks. When cream is over-whipped, it becomes butter; lightly whipped cream is easier to fold into other ingredients.

Soups

Cheese soup

IMPERIAL · METRIC	AMERICAN
1 small onion	1 small onion
1 stick celery	1 stalk celery
½ oz./15 g. butter	1 tablespoon butter
salt and pepper	salt and pepper
1 pint/6 dl. milk	2½ cups milk
¾ pint/4 dl. stock or water	scant 2 cups stock or water
½ oz./15 g. cornflour	2 tablespoons cornstarch
2 tablespoons water	3 tablespoons water
2 oz./50 g. cheese, grated	½ cup grated cheese

Chop the onion and celery finely. Melt the butter in a
saucepan and toss the onion and celery in this until all the fat
is absorbed. (Do not allow the vegetables to be fried or to brown.)
Add the seasoning, milk and stock. Simmer gently for about 30
minutes. Mix the cornflour to a smooth paste with 2 tablespoons
of water, slowly stir this into the mixture. Bring to the boil
and continue to cook for 5 minutes. Add the grated cheese and
simmer for a few minutes until it has melted.

Lancashire cheese is particularly good for this soup.

Lentil cream soup

IMPERIAL · METRIC	AMERICAN
4 oz./100 g. lentils, soaked	½ cup lentils, soaked
4 oz./100 g. carrots	¼ lb. carrots
4 oz./100 g. onions	¼ lb. onions
1 stick celery	1 stalk celery
small piece turnip	small piece turnip
1 oz./25 g. butter	2 tablespoons butter
1 pint/6 dl. stock	2½ cups stock
1 pint/6 dl. milk	2½ cups milk
salt and pepper	salt and pepper
¼ pint/1½ dl. double cream	⅔ cup whipping cream
chopped parsley	chopped parsley

Wash the lentils, prepare and slice the vegetables. Melt the
butter in a saucepan, add the vegetables and cook for
approximately 10 minutes, stirring to prevent them sticking.
Add the stock, milk and seasoning and bring to the boil.
Simmer gently until the vegetables are cooked. Sieve, return
the soup to the saucepan and add the cream. Reheat slowly.
Chopped parsley should be sprinkled on the top when the soup is
served.

If a thinner soup is preferred, add extra milk when adding the
cream.

Simple soup

This recipe can be varied by using different kinds of stock
instead of water, or different vegetables.

IMPERIAL · METRIC	AMERICAN
8 oz./225 g. potatoes	½ lb. potatoes
8 oz./225 g. carrots	½ lb. carrots
8 oz./225 g. onions	½ lb. onions
8 oz./225 g. turnips	½ lb. turnips
1 parsnip	1 parsnip
1 swede	1 swede
2 oz./50 g. butter	¼ cup butter
1½ pints/scant litre water	3¾ cups water
1 oz./25 g. flour	¼ cup all-purpose flour
1 pint/6 dl. milk	2½ cups milk
salt and pepper	salt and pepper
chopped parsley	chopped parsley

Prepare the vegetables and cut them into small pieces. Melt the
butter in a large saucepan, add the vegetables, cook and stir for a
few minutes. Add nearly all the water and a little seasoning.
Bring to the boil and simmer until the vegetables are tender.
Blend the flour with the remaining water and add to the
vegetables. Cook for a few minutes. Put through a fine sieve and
return to the saucepan. Stir in the milk and adjust the seasoning
to taste. Bring to the boil. Serve hot, sprinkled with chopped
parsley.

Farmhouse broth

IMPERIAL·METRIC	AMERICAN
8 oz./225 g. mixed root vegetables	½ lb. mixed root vegetables
2 sticks celery	2 stalks celery
¾ pint/4 dl. water or stock	scant 2 cups water or stock
pinch salt	pinch salt
1 oz./25 g. plain flour	¼ cup all-purpose flour
1 pint/6 dl. milk	2½ cups milk
3 oz./75 g. Cheddar cheese, grated	¾ cup grated Cheddar cheese
1 oz./25 g. butter	2 tablespoons butter
chopped parsley	chopped parsley

Grate the root vegetables, or cut in small dice. Chop the celery sticks. Put into the water or stock with the salt and simmer for 15 minutes. Mix the flour to a smooth paste with a little of the milk and then work in the remaining milk. Add to the vegetables, bring to the boil and simmer for 5 minutes. Remove from the heat and stir in half the grated cheese and the butter. Adjust the seasoning to taste. Pour into a warm bowl and sprinkle on the remaining cheese and a little chopped parsley.

Hot and cold puddings

Milk jelly

IMPERIAL·METRIC	AMERICAN
2 oz./50 g. castor sugar	¼ cup granulated sugar
grated rind of 1 lemon	grated rind of 1 lemon
1 pint/6 dl. milk	2½ cups milk
¾ oz./20 g. gelatine	3 envelopes gelatin
2 tablespoons hot water	3 tablespoons hot water

Add the sugar and lemon rind to the milk and allow to infuse for 10 minutes over a gentle heat. Dissolve the gelatine in 2 tablespoons of hot water. Add the cooled milk. Strain into a wetted mould and leave to set.

Honeycomb mould

IMPERIAL · METRIC	AMERICAN
2 eggs	2 eggs
1½ oz./40 g. castor sugar	3 tablespoons granulated sugar
1 pint/6 dl. milk	2½ cups milk
vanilla essence	vanilla extract
½ oz./15 g. gelatine	2 envelopes gelatin
2 tablespoons hot water	3 tablespoons hot water

Separate the yolks and whites of the eggs. Beat the yolks and sugar together, then add the milk. Strain into a saucepan (a double saucepan is best) and stir over a gentle heat until the mixture thickens, but do not allow to boil. Flavour with vanilla essence. Dissolve the gelatine in 2 tablespoons of hot water and add to the egg custard. Cool slightly, then fold in the stiffly whisked egg whites. Pour into a rinsed mould and turn out when set. Serve plain, or with fruit and cream.

Velvet cream

IMPERIAL · METRIC	AMERICAN
cold custard made with ½ pint/ 3 dl. milk etc.	1¼ cups cold custard pie filling
¼ pint/1½ dl. double cream	⅔ cup whipping cream
¼ oz./10 g. gelatine	1 envelope gelatin
2 tablespoons water	3 tablespoons water

For this recipe the custard should be creamy.

Blend the custard with most of the cream, leaving the remainder for decoration. Dissolve the gelatine in warm water and strain it into the custard mixture. Stir lightly until the mixture begins to set, then pour into a rinsed mould. When set, turn out and decorate with the reserved cream, whipped.

Lemon solid

IMPERIAL · METRIC	AMERICAN
1 oz./25 g. gelatine	4 envelopes gelatin
1½ pints/scant litre milk	3¾ cups milk
½ pint/3 dl. single cream	1¼ cups half-and-half
5 oz./150 g. granulated sugar	⅔ cup granulated sugar
2 lemons	2 lemons

Put the gelatine to soak in 1 pint (6 dl., 2½ cups) of the milk. Put the remaining milk and cream mixed, in a pan with the sugar. Heat until the sugar has melted, then bring to near boiling point. Add the grated rind of the lemons. Pour in the milk and gelatine mixture and slowly stir in the juice of the lemons. The mixture will slightly curdle. Pour into a rinsed mould; when set, turn out.

Scots cream-crowdie

IMPERIAL · METRIC	AMERICAN
2 oz./50 g. coarse oatmeal	⅓ cup oatmeal flour
1 pint/6 dl. double cream	2½ cups heavy cream
2 oz./50 g. castor sugar	¼ cup granulated sugar
1 tablespoon rum	1 tablespoon rum
4 oz./100 g. fresh raspberries or blackberries	about 1 cup raspberries or blackberries

Toss the oatmeal in a thick-bottomed saucepan over the heat until crisp. Beat the cream to a thick froth and stir in the oatmeal, sugar, rum and fruit. Serve at once.

Norfolk syllabub

IMPERIAL · METRIC	AMERICAN
4 fl. oz./1 dl. white wine	½ cup white wine
1 tablespoon sherry	1 tablespoon sherry
2 tablespoons brandy	3 tablespoons brandy
1 lemon	1 lemon
2 oz./50 g. castor sugar	¼ cup granulated sugar
½ pint/3 dl. double cream	1¼ cups heavy cream

Put the wine, sherry and brandy into a basin. Peel the lemon very thinly and squeeze out the juice. Put the peel and juice into the wine mixture. Leave overnight, then remove the peel. Stir in the sugar until it dissolves. Add the cream and whip until the mixture forms soft peaks. Put into tall glasses.

This syllabub will hold its shape for up to 12 hours.

Cider syllabub

IMPERIAL·METRIC	AMERICAN
½ pint/3 dl. double cream	1¼ cups heavy cream
grated rind and juice of 1 lemon	grated rind and juice of 1 lemon
3 oz./75 g. castor sugar	6 tablespoons granulated sugar
3 tablespoons cider	scant ¼ cup cider

Whip the cream until thick. Add the rind and juice of the lemon, the sugar and the cider, folding it in gently. Spoon into glasses and leave in a cool place until serving time. Serve with small sweet biscuits.

Baked coffee custard

IMPERIAL·METRIC	AMERICAN
little castor sugar	little granulated sugar
4 eggs	4 eggs
3 oz./75 g. sugar	6 tablespoons sugar
¾ pint/4 dl. milk	scant 2 cups milk
2 tablespoons coffee essence	3 tablespoons strong black coffee

Lightly grease a 7-inch (18-cm.) straight-sided ovenware dish and sprinkle the inside completely with castor sugar. Whisk the eggs and sugar together. Warm the milk, then gradually beat into the eggs and stir in the coffee essence. Strain the mixture into the prepared dish. Place in a roasting tin containing some water and bake in a moderate oven (350°F., 180°C., Gas Mark 4) for 50 minutes, until just set. Remove from the oven and roasting tin and serve hot. Alternatively, leave to cool and decorate with whipped double cream.

Junket

IMPERIAL · METRIC	AMERICAN
1 pint/6 dl. creamy milk	2½ cups milk
2 teaspoons sugar	2 teaspoons sugar
2 tablespoons rum or brandy	3 tablespoons rum or brandy
1 teaspoon rennet	1 teaspoon essence of rennet
nutmeg	nutmeg

Heat the milk gently to blood heat. Mix the sugar and rum or brandy in a shallow serving dish. Pour the warm milk into the bowl and gently stir in the rennet. Leave undisturbed until set. The junket must not be put in a cold place. Grate on a little nutmeg before serving.

Clotted cream is the perfect accompaniment to junket.

Brown bread cream

IMPERIAL · METRIC	AMERICAN
¾ pint/4 dl. milk	scant 2 cups milk
3 egg yolks	3 egg yolks
1 tablespoon sugar	1 tablespoon sugar
1 tablespoon gelatine	1 tablespoon gelatin
3 tablespoons water	scant ¼ cup water
3 tablespoons fresh brown breadcrumbs	4 tablespoons fresh soft wholewheat bread crumbs
grated rind of ½ lemon	grated rind of ½ lemon
3 tablespoons whipped cream	4 tablespoons whipped cream

Heat the milk, but do not boil. Cream the egg yolks and sugar together. Dissolve the gelatine in the water. Spread the crumbs on a baking sheet and put in a moderate oven (325°F., 160°C., Gas Mark 3) until crisp and lightly coloured. Pour the milk on to the egg mixture and heat gently until the mixture coats the back of a spoon. Remove from the heat, stir in the gelatine, and continue stirring until the gelatine has melted. Strain into a bowl and leave to cool. Stir in the lemon rind, breadcrumbs and cream just before the mixture is completely cold.

This sweet is very good served with a lightly sweetened fruit purée (strawberry, raspberry, blackcurrant are all good flavours) and some extra whipped cream.

Granny's milk pudding

IMPERIAL·METRIC	AMERICAN
1 pint/6 dl. milk	2½ cups milk
2 oz./50 g. semolina	⅓ cup semolina flour
1 oz./25 g. castor sugar	2 tablespoons granulated sugar
4 tablespoons bramble jelly	5 tablespoons blackberry jelly
¼ pint/1½ dl. double cream	⅔ cup whipping cream

Warm the milk to blood heat and sprinkle in the semolina.
Stir over the heat until thick. Remove from the heat, stir in the
sugar and pour into a bowl. Leave until set. Gently warm the
jelly and pour over the top. Leave until cold and then cover
with whipped cream.

Raspberry fluff

IMPERIAL·METRIC	AMERICAN
3 large eggs	3 large eggs
3 oz./75 g. castor sugar	6 tablespoons granulated sugar
½ pint/3 dl. thick raspberry purée	1¼ cups thick raspberry purée
½ oz./15 g. gelatine	2 envelopes gelatin
3 tablespoons water	scant ¼ cup water
¼ pint/1½ dl. double cream	⅔ cup whipping cream

Prepare a 1¼-pint (¾-litre) straight-sided dish by placing a collar
of greaseproof paper around the outside of the dish, to come
2 inches (5 cm.) above the rim.

Put the egg yolks and sugar in a basin over hot water and
whisk until the mixture is thick and creamy. Stir in the
raspberry purée. Dissolve the gelatine in the water, and whisk
into the raspberry and egg mixture. Leave to cool. Lightly whip
the cream and fold into the mixture. Whisk the egg whites until
a stiff snow and fold in. Leave for 10 minutes, then pour into
the prepared dish. When set, remove the paper collar.

If you prefer, you can use a 2-pint (1-litre) serving dish, in
which case it is not necessary to tie the paper round. As soon as
the fluff is made pour it into the dish.

Chocolate crumb pudding

IMPERIAL·METRIC	AMERICAN
2 oz./50 g. plain chocolate	⅓ cup semi-sweet chocolate pieces
½ pint/3 dl. milk	1¼ cups milk
1 egg	1 egg
2 oz./50 g. castor sugar	¼ cup granulated sugar
pinch salt	pinch salt
½ teaspoon vanilla essence	½ teaspoon vanilla extract
4 oz./100 g. white breadcrumbs	2 cups fresh soft bread crumbs
2 tablespoons flaked almonds	3 tablespoons flaked almonds
¼ pint/1½ dl. double cream	⅔ cup heavy cream

In a double boiler or a basin standing over a saucepan of hot water, heat the chocolate and milk, stirring until the chocolate melts. Beat the egg until frothy, then beat in the sugar, salt and vanilla essence. Blend in the hot milk mixture. Stir in the breadcrumbs and almonds and pour into a buttered 2-pint (1-litre) baking dish. Set dish in a roasting tin with 1 inch (2·5 cm.) of water. Bake in a moderate oven (350°F., 180°C., Gas Mark 4) for 1 hour. Serve hot with whipped cream.

Orange pudding

IMPERIAL·METRIC	AMERICAN
1 orange	1 orange
½ oz./15 g. butter	1 tablespoon butter
½ pint/3 dl. milk	1¼ cups milk
1 oz./25 g. sugar	2 tablespoons sugar
2 oz./50 g. white breadcrumbs	1 cup fresh soft bread crumbs
2 eggs	2 eggs
2 oz./50 g. castor sugar	¼ cup granulated sugar

Grate the rind of the orange. Peel and slice the orange into rings, across the segments. Heat the rind, butter and milk together until the butter has melted. Remove from the heat. Add the 1 oz. (25 g., 2 tablespoons) sugar and the breadcrumbs and allow to cool. Separate the eggs. Blend the egg yolks into the crumb mixture. Pour into a 1-pint (½-litre) greased ovenproof dish. Bake in a moderate oven (325°F., 160°C., Gas Mark 3) for 30–40 minutes. Remove from the oven and when cool cover with a layer of orange rings. Whisk the egg whites until stiff. Add the sugar, little by little, beating well. Pile the meringue on top of the pudding and brown quickly in a hot oven (425°F., 220°C., Gas Mark 7).

Custard sauce

IMPERIAL · METRIC	AMERICAN
2 eggs	2 eggs
½ pint/3 dl. milk	1¼ cups milk
½ oz./15 g. castor sugar	1 tablespoon granulated sugar
vanilla essence (optional)	vanilla extract (optional)

Whisk the eggs together in a basin. Heat the milk, without boiling, and gradually stir into the eggs. Strain into a clean basin and stand it over a pan of simmering water. Stir until the custard is pale and creamy, although quite runny. Mix in the sugar and essence, to taste, if used. Serve warm or cold.

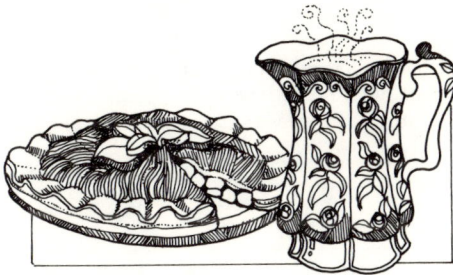

Drinks

Honey lemon cup

IMPERIAL · METRIC	AMERICAN
1 pint/6 dl. milk	2½ cups milk
2 tablespoons clear honey	3 tablespoons clear honey
2 teaspoons lemon juice	2 teaspoons lemon juice

Heat the milk with the honey. Remove from the heat, add the lemon juice and serve immediately.

Chocolate nog

IMPERIAL · METRIC	AMERICAN
2 egg whites	2 egg whites
2 teaspoons brown sugar	2 teaspoons brown sugar
2 teaspoons chocolate powder	2 teaspoons sweetened cocoa
1 pint/6 dl. milk	$2\frac{1}{2}$ cups milk
1 tablespoon brandy	1 tablespoon brandy

Whisk the egg whites and add the sugar and chocolate powder.
Heat the milk and fold in the egg white mixture. Add the
brandy and serve immediately.

Blenshaw

IMPERIAL · METRIC	AMERICAN
2 teaspoons oatmeal	2 teaspoons oatmeal
2 teaspoons Demerara sugar	2 teaspoons brown sugar
1 pint/6 dl. milk	$2\frac{1}{2}$ cups milk
nutmeg	nutmeg

Put the oatmeal and sugar into tumblers or mugs and blend
in a little of the milk. Heat the remaining milk, pour into the
tumblers and dust the tops with nutmeg. Serve when just
lukewarm.

Posset

IMPERIAL · METRIC	AMERICAN
$\frac{3}{4}$ pint/4 dl. milk	scant 2 cups milk
1 tablespoon golden syrup	1 tablespoon maple syrup
nutmeg	nutmeg

Bring the milk to the boil and stir in the syrup. Pour into mugs,
dust the tops with nutmeg and serve hot.

Vegetables

Potatoes

Potatoes don't have to be either boiled or boring. It is worth cooking them in the oven, baking them in their jackets or making them into salads, and why not try some filling home-made soups, and even some teatime treats? (Potatoes help to make delicious pastry, scones and cakes.)

Peel potatoes thinly, preferably using a proper potato peeling knife. Thick peeling is wasteful and also means the loss of nutrients, many of which are contained immediately under the skin. Before boiling, cut potatoes into even-sized pieces, so they will all be cooked at the same time, saving gas or electricity. Potatoes can also be boiled and served in their skins. Always boil potatoes gently, or as an alternative, steam them. Potatoes rarely break up, or go to mush if they are simmered gently or steamed. If potatoes show a tendency to go black during cooking, add a teaspoonful of vinegar or lemon juice to the water. The water in which potatoes have been boiled can be used for making soups and gravies as it contains valuable vitamins.

Jacket-baked potatoes can be served frequently. They are highly nutritious and usually very popular besides being easy to prepare and to cook. Whenever using the oven for general baking, save money by popping some well washed and scrubbed potatoes on a greased baking sheet. Large potatoes will bake more quickly when cut into halves.

Perfect mashed potatoes

Cut old potatoes into even-sized pieces and place in cold water with a teaspoon of vinegar or lemon to keep the potatoes white. Simmer gently for 20–30 minutes. Mash the potatoes with a fork, masher or electric beater. Add 2 oz. (50 g., ½ cup) butter and 2 tablespoons milk for each lb. (½ kg.) potatoes, beat in and season.

Perfect roast potatoes

Peel potatoes, halve or quarter if large. Parboil – cover with
cold water and add a teaspoon of salt. Put on a lid and bring
to the boil. Simmer for 5 minutes. Drain, dry off in the pan.
Roast in a roasting tin with very hot dripping or lard in a hot
oven (425°F., 220°C., Gas Mark 7). Baste and cook until
brown, about 1 hour. If roasted around meat in a moderate
oven (350°F., 180°C., Gas Mark 4) the potatoes will take about
$1\frac{1}{2}$ hours.

Perfect jacket potatoes

Scrub large potatoes and prick the skin with a fork. Rub with a
little oil or butter. Bake in a hot oven (425°F., 220°C., Gas Mark
7) until soft when pressed, about $1-1\frac{1}{2}$ hours. Slit the top and add
butter and seasonings or any other savoury fillings.

Perfect sauté potatoes

Parboil as for roast potatoes. Drain, cut into $\frac{1}{4}$ inch ($\frac{1}{2}$ cm.)
thick slices. Fry in 2 oz. (50 g., $\frac{1}{4}$ cup) fat (butter with oil to
stop the butter burning gives a delicious flavour) for 7–10
minutes. Drain on absorbent paper.

Perfect chipped potatoes

Peel potatoes and slice into chips. Soak to remove the excess
starch. Rinse and dry carefully. Heat oil or fat in wide deep pan
a third full. When a cube of bread turns golden in 20 seconds,
the oil or fat is hot enough. Place a few chips at a time in
uncovered pan – don't allow the fat to froth. Fry until golden,
about 7–10 minutes. Drain on absorbent paper.

Perfect potato salad

Use firm white potatoes for this and cook them until they are
only just done, so that they do not break up. If you want the
flavour of the dressing to be absorbed by the potatoes, add it
while they are still hot. To keep the potato flavour distinct, add
the dressing when the potatoes are cold. A scraping of onion,
or scattering of chives improves a potato salad. As a change from
mayonnaise or salad dressing, use an oil and vinegar dressing,
or hot bacon fat with a dash of vinegar.

Potato and celery soup

IMPERIAL · METRIC	AMERICAN
1 oz./25 g. butter	2 tablespoons butter
½ head celery, cut into 1-inch (2·5-cm.) pieces	½ head celery, cut into 1-inch pieces
2 medium onions	2 medium onions
1 lb./450 g. potatoes, quartered	1 lb. potatoes, quartered
1 pint/6 dl. stock or water	2½ cups stock or water
salt and black pepper	salt and black pepper
¼ pint/1½ dl. milk	⅔ cup milk
2–3 oz./50–75 g. Double Gloucester cheese, grated	½–¾ cup grated cheese

Melt the butter in a saucepan, add the celery and chopped onions, and cook gently without browning. Put in the potatoes, stock and seasoning. Bring to the boil and simmer until all are tender. Sieve or liquidise. Add the milk, reheat and adjust the seasoning. Serve very hot sprinkled with the grated cheese.

Potato and leek soup

IMPERIAL · METRIC	AMERICAN
3 medium potatoes	3 medium potatoes
4 medium leeks	4 medium leeks
1 onion	1 onion
2 oz./50 g. butter	¼ cup butter
salt and pepper	salt and pepper
2 pints/generous litre chicken stock	5 cups chicken stock
2 tablespoons cream or top of the milk	3 tablespoons half-and-half

Peel, wash and slice the vegetables. Add to the melted butter in a pan and cook gently for about 5 minutes. Season. Add the stock, cover and simmer for about 45 minutes, or until the vegetables are tender. Sieve or liquidise. Reheat and add the cream just before serving.

Hashed potatoes

IMPERIAL · METRIC	AMERICAN
8 medium potatoes	8 medium potatoes
8 lean bacon rashers	8 bacon slices (preferably Canadian bacon slices)
3 medium onions	3 medium onions
¼ teaspoon salt	¼ teaspoon salt
shake black pepper	shake black pepper
pinch chopped sage	pinch chopped sage
pinch chopped thyme	pinch chopped thyme

Grate the potatoes coarsely and blot the moisture with kitchen paper. Put the bacon rashers in pan and toss until crisp and brown over a medium heat. Remove the bacon and reserve, along with half the bacon fat. Spread the potatoes in the fat in the pan and brown lightly on one side. Peel and grate the onions, reserving the onion juices. Use a spatula to flatten the potatoes, then scatter the onions, onion juice, seasonings and herbs over them. When the potatoes are crisp and brown, cut the potato pancake into eight wedges. Lift each wedge carefully from the pan and put on a plate. Add the remaining bacon fat to the pan, turn the wedges over carefully and return to pan, uncooked side down. Top each wedge with a rasher of bacon and cook until the underside is brown. Serve at once.

Potato slices baked with salt pork

IMPERIAL · METRIC	AMERICAN
2 large onions, sliced	2 large onions, sliced
2 large potatoes, sliced	2 large potatoes, sliced
butter	butter
salt and black pepper	salt and black pepper
2 ¼-inch (½-cm.) slices salt pork, cut in strips	2 ¼-inch slices salt pork, cut in strips

Arrange the onion and potato slices in alternate layers in a large, well buttered casserole. Sprinkle with salt and pepper and add just enough water barely to cover the top layer. Arrange the strips of salt pork over the top. Bake in a cool oven (300°F., 150°C., Gas Mark 2) for 2½ hours.

Bacon and onion potatoes

IMPERIAL · METRIC	AMERICAN
6 large potatoes	6 large potatoes
3 oz./75 g. butter	6 tablespoons butter
6 streaky bacon rashers, chopped and lightly fried	6 bacon slices, chopped and lightly fried
1 large onion, finely sliced and fried	1 large onion, finely sliced and fried
salt and pepper	salt and pepper

Scrub the potatoes and prick with a fork. Put on a baking sheet and bake in a moderately hot oven (400°F., 200°C., Gas Mark 6) for 1 hour. Slit the tops of the potatoes across and scoop out the pulp into a bowl. Mash the pulp and add the butter, bacon, onion and seasoning. Pile the mixture into the potato shell and bake for a further 15 minutes.

New potato surprise

IMPERIAL · METRIC	AMERICAN
1½ lb./¾ kg. new potatoes	1½ lb. new potatoes
6 tomatoes	6 tomatoes
6 oz./75 g. cheese, grated	1½ cups grated cheese
3 eggs	3 eggs
¾ pint/4 dl. milk	scant 2 cups milk
salt and pepper	salt and pepper

Cook and cool the potatoes, then slice them. Arrange skinned and sliced tomatoes, potatoes and cheese in layers in a lightly greased ovenproof dish. Beat the eggs with the milk and add salt and pepper. Strain and pour over the other ingredients. Bake in a moderately hot oven (375°F., 190°C., Gas Mark 5) for about 35–45 minutes, until set. Serve hot, accompanied by a crisp green salad.

Stovies

IMPERIAL · METRIC	AMERICAN
1 oz./25 g. bacon fat or dripping	2 tablespoons bacon drippings
8 oz./225 g. onions	½ lb. onions
2 lb./1 kg. potatoes	2 lb. potatoes
½ pint/3 dl. hot water	1¼ cups hot water
salt and pepper	salt and pepper

Melt the fat. Slice and fry onions without browning. Add the sliced potatoes, hot water and seasoning. Cover and cook very slowly for 1–1½ hours, stirring or shaking the pan occasionally to prevent browning. Serve with minced beef or casseroles.

Cider-baked potatoes

IMPERIAL · METRIC	AMERICAN
1 lb./450 g. potatoes	1 lb. potatoes
salt and pepper	salt and pepper
1 oz./25 g. cheese, grated	¼ cup grated cheese
1 oz./25 g. butter	2 tablespoons butter
¼ pint/1½ dl. cider	⅔ cup cider

Cut the potatoes in slices and put them into a lightly greased ovenproof dish. Season and sprinkle a little cheese between each layer. Repeat until the dish is full. Dot with the butter and pour the cider over. Bake in a moderately hot oven (375°F., 190°C., Gas Mark 5) for 1½ hours.

Kidney potatoes

IMPERIAL · METRIC	AMERICAN
4 large potatoes	4 large potatoes
4 thin streaky bacon rashers	4 bacon slices
4 lamb's kidneys	4 lamb kidneys
salt and pepper	salt and pepper
1 oz./25 g. butter	2 tablespoons butter

Scrub the potatoes and rub salt into the skins. Bake in a moderate oven (350°F., 180°C., Gas Mark 4) until just soft, for approximately 1¼ hours. Remove the rind and bone from the bacon rashers and flatten out. Skin and core the kidneys. Wrap each kidney in a rasher of bacon. Cut off the tops of the potatoes and scoop out enough potato to make room for the kidney. Season the insides with pepper and add a knob of butter. Put in the kidneys and replace the tops. Return to the oven for a further 20 minutes, or until the kidneys are cooked. After 10 minutes, remove the lids to allow the bacon to become crispy. Serve hot.

Potato dumplings

IMPERIAL · METRIC	AMERICAN
7 medium potatoes	7 medium potatoes
2 medium onions	2 medium onions
12 slices white bread	12 slices white bread
¾ teaspoon salt	¾ teaspoon salt
pinch black pepper	pinch black pepper
¾ teaspoon fresh or dried dill	¾ teaspoon fresh or dried dill
3 eggs	3 eggs
6 oz./175 g. self-raising flour	1½ cups all-purpose flour sifted with 1½ teaspoons baking powder

Grate the potatoes coarsely, squeeze out the moisture, and dry in kitchen paper. Grate the onions and press out the juices through a sieve. Mix the onion juice and 3 tablespoons onion pulp with the potatoes. Soak the bread slices in water. Squeeze out the liquid and put the bread in a bowl. Add the salt, pepper and dill and stir in the potato and onion mixture; mix in the eggs. Blend all the ingredients thoroughly and form into balls. Bring 9 pints (5 litres, 11½ pints) salted water to a low rolling boil in a large pan. Roll the dumplings in flour until they are thickly covered. Cook with the lid on the pan for 15 minutes. Drain and serve piping hot, with butter, or serve with stews.

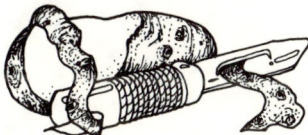

Cheese and mushroom flan

(with potato pastry)

IMPERIAL · METRIC	AMERICAN
Potato pastry	*Potato pastry*
2 oz./50 g. butter	¼ cup butter
4 oz./100 g. plain flour	1 cup all-purpose flour
pinch salt	pinch salt
4 oz./100 g. cooked potato, sieved	½ cup cooked sieved potato
Filling	*Filling*
3 eggs	3 eggs
3 oz./75 g. cheese, grated	¾ cup grated cheese
salt and pepper	salt and pepper
4 oz./100 g. mushrooms	1 cup mushrooms
3 tomatoes	3 tomatoes

To make the pastry, rub the butter into the sifted flour and salt. Work in the potato to bind the dough together. Roll out on a floured board in the usual way. Line a shallow tin with the pastry and flute the edges. Reserve the pastry trimmings.

Beat the eggs and add the grated cheese and seasoning and spread over the pastry. Place strips of pastry diagonally over the filling, with the prepared mushrooms and sliced tomatoes in the alternate spaces. Bake in a moderately hot oven (375°F., 190°C., Gas Mark 5) for 25–30 minutes. Garnish with parsley before serving.

Farmhouse potatoes

IMPERIAL · METRIC	AMERICAN
1½ lb./¾ kg. potatoes	1½ lb. potatoes
4 oz./100 g. mushrooms	1 cup sliced mushrooms
4 oz./100 g. cheese, grated	1 cup grated cheese
8 fl. oz./2½ dl. double cream	1 cup whipping cream
2 oz./50 g. butter	¼ cup butter
salt and pepper	salt and pepper
chopped parsley	chopped parsley

Peel the potatoes thinly and cut into slices about ⅛ inch (¼ cm.) thick. Wash the mushrooms, dry and cut into slices. Lay the potatoes on a large sheet of foil, cover evenly with the mushrooms, sprinkle with the cheese, pour over the cream and dot with pats of butter. Season well with salt and pepper. Make a parcel of the foil and place in a roasting tin. Bake in a moderately hot oven (400°F., 200°C., Gas Mark 6) for about 1–1½ hours, until the potatoes are cooked. Serve piping hot, sprinkled with chopped parsley.

Stelk

IMPERIAL · METRIC	AMERICAN
2 lb./1 kg. potatoes	2 lb. potatoes
2 oz./50 g. butter	¼ cup butter
bunch spring onions	bunch scallions
milk	milk
salt and pepper	salt and pepper

Peel the potatoes and boil them in salted water. Mash them and add the butter. Keep hot. Chop the spring onions and cook in a little milk until tender. Add to the potatoes, together with the milk and seasoning and beat until fluffy. Pile on to serving plates and make a well in the centre. Put a big knob of butter in each well just before serving. Eat the potatoes from the outside, dipping each mouthful into the pool of butter.

Pan haggerty

IMPERIAL · METRIC	AMERICAN
2 lb./1 kg. potatoes	2 lb. potatoes
1 lb./450 g. onions	1 lb. onions
4 oz./100 g. Cheddar cheese	1 cup grated Cheddar cheese
3 oz./75 g. dripping	6 tablespoons drippings
salt and pepper	salt and pepper

Peel the potatoes and cut them into ⅛-inch (¼-cm.) slices. Slice the onions in the same way and grate the cheese. Melt the dripping in a thick frying pan and put in layers of potatoes, onions, cheese and seasoning, topping with potatoes. Fry gently with a lid on the pan until the potatoes are tender. Turn from time to time with a fish slice to brown all sides.

   This is a good dish on its own, or with cold meats.

Country potato bake

IMPERIAL · METRIC	AMERICAN
1 lb./450 g. potatoes	1 lb. potatoes
¼ cabbage	¼ cabbage
8 oz./225 g. lean bacon	½ lb. Canadian bacon
4 oz./100 g. mushrooms	1 cup sliced mushrooms
2 tablespoons oil or butter	3 tablespoons oil or butter
salt and pepper	salt and pepper
8 oz./225 g. cheese, grated	2 cups grated cheese
little stock	little stock

Peel the potatoes very thinly, and parboil in salted water for about 5 minutes. Drain off the water, and cut the potatoes into slices. Shred the cabbage, cut the bacon into small pieces and slice the mushrooms. Toss the cabbage, bacon and mushrooms in the oil or butter until soft – do not brown. Place the potatoes, cabbage, mushrooms and bacon in an ovenproof dish, season well and sprinkle with cheese. Pour in a little stock and bake in a moderate oven (350°F., 180°C., Gas Mark 4) for 1¼ hours.

Rumbledethumps

IMPERIAL · METRIC	AMERICAN
1 lb./450 g. cooked cabbage	2 cups cooked cabbage
1 small onion	1 small onion
4 oz./100 g. Cheddar cheese	1 cup grated Cheddar cheese
1 lb./450 g. mashed potatoes	2 cups mashed potato
salt and pepper	salt and pepper

Shred the cabbage, chop the onion and grate the cheese. Mix together the potatoes, cabbage, onion, salt and pepper, and put into a greased ovenproof dish. Cover with grated cheese and bake in a moderately hot oven (400°F., 200°C., Gas Mark 6) until the cheese is golden.

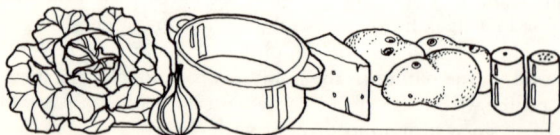

Boxty

IMPERIAL · METRIC	AMERICAN
2 large raw potatoes	2 large raw potatoes
12 oz./350 g. mashed potatoes	1½ cups mashed potato
1 teaspoon salt	1 teaspoon salt
1 teaspoon bicarbonate of soda	1 teaspoon baking soda
2 tablespoons plain flour	3 tablespoons all-purpose flour

Grate the raw potatoes and squeeze out the liquid. Add to the
mashed potatoes and salt. Mix the bicarbonate of soda with the
flour and add to the potatoes. Roll out in a circle ½ inch (1 cm.)
thick. Cut in four quarters and put on an ungreased griddle or
in a thick frying pan. Cook gently for 30 minutes, turning once,
until well browned on both sides.

Potato scones

IMPERIAL · METRIC	AMERICAN
8 oz./225 g. cold cooked potatoes	1 cup cold cooked potato
½ oz./15 g. butter	1 tablespoon butter
salt	salt
2 oz./50 g. flour	½ cup all-purpose flour
pinch baking powder	pinch baking powder

Mash the potatoes and melt the butter. Mix the butter and
potato together, add the salt and work in as much flour, sieved
with the baking powder, as the paste will take. Turn on to a
floured board and roll out very thinly. Cut into triangles and
place on a hot, greased griddle. Prick well and cook for about
3 minutes on each side. Cool in a clean tea towel.

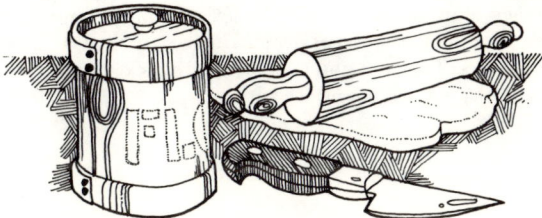

Potato oatcakes

IMPERIAL · METRIC	AMERICAN
1 lb./450 g. mashed potatoes	2 cups mashed potato
6 oz./175 g. fine oatmeal	1 cup fine oatmeal
salt	salt
little milk	little milk

Mix the potatoes, oatmeal and salt together. Add enough milk to make a fairly stiff dough. Roll out on a floured board about ⅛ inch (¼ cm.) thick. Prick with a fork and cut into rounds or triangles. Cook quickly in a lightly greased, heavy frying pan or on a griddle. Cook on both sides until golden and serve with plenty of butter.

Chocolate potato cake

IMPERIAL · METRIC	AMERICAN
4 oz./100 g. butter	½ cup butter
6 oz./175 g. sugar	¾ cup sugar
3 oz./75 g. mashed potatoes	scant ½ cup mashed potato
1½ oz./40 g. plain chocolate	¼ cup semi-sweet chocolate pieces
2 eggs	2 eggs
pinch salt	pinch salt
6 oz./175 g. self-raising flour	1½ cups all-purpose flour sifted with 1½ teaspoons baking powder
about 4 tablespoons milk	about ⅓ cup milk

Cream the butter and sugar until light and fluffy and gradually work in the potatoes and the grated chocolate. Add the beaten eggs, salt and flour, and enough milk to make a soft dropping consistency. Put into two greased 7-inch (18-cm.) sponge tins and bake in a moderately hot oven (375°F., 190°C., Gas Mark 5) for 30 minutes. Turn out and cool on a wire rack. Fill with apricot or raspberry jam and ice with 4 oz./100 g. (4 squares) melted chocolate.

Potato fritters

IMPERIAL · METRIC	AMERICAN
1 lb./450 g. boiled potatoes	1 lb. boiled potatoes
4 oz./100 g. plain flour	1 cup all-purpose flour
salt	salt
1 egg	1 egg
¼ pint/1½ dl. milk	⅔ cup milk
oil for deep frying	oil for deep frying

See that the potatoes are slightly undercooked. Cut them into ¼-inch (½-cm.) slices. Sieve the flour and salt together and work in the egg and the milk gradually, beating until thick and creamy. Dip the potato slices into the batter and fry in hot oil until golden. Drain on absorbent paper and serve very hot.

As a change, try putting two slices of potato together with a piece of cheese in between before dipping in the batter.

Devonshire potato cake

IMPERIAL · METRIC	AMERICAN
1 lb./450 g. boiled potatoes	1 lb. boiled potatoes
2 oz./50 g. butter	¼ cup butter
2 oz./50 g. sugar	¼ cup sugar
2 oz./50 g. dried fruit	6 tablespoons dried fruit
pinch cinnamon	pinch cinnamon
6 oz./175 g. self-raising flour	1½ cups all-purpose flour sifted with 1½ teaspoons baking powder

Sieve the potatoes while hot and add the butter, sugar, fruit and cinnamon. Knead in the flour to make a stiff dough, and roll out to a circle 1½ inches (3·5 cm.) thick. Shape into a round and mark into segments across the top, but do not cut right through. Place on a baking sheet and bake in a moderately hot oven (375°F., 190°C., Gas Mark 5) for 30 minutes. Sprinkle with castor sugar and serve hot.

Root vegetables

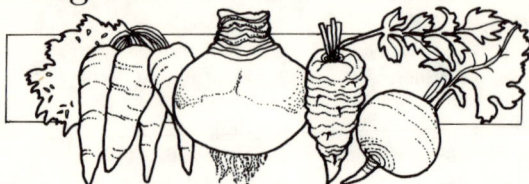

Just because root vegetables look rather dull and are usually cheap, we tend to despise them, but they make wonderfully satisfying dishes, and hearty soups.

Carrots and turnips are nicest when eaten young and tender, but parsnips are better when they have stayed longer in the ground and had a 'touch of frost'. All the root vegetables are good if they are boiled, then mashed with butter or cream and plenty of seasoning. When you are roasting a joint, half-boil parsnips, artichokes, swedes or turnips and finish them off in the fat around the joint.

Turnip soup

IMPERIAL·METRIC	AMERICAN
1 lb./450 g. turnips	1 lb. turnips
2 large potatoes	2 large potatoes
2 bacon rashers	2 bacon slices
2 oz./50 g. onion	½ cup chopped onion
creamy milk	milk
salt and pepper	salt and pepper
nutmeg	nutmeg

Dice the turnips and potatoes. Cut the bacon into small pieces and fry them in their own fat until crisp. Take out the bacon pieces and keep aside. Chop the onion and toss it in the bacon fat until it becomes soft and yellow. Add the turnips and potatoes and cook for 3 minutes, stirring gently. Add 4 tablespoons water, cover and cook gently until the vegetables are soft. Press through a sieve. Add enough milk to give a soup consistency and reheat gently. Season to taste with salt, pepper and nutmeg. Serve very hot sprinkled with the bacon pieces.

Artichoke soup

IMPERIAL · METRIC	AMERICAN
1 lb./450 g. Jerusalem artichokes	1 lb. Jerusalem artichokes
3 potatoes	3 potatoes
1 leek or onion	1 leek or onion
salt and pepper	salt and pepper
½ pint/3 dl. chicken stock	1¼ cups chicken stock
1 pint/6 dl. creamy milk	2½ cups milk
cream or butter	cream or butter
chopped parsley	chopped parsley

Scrape the artichokes and cut them up, together with the potatoes and the leek or onion. Just cover with water and add salt and pepper. Simmer for 30 minutes, then put through a sieve. Add the stock and milk and heat for 15 minutes. Add a spoonful of cream or a knob of butter at the end, and a good scattering of chopped parsley.

Carrot soup

IMPERIAL · METRIC	AMERICAN
2 lb./1 kg. carrots	2 lb. carrots
2 onions	2 onions
2 oz./50 g. butter	¼ cup butter
2 pints/generous litre stock	5 cups stock
1 bay leaf	1 bay leaf
salt and pepper	salt and pepper

Scrape and slice the carrots, and peel and chop the onions. Heat the butter and fry the vegetables for a few minutes. Pour in the stock, add the bay leaf and bring to the boil. Reduce the heat and then simmer for about 1 hour, until carrots are soft. Sieve the soup and press carrots through as well. Return to the pan and add salt and pepper to taste. Reheat before serving.

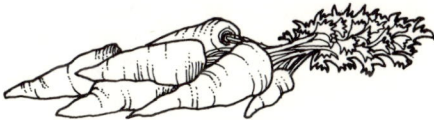

Celery soup

IMPERIAL · METRIC	AMERICAN
1 head celery	1 head celery
2 onions	2 onions
2 medium potatoes	2 medium potatoes
2 pints/generous litre stock	5 cups stock
salt and pepper	salt and pepper
pinch mixed herbs	pinch mixed herbs

Wash the celery and cut into small pieces. Peel and chop the onions and potatoes. Place the vegetables in a pan and add the stock, seasoning and herbs. Bring to the boil, cover the pan and simmer for about 1 hour. Sieve, before serving, if a creamy soup is preferred.

Celery bake

IMPERIAL · METRIC	AMERICAN
1 lb./450 g. celery	1 lb. celery
juice of ½ lemon	juice of ½ lemon
1 bay leaf	1 bay leaf
1 sprig parsley	1 sprig parsley
1¼ pints/¾ litre beef stock	generous 3 cups beef stock
¼ pint/1½ dl. single cream	⅔ cup half-and-half
4 oz./100 g. cheese, grated	1 cup grated cheese
3 oz./75 g. coarse breadcrumbs	1½ cups coarse bread crumbs
1 oz./25 g. butter	2 tablespoons butter

Put the celery into a pan with the lemon juice, bay leaf, parsley and stock. Simmer until just tender. Drain off the liquid and reduce the liquid over a high heat to about ¼ pint (1½ dl., ⅔ cup). Stir in the cream and season to taste. Put half the celery into a shallow, greased ovenproof dish. Pour on half the creamy sauce and sprinkle with half the cheese. Put on the rest of the celery and the remaining sauce. Sprinkle with the remaining cheese and the crumbs mixed together. Melt the butter and sprinkle it on top of the dish. Bake in a hot oven (450°F., 230°C., Gas Mark 8) for 10 minutes. Serve very hot with poultry, game, veal or pork.

Carrots and celery in cider

IMPERIAL · METRIC	AMERICAN
1 pint/6 dl. cider	2½ cups cider
1 lb./450 g. carrots	1 lb. carrots
½ head celery	½ head celery
salt and pepper	salt and pepper
chopped parsley	chopped parsley

Bring the cider to boiling point. Prepare the vegetables and cut into 2-inch (5-cm.) strips. (The outside stalks of the celery should be used.) Add the carrots to the cider and simmer for 15 minutes. Add the celery with the seasonings and cook for a further 30 minutes. Retaining the liquid, drain the vegetables and keep hot. Boil the cider quickly until reduced to about 4 tablespoons. Pour over the vegetables, sprinkle with parsley and serve.

Turnips and parsley

IMPERIAL · METRIC	AMERICAN
2 lb./1 kg. white turnips	2 lb. white turnips
3 oz./75 g. butter	6 tablespoons butter
salt	salt
1 teaspoon castor sugar	1 teaspoon granulated sugar
2 tablespoons chopped parsley	3 tablespoons chopped parsley

Peel the turnips thinly and cut into ½-inch (1-cm.) thick rings. Parboil for 5 minutes in boiling salted water. Drain thoroughly and cool. Melt the butter in a frying pan and over a low heat, gently fry the turnip rings, turning frequently. Sprinkle with a little salt and the sugar. Turn into a serving dish and sprinkle very liberally with parsley before serving.

This dish is very good served with beef or duck.

Punchnep

IMPERIAL · METRIC	AMERICAN
2 lb./1 kg. white turnips	2 lb. white turnips
2 lb./1 kg. potatoes	2 lb. potatoes
2 oz./50 g. butter	¼ cup butter
salt and pepper	salt and pepper
¼ pint/1½ dl. single cream	⅔ cup half-and-half

Peel the turnips and potatoes and cook in separate pans of boiling salted water until tender. Drain both very thoroughly and mash with the butter. Season, mix together and turn into a serving dish. Smooth over the top, make holes in the mixture and pour warmed cream into the holes. Serve hot with grilled or roast meats.

Crisp-topped turnips

IMPERIAL · METRIC	AMERICAN
8 large white turnips	8 large white turnips
2 oz./50 g. butter	¼ cup butter
2 oz./50 g. fresh breadcrumbs	1 cup fresh soft bread crumbs
2 hard-boiled eggs	2 hard-cooked eggs
2 oz./50 g. Lancashire cheese	½ cup grated cheese
chopped parsley	chopped parsley

Peel the turnips and cut into large chunks. Cook in boiling salted water for about 10–15 minutes, until tender. Drain well and toss in half the butter, melted. Turn into a pie dish. Fry the crumbs in the remaining butter until light golden. Drain and mix with finely chopped hard-boiled egg and grated cheese. Sprinkle over the top of the turnips and place under a hot grill to crisp the top slightly. Garnish with chopped parsley and serve.

Carrot-stuffed onions

IMPERIAL · METRIC	AMERICAN
4 large onions	4 large onions
4 large carrots	4 large carrots
½ oz./15 g. butter	1 tablespoon butter
salt and pepper	salt and pepper
½ pint/3 dl. white sauce	1¼ cups white sauce
3 oz./75 g. fine white breadcrumbs	1½ cups fresh soft bread crumbs

Boil the onions until tender and scoop out the centres carefully. Cook the carrots and cut into small pieces. Dip into melted butter, season with salt and pepper, and mix them with the scraped-out onion pieces. Put the whole onions into a buttered ovenproof dish, fill with the mixture of carrots and onions, and pour on the white sauce. Sprinkle with the breadcrumbs and dot with a few bits of butter. Cook in a moderate oven (350°F., 180°C., Gas Mark 4) for 25 minutes, until the breadcrumbs are just brown. Serve very hot.

Swede supper

IMPERIAL · METRIC	AMERICAN
1 lb./450 g. swedes	1 lb. swedes
8 oz./225 g. potatoes	½ lb. potatoes
¾ pint/4 dl. beef stock	scant 2 cups beef stock
salt	salt
2 teaspoons sugar	2 teaspoons sugar
pepper	pepper
4 oz./100 g. cheese, grated	1 cup grated cheese
1 tablespoon minced onion	1 tablespoon ground onion
chopped parsley	chopped parsley

Peel and cut the swedes and potatoes into pieces. Put into a pan with the stock, salt and sugar. Cover and boil for 12 minutes, until the vegetables are tender. Drain and mash with the pepper, cheese and onion and beat until light and fluffy. Serve very hot with a sprinkling of chopped parsley.

This dish is excellent served with cold meat or ham.

Parsnip cakes

IMPERIAL · METRIC	AMERICAN
6 large parsnips	6 large parsnips
3 oz./75 g. butter	6 tablespoons butter
salt and pepper	salt and pepper
pinch nutmeg	pinch nutmeg
3 tablespoons plain flour	4 tablespoons all-purpose flour
2 tablespoons single cream	3 tablespoons half-and-half
1 egg	1 egg
1 oz./25 g. onion, grated	¼ cup grated onion
fine breadcrumbs	fine bread crumbs
grated cheese	grated cheese
oil, butter or dripping for frying	oil, butter or drippings for frying

Cook the parsnips and mash them with the butter, salt and pepper, nutmeg, flour, cream, egg and onion. Form the mixture into 12 flat cakes and coat them with crumbs and cheese. Fry until golden brown in oil, butter or dripping. Drain on absorbent paper and serve with bacon or beef.

Onions and leeks

You can take some of the pain out of preparing onions by adopting these measures. With large onions cut off the tops and roots, then, with a sharp vegetable knife, remove the brown outer-skin under cold, running water. Small onions, after being topped and tailed, can be skinned more easily if immersed in boiling water for a minute or two. Don't be heavy-handed, though. Much of their valuable vitamins and mineral salts lies close to the skin.

When it comes to chopping an onion you won't cry nearly so much if you cut it in half from root to stem (after peeling it first) and then, with cut sides down on a board you slice it through lengthwise, not quite to the root. Next, make three or four cuts across the other way. You get neat little pieces, too.

Whatever their size, onions should be firm and the skins feathery. They are never good if discoloured and soft. If you like a mild onion flavour, try using leeks instead. Be sure to clean them well as they can be very gritty. They are particularly good in a white or cheese sauce served as a vegetable, and go well with chicken stock to make a delicious soup.

Fried onions

IMPERIAL · METRIC	AMERICAN
onions	onions
salt and pepper	salt and pepper
flour	flour
oil or fat for frying	oil or shortening for frying
lemon juice	lemon juice

Cut the onions into slices about $\frac{1}{8}$ inch ($\frac{1}{4}$ cm.) thick and shake out into separate rings. Season with salt, dredge with flour and cook in very hot oil or fat. Drain on absorbent paper and sprinkle with salt before serving.

A pleasant alternative is onions fried in batter. Prepare the rings as above, sprinkle with salt, pepper, oil and lemon juice. Leave for 30 minutes. Immediately before frying, dip the rings in a light batter (see page 57) and fry in deep hot fat or oil. Drain on absorbent paper.

Braised onions

IMPERIAL · METRIC	AMERICAN
4 large onions	4 large onions
3 tablespoons oil	scant $\frac{1}{4}$ cup oil
$\frac{1}{2}$ pint/3 dl. dry cider	$1\frac{1}{4}$ cups dry cider
salt and pepper	salt and pepper

Put the peeled onions into an ovenproof dish with the oil, and cook in a moderately hot oven (400°F., 200°C., Gas Mark 6) for 15 minutes, or until the onions begin to exude juice. Add the cider and cook until the onions are tender. Season with salt and pepper.

Onion soup

IMPERIAL · METRIC	AMERICAN
8 oz./225 g. onions	$\frac{1}{2}$ lb. onions
1 oz./25 g. butter	2 tablespoons butter
2 tablespoons flour	3 tablespoons all-purpose flour
salt and pepper	salt and pepper
2 pints/generous litre stock or water	5 cups stock or water

Slice the onions thinly and fry in a saucepan with the butter over a gentle heat, to cook them thoroughly but without discolouring them. When nearly cooked, sprinkle the onions with the flour and stir with a wooden spoon. Add the seasoned stock or water and cook for about 30 minutes.

The ideal way to serve this soup is to place a slice of bread on each soup plate and sprinkle with chopped watercress or chopped parsley, pour on the soup and serve at once. Another alternative is to sprinkle the bread with grated cheese.

Crispy onion omelette

IMPERIAL · METRIC	AMERICAN
1 medium onion	1 medium onion
1 tablespoon oil and vinegar dressing	1 tablespoon oil and vinegar dressing
2 eggs	2 eggs
salt and pepper	salt and pepper
1 teaspoon chopped parsley	1 teaspoon chopped parsley
2 tablespoons double cream	3 tablespoons whipping cream

Peel the onion, chop finely and mix with the oil and vinegar dressing. Beat the egg yolks with seasoning. Beat the whites until stiff and fold into the yolks. Pour into a warmed, greased omelette pan. Cook over a medium heat for a few minutes. Put the pan under a hot grill to cook the top. Put the onion mixture on one half of the omelette, fold over and slide on to a plate. Quickly mix the parsley into lightly whipped cream and spoon over the omelette. Serve immediately.

Stuffed onions

IMPERIAL · METRIC	AMERICAN
4 medium onions	4 medium onions
6 oz./175 g. pork, veal, beef or lamb, minced	¾ cup ground pork, veal, beef or lamb
salt and pepper	salt and pepper
chopped fresh herbs	chopped fresh herbs
¾ pint/4 dl. brown gravy	scant 2 cups brown gravy
breadcrumbs	bread crumbs

Peel the onions, taking care not to damage the first white layer. Cut off the tops about three-quarters down and plunge the onions into salted water to blanch them. Drain and remove the insides, leaving only two layers of the onion intact. Chop up the scooped out parts very carefully and mix with the minced meat, flavoured with salt, pepper and herbs. Stuff the onion cases with this mixture and put them into a buttered flameproof dish. Add the gravy, bring to the boil, with the lid on, and then cook in a moderate oven (350°F., 180°C., Gas Mark 4), until the onions are tender, basting from time to time to glaze the onions. Just before taking them out of the oven, sprinkle the tops with toasted or fresh breadcrumbs and brown under the grill.

Onion pie

IMPERIAL · METRIC	AMERICAN
2 lb./1 kg. potatoes	2 lb. potatoes
6 large onions	6 large onions
2 oz./50 g. butter	¼ cup butter
salt and pepper	salt and pepper
8 oz./225 g. cooked meat, minced	1 cup ground cooked meat

Prepare a 7-inch (18-cm.) cake tin by greasing it well with butter. Peel and slice the potatoes. Peel and cut the onions into rings. Place a layer of potatoes on the bottom of the tin and season well, placing pats of butter on top. Arrange a layer of onions together with some of the minced meat. Season well and continue in this way until the tin is nearly full, ending with a layer of potatoes. Cover with foil and bake in a moderately hot oven (375°F., 190°C., Gas Mark 5) for 1 hour. Serve with gravy.

Onion dumplings

IMPERIAL · METRIC	AMERICAN
8 oz./225 g. self-raising flour	2 cups all-purpose flour sifted with 2 teaspoons baking powder
4 oz./125 g. shredded suet	scant 1 cup shredded suet
pinch salt	pinch salt
4 large onions	4 large onions
2–3 oz./50–75 g. cooked ham or bacon	$\frac{1}{4}$–$\frac{1}{2}$ cup chopped cooked ham or bacon
1 tablespoon chopped parsley	1 tablespoon chopped parsley

Make up the suet pastry with the flour, suet and salt and enough cold water to make a firm paste. Roll out and cut into four large squares which will enclose the onions. Scoop out the centre of each onion and fill with a mixture of finely chopped ham or bacon and parsley. Wrap each onion in a piece of suet pastry. Tie in cloths and boil for $1\frac{1}{2}$ hours. Serve with a rich brown gravy.

Onion flan

IMPERIAL · METRIC	AMERICAN
4 oz./100 g. flour	1 cup all-purpose flour
pinch salt	pinch salt
3 oz./75 g. butter	6 tablespoons butter
1 egg yolk	1 egg yolk
Filling	*Filling*
1 lb./450 g. onions	1 lb. onions
$1\frac{1}{2}$ oz./40 g. butter	3 tablespoons butter
1 tablespoon olive oil	1 tablespoon olive oil
2 eggs	2 eggs
$\frac{1}{4}$ pint/$1\frac{1}{2}$ dl. cream	$\frac{2}{3}$ cup half-and-half
salt and pepper	salt and pepper
nutmeg	nutmeg
2 oz./50 g. cheese, grated	$\frac{1}{2}$ cup grated cheese

Sift the flour with the salt and rub in the butter. Beat the egg yolk with 2 teaspoons cold water and bind the mixture with this. You may need a little more water but do not make the pastry too wet – it should just come away cleanly from the bowl. Roll out thinly on a floured board and use to line a 9-inch (23-cm.) flan tin.

Chop the onions finely. Melt the butter with the oil in a large frying pan. Put in the onions, cover and cook over a low heat until they are quite soft, transparent and very pale gold. Beat the eggs with the cream and mix well into the onions. Stir in the seasonings and cheese and pour into the pastry case. Bake in a moderately hot oven (375°F., 190°C., Gas Mark 5) for about 35 minutes.

Baked onions

IMPERIAL · METRIC	AMERICAN
4 large onions	4 large onions
1 oz./25 g. butter	2 tablespoons butter
1 pint/6 dl. milk	2½ cups milk
salt	salt
½ teaspoon black pepper	½ teaspoon black pepper
little cayenne pepper	little cayenne pepper
2 oz./50 g. Cheddar cheese, grated (optional)	½ cup grated Cheddar cheese (optional)
1 tablespoon chopped parsley	1 tablespoon chopped parsley

Peel the onions and cut a bit off the top and bottom of each onion. Grease an ovenproof dish with the butter. Place in the onions to fit tightly. Pour over the milk until it comes to half the depth of the onions. Season with salt and pepper and cover. Bake in a moderate oven (350°F., 180°C., Gas Mark 4) for 45 minutes, until the onions are cooked. The onions should not be soupy, but nearly dry when done. If too wet, uncover for the last 5–10 minutes of baking. If cheese is liked, uncover the dish and sprinkle over the cheese about 15 minutes before serving. Brown under the grill until the cheese bubbles. Sprinkle with chopped parsley.

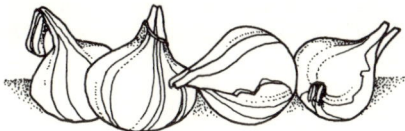

Cheese and leek broth

IMPERIAL·METRIC	AMERICAN
4 streaky bacon rashers	4 bacon slices
2 lb./1 kg. leeks	2 lb. leeks
1½ pints/scant litre chicken stock	3¾ cups chicken stock
2 oz./50 g. pearl barley	¼ cup pearl barley
salt and pepper	salt and pepper
chopped parsley	chopped parsley

Remove the rinds and chop the bacon. Wash and finely slice
the leeks. Fry the bacon in a large saucepan, add the leeks and
fry for a further few minutes. Pour in the stock; add the pearl
barley, salt and pepper. Bring to the boil, cover and simmer for
1 hour. Sprinkle with chopped parsley before serving.

Leek and cheese pudding

IMPERIAL·METRIC	AMERICAN
8½ oz./240 g. self-raising flour	2 cups plus 2 tablespoons all-purpose flour sifted with 2 teaspoons baking powder
4 oz./125 g. shredded suet	scant 1 cup shredded suet
salt	salt
1 lb./450 g. leeks	1 lb. leeks
½ oz./15 g. butter	1 tablespoon butter
¼ pint/3 dl. milk	1¼ cups milk
10 oz./275 g. Cheddar cheese	2½ cups grated Cheddar cheese

Make a suet pastry with 8 oz. (225 g., 2 cups) flour, the suet,
a pinch of salt and cold water. Use two-thirds of this pastry to
line a greased pudding basin. Clean the leeks and cut them into
rounds. Make a cheese sauce with the butter, the remaining
flour, milk and the grated cheese. Fill the basin with alternate
layers of leeks and cheese sauce, ending with a layer of leeks.
Put on a lid of the remaining pastry. Cover with greaseproof
paper and foil and boil in a large pan of water for 2 hours.
Serve very hot.

Green vegetables

No one likes to eat overcooked, watery cabbage or sprouts, damp spinach or soggy cauliflower. All greens are at their best if they are lightly cooked until they are only just tender, then drained well and tossed in butter, salt and pepper. But why stop at plain boiled vegetables? Try some unusual soups or some tempting supper dishes as well.

Brussels sprouts soup

IMPERIAL · METRIC	AMERICAN
1½ lb./¾ kg. Brussels sprouts	1½ lb. Brussels sprouts
2½ pints/1¼ litres chicken stock	3 pints chicken stock
½ oz./15 g. butter	1 tablespoon butter
1 tablespoon cornflour	1 tablespoon cornstarch
1 tablespoon lemon juice	1 tablespoon lemon juice
pinch nutmeg	pinch nutmeg
½ teaspoon brown sugar	½ teaspoon brown sugar
grated cheese	grated cheese

Take two or three of the larger outer leaves from each sprout and simmer the leaves in the stock for 10 minutes. Put through a sieve, reserving the liquid. Cook the remaining sprouts in the butter and about 3 tablespoons water until just tender. Mix the cornflour with a little water and add to the sieved sprouts and stock. Simmer, stirring, until the mixture begins to thicken, then add the whole sprouts and their cooking liquid, the lemon juice, nutmeg and sugar. Simmer for 5 minutes and then serve hot, with a few sprouts in each bowl and a little grated cheese on top.

Spinach soup

IMPERIAL · METRIC	AMERICAN
1 medium onion	1 medium onion
2 oz./50 g. butter	$\frac{1}{4}$ cup butter
1$\frac{1}{2}$ lb./$\frac{3}{4}$ kg. spinach	1$\frac{1}{2}$ lb. spinach
1 teaspoon sugar	1 teaspoon sugar
salt and pepper	salt and pepper
1 teaspoon basil or tarragon	1 teaspoon basil or tarragon
$\frac{1}{4}$ pint/1$\frac{1}{2}$ dl. single cream	$\frac{2}{3}$ cup half-and-half
milk	milk

Chop the onion and put with the butter in the bottom of a heavy pan. Heat gently for 3 minutes, then add the spinach, sugar, salt, pepper and basil or tarragon. Cover tightly and cook gently until the spinach is soft. Put through a sieve, or blend in a liquidiser. Add the cream and enough milk to thin to taste – the soup should be the consistency of cream. Leave to stand for 1–2 hours, then heat to serve.

This soup can also be thoroughly chilled and then put into individual bowls and served with a garnish of yogurt and chopped chives or dill.

Hot cabbage salad

IMPERIAL · METRIC	AMERICAN
1 small firm white cabbage	1 small firm white cabbage
2 egg yolks	2 egg yolks
$\frac{1}{2}$ oz./15 g. butter	1 tablespoon butter
2 tablespoons cold water	3 tablespoons cold water
2 tablespoons hot vinegar	3 tablespoons hot vinegar
$\frac{1}{2}$ teaspoon salt	$\frac{1}{2}$ teaspoon salt

Shred the cabbage finely and put it into ice-chilled water while you make the sauce.

Beat the egg yolks lightly, and put into a double saucepan with the remaining ingredients. Cook over hot water, stirring well until the sauce is thick. Drain the cabbage and add it to the sauce. Heat through and serve hot with cold meat or ham.

Braised cabbage

IMPERIAL · METRIC	AMERICAN
1 medium cabbage	1 medium cabbage
6 streaky bacon rashers	6 bacon slices
1 carrot	1 carrot
1 small onion	1 small onion
2 cloves	2 cloves
1 bay leaf	1 bay leaf
1 sprig parsley	1 sprig parsley
1 sprig thyme	1 sprig thyme
½ pint/3 dl. beef stock	1¼ cups beef stock

Cut the cabbage into quarters and cook in boiling salted water until just tender. Drain well and press out all the moisture. Put half the bacon rashers into a casserole. Cover with the cabbage, sliced carrot and onion, herbs and stock. Cover with the remaining bacon and put on a tight lid. Cook in a cool oven (300°F., 150°C., Gas Mark 2) for 2 hours.

This is very good served with sausages.

Cabbage rolls

IMPERIAL · METRIC	AMERICAN
1 lb./450 g. cooked meat, minced	2 cups ground cooked meat
1 oz./25 g. butter	2 tablespoons butter
1 small onion	1 small onion
2 tablespoons cooked rice	3 tablespoons cooked rice
1 teaspoon chopped parsley	1 teaspoon chopped parsley
salt and pepper	salt and pepper
stock	stock
12 medium-sized cabbage leaves	12 medium-sized cabbage leaves

Sauté the meat in the butter together with the finely chopped onion until the meat begins to colour. Mix in the rice, parsley, salt and pepper and enough stock to moisten. Cook for 5 minutes. Blanch the whole cabbage leaves in boiling water for 2 minutes and drain well. Put a spoonful of filling on each leaf and form into a parcel. Put the parcels close together in an ovenproof dish. Pour in stock to cover; cover with a lid and cook in a moderate oven (350°F., 180°C., Gas Mark 4) for 45 minutes.

Sweet and sour red cabbage

IMPERIAL·METRIC	AMERICAN
½ oz./15 g. butter	1 tablespoon butter
2 small onions	2 small onions
1 tablespoon brown sugar	1 tablespoon brown sugar
1 tablespoon cider vinegar	1 tablespoon cider vinegar
1 red cabbage, weighing about 2 lb. (1 kg.)	1 red cabbage, weighing about 2 lb.
¼ pint/1½ dl. cider	⅔ cup cider
salt and pepper	salt and pepper
2 small tart apples	2 small tart apples

Use a strong pan, not an iron one, with a well-fitting lid.

Melt the butter and fry the onions, halved and sliced, until soft. Stir in the sugar and vinegar. Trim the cabbage, cut into quarters and remove the centre core; shred finely, wash and drain very well. Add to the pan with the cider and seasoning; stir well. Simmer slowly for 1 hour. Peel and core the apples and cut each into eighths. Stir into the cabbage and cook for a further 1 hour. Serve hot with sausages or pork.

Cauliflower pie

IMPERIAL·METRIC	AMERICAN
1 large cauliflower	1 large cauliflower
2 oz./50 g. cheese, grated	½ cup grated cheese
2 teaspoons chopped parsley	2 teaspoons chopped parsley
2 oz./50 g. butter	¼ cup butter
4 tablespoons milk	⅓ cup milk
salt and pepper	salt and pepper
1 large onion	1 large onion
1 lb./450 g. tomatoes	1 lb. tomatoes
1 lb./450 g. potatoes	1 lb. potatoes
butter or dripping	butter or drippings

Trim off the green stalks from the cauliflower to use as a vegetable. Cook the florets until tender. Drain and beat until creamy with the cheese, parsley, butter and half the milk. Season to taste and put into a deep casserole. Peel and chop the onion finely, and peel and slice the tomatoes. Put the tomatoes and onions on the cauliflower mixture and season lightly. Boil and mash the potatoes with the remaining milk and spread on top. Dot with a little butter or dripping and bake in a moderate oven (350°F., 180°C., Gas Mark 4) for 30 minutes.

Cauliflower cheese

IMPERIAL·METRIC	AMERICAN
1 lb./450 g. cauliflower sprigs	1 lb. cauliflower sprigs
1 large onion	1 large onion
flour	flour
oil for deep frying	oil for deep frying
¾ pint/4 dl. cheese sauce	scant 2 cups cheese sauce
pinch paprika pepper	pinch paprika pepper
1 tablespoon chopped parsley	1 tablespoon chopped parsley

Cook the cauliflower sprigs in boiling salted water until just tender; drain well. Put in a buttered ovenproof dish. Cut the onion into very thin rings, dip in a little flour and fry until crisp and golden. Drain on absorbent paper and stir half the onions into the hot cheese sauce. Pour over the cauliflower and sprinkle with paprika pepper. Cover and bake in a moderately hot oven (400°F., 200°C., Gas Mark 6) for 15 minutes. Remove the cover, sprinkle with the remaining onions and the parsley and bake for a further 5 minutes. Serve very hot.

Creamed spinach

IMPERIAL·METRIC	AMERICAN
2 lb./1 kg. spinach	2 lb. spinach
1 oz./25 g. butter	2 tablespoons butter
½ oz./15 g. cornflour	2 tablespoons cornstarch
4 tablespoons creamy milk	⅓ cup milk
1 teaspoon lemon juice	1 teaspoon lemon juice

Wash the spinach and cook it with a little salt but no water. Drain and chop finely. Make a thick sauce with the butter, cornflour, milk and lemon juice. Stir in the spinach and simmer for 5 minutes. Serve with meat, fish or eggs.

Brussels sprouts in chicken stock

IMPERIAL · METRIC	AMERICAN
1½ lb./¾ kg. Brussels sprouts	1½ lb. Brussels sprouts
1 oz./25 g. butter	2 tablespoons butter
1 medium onion	1 medium onion
4 tablespoons chicken stock	⅓ cup chicken stock
salt and pepper	salt and pepper
1 teaspoon chopped parsley	1 teaspoon chopped parsley
½ teaspoon chopped chives	½ teaspoon chopped chives

Cook the sprouts in a little boiling water for 5 minutes. Drain very thoroughly. Melt the butter in a heavy saucepan and in it cook the very thinly sliced onion until soft. Add the stock, sprouts and salt and pepper. Simmer for 5 minutes, basting the vegetables with the liquid. Serve very hot, with a sprinkling of parsley and chives, with poultry or veal.

Kale cakes

IMPERIAL · METRIC	AMERICAN
12 oz./350 g. kale	¾ lb. kale
3 oz./75 g. cottage cheese	scant ½ cup cottage cheese
½ teaspoon basil	½ teaspoon basil
½ teaspoon fennel	½ teaspoon fennel
1 tablespoon plain flour	1 tablespoon all-purpose flour
2 tablespoons grated cheese	3 tablespoons grated cheese
1 egg	1 egg
salt and pepper	salt and pepper
butter for frying	butter for frying

Cook the kale very lightly in salted water until just tender. Drain well, cool slightly and then put through a mincer or into a liquidiser until it is a thick purée. Sieve the cottage cheese and blend in the herbs, flour, grated cheese and beaten egg. Season and mix well with the kale to form a soft dropping consistency (add a little more flour if the mixture is not firm enough). Drop spoonfuls into hot butter and fry until golden brown on both sides. Drain on absorbent paper and serve with bacon, sausages or fish, and a light cream sauce.

Broccoli with sour cream

IMPERIAL · METRIC
1 lb./450 g. broccoli
1 tablespoon flour
8 fl. oz./2½ dl. soured cream
2 teaspoons grated horseradish
½ teaspoon vinegar
salt and black pepper

AMERICAN
1 lb. broccoli
1 tablespoon flour
1 cup sour cream
2 teaspoons grated horseradish
½ teaspoon vinegar
salt and black pepper

Cook the broccoli in boiling water and drain thoroughly. Mix
the flour and soured cream. (See that the cream is at room
temperature or it will curdle when heated.) Put the flour and
cream into a double boiler, or into a bowl over a pan of boiling
water, and cook until smooth, stirring constantly. Add the
horseradish, vinegar, salt and pepper and mix well. Pour over the
hot broccoli and serve with pork, veal or chicken.

Peas and beans

It seems a pity to contrive too many dishes with peas and beans
because they are so delicious when young, cooked simply,
dressed with salt and pepper, butter and a sprinkling of herbs.
Broad beans are good served in a parsley sauce with ham or
bacon. Cooked French beans are delicious when cold and mixed
with tomatoes in an oil and vinegar dressing. Runner beans do
not lend themselves to inventive dishes. They are best cooked
when young, and sliced rather thickly instead of being shredded.

Green pea soup

IMPERIAL · METRIC	AMERICAN
2 lb./1 kg. green peas	2 lb. green peas
1 oz./25 g. butter	2 tablespoons butter
1 small onion	1 small onion
1 small lettuce	1 small lettuce
mixed herbs	mixed herbs
3 pints/1½ litres stock	4 pints stock
salt and pepper	salt and pepper
chopped mint or crisply cooked bacon, chopped	chopped mint or crisply cooked bacon, chopped

Put the peas, butter, grated onion, shredded lettuce, and a small bunch of herbs in a pan with a tight-fitting lid. Cook slowly for 10 minutes. Add the stock, salt and pepper, and simmer for 1½ hours. Put through a sieve and reheat. Serve with a little chopped mint or chopped crisply cooked bacon.

Peas with onions

IMPERIAL · METRIC	AMERICAN
4 oz./100 g. lean salt pork	¼ lb. lean salt pork
12 small white onions	12 small white onions
1 teaspoon flour	1 teaspoon flour
½ pint/3 dl. chicken stock	1¼ cups chicken stock
2 lb./1 kg. shelled peas	2 lb. shelled peas
2 tablespoons chopped parsley	3 tablespoons chopped parsley
salt and pepper	salt and pepper

Cut the salt pork into very small dice and boil in a little water for 2 minutes. Drain thoroughly and fry in its own fat in a heavy pan with a lid. When the pork begins to brown add the peeled onions and cook until the onions are tender and the pork is crisp. Drain off the surplus fat. Work the flour into the mixture and cook for 1 minute. Add the stock and bring to the boil. Cover and simmer until the onions are tender. Add the peas, parsley, salt and pepper and cover and simmer until the peas are just tender.

Braised peas

IMPERIAL · METRIC	AMERICAN
1 large lettuce	1 large lettuce
2 lb./1 kg. shelled peas	2 lb. shelled peas
1 teaspoon sugar	1 teaspoon sugar
¼ pint/1½ dl. boiling water	⅔ cup boiling water
salt and pepper	salt and pepper
butter	butter

Line a heavy saucepan with a tight-fitting lid with some of the washed lettuce leaves. Add the peas and sprinkle with the sugar. Add the boiling water. Cover with the remaining washed lettuce leaves, put on the lid, and cook over a medium heat for 15 minutes, until the peas are just tender. Remove the lettuce leaves. Season the peas with salt and pepper and toss in butter.

French beans with cream

IMPERIAL · METRIC	AMERICAN
1½ lb./¾ kg. French beans	1½ lb. French beans
2 bacon rashers	2 bacon slices
2 oz./50 g. onion	½ cup chopped onion
2 oz./50 g. green pepper	½ cup chopped green sweet pepper
¼ pint/1½ dl. water	⅔ cup water
salt and pepper	salt and pepper
3 tablespoons single cream	4 tablespoons half-and-half

Prepare the beans by stringing them and cut them in pieces if large. Cut the bacon in small pieces and put into a heavy pan. Heat for a minute until the fat begins to run. Add the finely chopped onion and green pepper and cook gently for 4 minutes. Add the beans and the water and cover tightly. Simmer for 15 minutes, until the beans are tender – see that they do not burn. Season with salt and pepper, stir in the cream and serve hot.

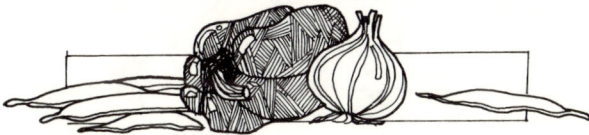

Beans in their jackets

IMPERIAL·METRIC	AMERICAN
1½ lb./¾ kg. young broad beans in pods	1½ lb. young lima or fava beans, unshelled
salt and pepper	salt and pepper
squeeze of lemon juice	squeeze of lemon juice
1 oz./25 g. butter	2 tablespoons butter
3 tablespoons double cream	scant ¼ cup heavy cream
1 tablespoon chopped parsley	1 tablespoon chopped parsley

Use only very young beans with tender pods.

Wash the pods, top and tail them, and trim the sides. Cook whole in unsalted boiling water for 15 minutes and drain. Season with salt and pepper and lemon juice, and toss in the butter, cream and parsley. Heat through gently and serve.

Broad bean salad

IMPERIAL·METRIC	AMERICAN
1 lb./450 g. shelled broad beans	1 lb. shelled lima or fava beans
1 teaspoon French mustard	1 teaspoon French mustard
1 teaspoon paprika pepper	1 teaspoon paprika pepper
1 clove garlic	1 clove garlic
salt and black pepper	salt and black pepper
1 tablespoon chopped parsley	1 tablespoon chopped parsley
1 tablespoon vinegar	1 tablespoon vinegar
3 tablespoons olive oil	scant ¼ cup olive oil

Cook the beans and slip them from their outer skins before the dressing is added. In a serving bowl, put the mustard, paprika pepper, crushed garlic, salt, pepper and parsley. Add the vinegar and oil and work the mixture together until well blended. Add the beans and toss them in the dressing just before serving.

Cucumbers, marrows and pumpkins

Cucumbers are usually only eaten cold, marrow is despised, and pumpkin rarely used except for a Harvest Festival display. They are all delicious vegetables if treated with care. Cucumbers, in particular, are very good cooked, as well as in the traditional thin bread and butter sandwich.

Cucumbers
Contrary to general opinion, they are more digestible if the peel is left on for sandwiches and salads. For cooking though, the cucumber is usually peeled.

Cucumber salad
Slice the cucumber very thinly and put into a half-and-half mixture of water and vinegar, seasoned with salt and pepper and a pinch of sugar. Leave in a cool place for 2 hours, drain well, and sprinkle with chopped parsley.

Cucumber fritters
Peel a cucumber and slice it thickly. Dip the slices in a coating of batter (flavoured with a little grated cheese if you like) and deep fry in hot oil. Drain on absorbent paper.

Creamed cucumber
Peel a cucumber and cut it in finger-lengths. Simmer gently in chicken or veal stock until just tender. Thicken the cooking liquid with a little butter and flour to coat the cucumber. Serve as a vegetable, or put the cucumber and sauce into a shallow dish, sprinkle with grated cheese and breadcrumbs and brown under the grill.

Cucumber soup

IMPERIAL · METRIC	AMERICAN
1 cucumber	1 cucumber
1 oz./25 g. butter	2 tablespoons butter
flour	flour
1 pint/6 dl. white stock or water	2½ cups white stock or water
salt and pepper	salt and pepper
½ pint/3 dl. milk	1¼ cups milk
1 egg	1 egg
3–4 tablespoons double cream	¼–⅓ cup whipping cream
chopped parsley	chopped parsley

Peel the cucumber and cut it in half lengthways. Remove the seeds and cut the flesh into small pieces. Melt the butter in a thick pan and thicken with a little flour. Gradually add the stock and bring to the boil, stirring. Add the cucumber, salt and pepper to taste and simmer until cucumber is tender. Pour the soup through a sieve, pressing the cucumber through to form a thin purée. Return to the pan. In a small pan, bring the milk to the boil and stir it into the soup. Beat the egg and cream together, remove the soup from the heat and stir in egg and cream. Serve immediately garnished with chopped parsley.

Savoury marrow

IMPERIAL · METRIC	AMERICAN
1 large marrow	1 large summer squash
1 lb./450 g. cold cooked meat	2 cups ground cooked meat
2 oz./50 g. bacon	3 bacon slices
1 small onion	1 small onion
1 oz./25 g. flour	¼ cup all-purpose flour
1 teaspoon salt	1 teaspoon salt
½ teaspoon pepper	½ teaspoon pepper
3 tablespoons breadcrumbs	4 tablespoons bread crumbs
1 teaspoon chopped parsley	1 teaspoon chopped parsley
2 tomatoes	2 tomatoes
stock	stock
1 oz./25 g. dripping	2 tablespoons drippings

Cut the marrow through about 2 inches (5 cm.) from the end.
Remove the seeds and pulp. Peel the large piece of marrow and
boil it for 5 minutes. Mince the meat, bacon and onion and mix
with flour, salt and pepper, breadcrumbs and parsley. Skin and
chop the tomatoes and add to the mixture and moisten with a
little stock. Stuff the marrow with the mixture and replace peeled,
cut-off end. Put in an ovenproof dish, dot with dripping and bake
in a moderate oven (350°F., 180°C., Gas Mark 4) for 1 hour,
basting frequently. Serve with plenty of gravy.

Pumpkin soup

IMPERIAL·METRIC	AMERICAN
2 lb./1 kg. pumpkin flesh	2 lb. pumpkin flesh
8 oz./225 g. potatoes	½ lb. potatoes
8 oz./225 g. tomatoes	½ lb. tomatoes
1 stick celery	1 stalk celery
1½ pints/scant litre chicken stock	3¾ cups chicken stock
1 large onion	1 large onion
1 pint/6 dl. milk	2½ cups milk
salt and pepper	salt and pepper
2 oz./50 g. butter	¼ cup butter
3 tablespoons cream	4 tablespoons half-and-half
chopped parsley (optional)	chopped parsley (optional)
crisply cooked bacon, chopped (optional)	crisply cooked bacon, chopped (optional)

Cut the pumpkin flesh into cubes, chop the potatoes, peel and
chop the tomatoes and chop the celery. Simmer in the stock for
15 minutes, then put through a sieve. Chop the onion very finely
and simmer in the milk until tender. Add the sieved purée and
season well with salt and pepper. Stir in the butter and cream
just before serving. A little chopped parsley, or crisp bacon pieces
may be added to give colour and flavour.

Cucumber fritters

IMPERIAL·METRIC	AMERICAN
1 cucumber	1 cucumber
flour	flour
salt and pepper	salt and pepper
oil for frying	oil for frying

Peel the cucumber and cut into ½-inch (1-cm.) slices. Pat the slices very dry with kitchen paper and toss in flour well seasoned with salt and pepper. Fry until golden in oil. Drain well on absorbent paper and serve very hot.

Cucumber slices are particularly delicious with lamb dishes and with veal.

For crisper cucumber slices, dip in flour first, then in egg and fine breadcrumbs before frying.

Stuffed marrow rings

IMPERIAL·METRIC	AMERICAN
1 medium marrow	1 medium summer squash
1 lb./450 g. cooked beef or lamb	2 cups ground cooked beef or lamb
6 oz./175 g. fresh white breadcrumbs	3 cups fresh soft bread crumbs
1 medium onion	1 medium onion
½ pint/3 dl. stock	1¼ cups stock
2 teaspoons tomato purée (optional)	2 teaspoons tomato paste (optional)
salt and pepper	salt and pepper

Cut marrow into 2-inch (5-cm.) slices, removing the seeds and pith. Cook in boiling water for 3 minutes. Drain well and arrange in a greased ovenproof dish. Mince the meat and mix with the breadcrumbs, the onion which has been chopped and softened in a little fat, stock, tomato purée (if used) and seasoning. (The stock may be thickened with a little cornflour if a firmer mixture is liked.) Cook the mixture together for 10 minutes, then use to fill the marrow rings. Cook in a moderately hot oven (375°F., 190°C., Gas Mark 5) for 45 minutes.

Pumpkin pie

IMPERIAL·METRIC	AMERICAN
8 oz./225 g. shortcrust pastry	basic pie dough made with 2 cups all-purpose flour etc.
1 lb./450 g. pumpkin flesh	1 lb. pumpkin flesh
6 oz./175 g. brown sugar	¾ cup brown sugar
¼ teaspoon ground cloves	¼ teaspoon ground cloves
1¼ teaspoons ground cinnamon	1¼ teaspoons ground cinnamon
1¼ teaspoons ground ginger	1¼ teaspoons ground ginger
½ teaspoon salt	½ teaspoon salt
2 eggs	2 eggs
½ pint/3 dl. milk	1¼ cups milk
1 tablespoon grated orange rind	1 tablespoon grated orange rind

Line a flan ring or pie plate with the pastry and bake blind in a moderately hot oven (400°F., 200°C., Gas Mark 6) until just beginning to colour. Dice the pumpkin flesh, steam until soft, then put through a sieve. Leave to cool, then stir in sugar, spices, salt, beaten eggs, milk and orange rind. Pour into the flan case and return to the oven for a further 30 minutes.

Mushrooms

Mushrooms don't need to be peeled, just wiped over with a damp cloth. The tiny, unopened ones are known as button mushrooms. These are the ones to use for a white sauce or to serve whole, or sliced raw, in a fresh crisp salad. They are also good for garnishing and for pickling. The slightly riper ones, which are starting to open, are cups and are fine for adding, sliced, to soups and stews, or for using whole for baking or stuffing with a tasty mixture. Opens or flats are, as the names suggest, fully opened mushrooms. They have plenty of flavour to them and are the ones for grilling or frying.

Mushrooms can be stored, if necessary, for a few days. They dry out quickly, so put them, unwashed, into an airtight container and keep in a cool place, such as a cold larder or the lowest shelf of a refrigerator.

Grilled mushrooms

Allow 4 open mushrooms per person. Season with pepper and salt. Grill them, and turn them so that they can cook thoroughly. Place on a very hot platter, adding a small dab of butter in the centre of each mushroom. Serve sprinkled with lemon juice.

Baked mushrooms

Place stalked mushrooms upside down on a baking tin with a small piece of butter on the gills of each mushroom. Cover with an inverted deep plate and place in a hot oven (425°F., 220°C., Gas Mark 7) for about 15 minutes. Serve on a hot plate.

Mushrooms on toast

Slice large mushrooms, but also use those in the button stage whole. Make a pan hot, allow some butter to melt and add the mushrooms and seasoning. Cook over a medium heat for about 20 minutes. Cut rounds of bread and toast both sides. Place a generous portion of mushrooms on each slice, thicken the juice remaining in the pan with a small quantity of flour or a little cream and pour over the mushrooms.

Raw mushroom salad

Wash and drain 8 oz. (225 g., 2 cups) firm white mushrooms. Slice them fairly thinly and put in a bowl with olive oil, pepper, a little lemon juice and, if you like, a tiny piece of garlic. Add salt only just before serving.

Raw mushrooms are a delightful addition to any salad.

Mushroom cream sauce

IMPERIAL · METRIC	AMERICAN
2 oz./50 g. butter	$\frac{1}{4}$ cup butter
4 oz./100 g. button mushrooms	1 cup button mushrooms
$\frac{1}{4}$ pint/1$\frac{1}{2}$ dl. single cream	$\frac{2}{3}$ cup half-and-half
salt and pepper	salt and pepper

Melt the butter in a small, thick saucepan and soften the mushrooms. Add the cream and stir gently over a low heat, without boiling, for 5 minutes. Season well with salt and pepper, and serve with grilled meat or fish.

Spiced mushrooms

IMPERIAL · METRIC	AMERICAN
1 lb./450 g. button mushrooms	4 cups button mushrooms
juice of 1 lemon	juice of 1 lemon
1 teaspoon salt	1 teaspoon salt
¼ pint/1½ dl. wine vinegar	⅔ cup wine vinegar
1 small clove garlic	1 small clove garlic
1 small onion	1 small onion
1 bay leaf	1 bay leaf
sprig thyme	sprig thyme
freshly ground black pepper	freshly ground black pepper
1 tablespoon tomato sauce	1 tablespoon tomato sauce
3 tablespoons olive oil	scant ¼ cup olive oil

Wipe the mushrooms and just cover them with water. Add the lemon juice and a pinch of salt and simmer for 5 minutes. Meanwhile, simmer together the remaining salt, the vinegar, crushed garlic, finely chopped onion, bay leaf, thyme, pepper, sauce and oil for 5 minutes. Drain the mushrooms and put them in the vinegar mixture. Leave in the refrigerator for several hours before using. (They keep for up to a week.) Drain mushrooms, sprinkle with a little liquor and serve as a salad.

Savoury mushrooms

IMPERIAL · METRIC	AMERICAN
8 oz./225 g. mushrooms	2 cups mushrooms
2 oz./50 g. butter	¼ cup butter
salt and pepper	salt and pepper
1 small onion	1 small onion
2 tablespoons lemon juice	3 tablespoons lemon juice
1 teaspoon finely chopped parsley	1 teaspoon finely chopped parsley

Cut off all but ½ inch (1 cm.) of the mushroom stalk. Rinse in cold water and dry. Cut in thin slices through the stem. Heat the butter to near smoking. Add part of the mushroom slices and toss and turn in the butter. Add the rest, season and fry for a moment. Add the chopped onion and fry for 2 minutes. Cover closely, reduce the heat and simmer for 2–4 minutes. Add the lemon juice and parsley. Serve with meat dishes.

Cheese and mushroom flan

IMPERIAL · METRIC	AMERICAN
6 oz./175 g. shortcrust pastry	basic pie dough made with 1½ cups all-purpose flour etc.
6 oz./175 g. button mushrooms, lightly fried	1½ cups button mushrooms, lightly fried
2 eggs	2 eggs
2½ oz./65 g. Cheddar cheese, grated	generous ½ cup grated Cheddar cheese
2 oz./50 g. cooked bacon, chopped	¼ cup cooked chopped bacon
7 tablespoons milk	generous ½ cup milk
pinch cayenne pepper and salt	pinch cayenne pepper and salt

Line a 7-inch (18-cm.) flan ring with the pastry and bake blind in a hot oven (425°F., 220°C., Gas Mark 7) for 15 minutes. Slice half the fried mushrooms, keeping the smallest even-sized buttons for garnishing. Place in the base of the pastry case. Beat the eggs, add 2 oz. (50 g., ½ cup) of the cheese, the bacon, mushrooms, milk and seasonings. Mix well and pour over the mushrooms. Sprinkle over the remaining cheese and bake in a moderately hot oven (400°F., 200°C., Gas Mark 6) for 20–25 minutes, until golden brown and set. Garnish with the reserved mushrooms. Serve hot or cold.

Mushroom savoury

IMPERIAL · METRIC	AMERICAN
4 bacon rashers	4 bacon slices
8 oz./225 g. open mushrooms	½ lb. open mushrooms
8 oz./225 g. soft roes	½ lb. soft roes
1 oz./25 g. butter	2 tablespoons butter
4 slices toast	4 slices toast
salt and pepper	salt and pepper

Fry the bacon and then the mushrooms in one pan. Fry the roes in butter in another pan. When all are cooked, cover the toast with bacon, then the roes and lastly pile on the mushrooms. Season to taste and serve.

Gammon with mushroom stuffing

IMPERIAL · METRIC	AMERICAN
4 oz./100 g. mushrooms	1 cup chopped mushrooms
1 oz./25 g. butter	2 tablespoons butter
3 oz./75 g. breadcrumbs	1½ cups fresh soft bread crumbs
juice of ½ lemon	juice of ½ lemon
1 teaspoon chopped parsley	1 teaspoon chopped parsley
salt and pepper	salt and pepper
2 egg yolks	2 egg yolks
4 gammon rashers	4 ham steaks

Wash the mushrooms and chop them finely. Melt the butter in a
saucepan and cook the mushrooms in it. Add the breadcrumbs,
lemon juice, chopped parsley, salt and pepper. Mix well and
bind the mixture together with the egg yolks, lightly beaten.
Divide the stuffing into four portions and pile on to the grilled
slices of gammon. Brown in a moderate oven (350°F., 180°C.,
Gas Mark 4) for 15 minutes.

Stuffed mushrooms

IMPERIAL · METRIC	AMERICAN
4 large mushrooms	4 large mushrooms
1 teaspoon finely chopped onion	1 teaspoon finely chopped onion
½ oz./15 g. butter	1 tablespoon butter
1 tablespoon chopped cooked ham	1 tablespoon chopped cooked ham
1 tablespoon breadcrumbs	1 tablespoon bread crumbs
salt and pepper	salt and pepper
1 tablespoon white sauce	1 tablespoon white sauce
4 slices fried bread	4 slices fried bread
1 teaspoon chopped parsley	1 teaspoon chopped parsley

Wash the mushrooms. Trim to equal-sized rounds, with a cutter,
if necessary. Chop the trimmings finely. Fry the onion and the
trimmings in the butter for 10 minutes. Add the ham,
breadcrumbs and seasoning with sufficient sauce to bind. Pile the
mixture on the underside of the prepared mushrooms. Put on a
greased tin, cover with greased paper and bake in a moderate
oven (350°F., 180°C., Gas Mark 4) for about 20 minutes, until
soft. Serve on the fried bread and garnish with parsley.

Mushroom sandwiches

IMPERIAL · METRIC	AMERICAN
8 oz./225 g. open mushrooms	½ lb. open mushrooms
4 oz./100 g. butter	½ cup butter
squeeze lemon juice	squeeze lemon juice
salt and pepper	salt and pepper
pinch cayenne pepper	pinch cayenne pepper

Chop the mushrooms roughly and cook in 1 oz. (25 g., 2 tablespoons) of the butter with the lemon juice. Cook for 8 minutes, until very soft. Cool slightly, then chop the mushrooms finely. Pound the mushrooms to a paste with plenty of salt and pepper and a pinch of cayenne pepper and work in the remaining butter. Use in brown bread sandwiches, or make into toasted sandwiches with thin slices of toast.

Tomatoes

Tomatoes give their own special and refreshing flavour to so many dishes that they are worth preserving for winter. A tomato in a stew helps to soften tough meat, while tomatoes enrich the flavour of curry and moderate the bite of some curry powders. Fresh tomatoes make delicious salads, soups and sauces and are always a welcome garnish for meat, fish and cheese dishes. A pinch of sugar brings out the flavour of tomatoes, and they are good seasoned with sea salt and freshly ground black pepper, a little chopped basil, mint, parsley or chives.

Grilled tomatoes
Cut the tomatoes in halves and grill them, cut-side up facing the grill, until the tops are almost blackened.
If small tomatoes are used, leave them whole, but slash the tops in a cross and sprinkle with salt before grilling.

Fried tomatoes
Cut the tomatoes in halves and fry them, skin side down, in very little fat until the skin has almost burnt, but do not turn them over.

Baked tomatoes

Use small tomatoes of even size and leave them whole. Slash the tops in a cross and arrange them in a well greased ovenproof dish or baking tin. Bake in a hot oven (425°F., 220°C., Gas Mark 7) until the tops split and are slightly burned.

Stuffed tomatoes

Raw tomatoes can be scooped out and filled with cooked meat or fish, chopped egg or grated cheese. Bind the filling with a little mayonnaise or salad cream and add a few cooked vegetables such as peas or chopped carrots for colour.

Tomatoes can also be stuffed for cooking. Scoop out the insides and mix with minced cooked meat or flaked fish, binding with cooked rice or breadcrumbs and plenty of seasoning. Bake in a hot oven (425°F., 220°C., Gas Mark 7) until the skins begin to blacken.

Bottled tomatoes

Water method Carefully pack the tomatoes as tightly as possible into jars. It is wise to halve the larger tomatoes. Add $\frac{1}{2}$ teaspoon of sugar and $\frac{1}{2}$ teaspoon of salt to every 1 lb. (450 g.) of tomatoes. Fill the jar with tomato juice prepared by rubbing stewed tomatoes through a sieve. When the bottles are completely full, put on the rubber rings, tops and clips or screw bands (screw bands should be given a half-turn back to allow for glass expansion). Place in a large saucepan of water.

Heat very slowly to 190°F. (88°C.) and keep the water as near as possible to that temperature for 30 minutes. Then lift out the jars and tighten the screw bands. Next day remove the clip or band and see if the lid is tight. The tomato level will have dropped in the jar but on no account add any more.

Oven method Prepare and pack the tomatoes in the jars as before, but do not add any liquid. Do not put on any screw bands, but cover the jar tops with saucers or patty tins. Place the jars on an old mat or board and put in a very cool oven (250°F., 120°C., Gas Mark $\frac{1}{2}$). While the jars are in the oven (they should stay there for approximately $1\frac{1}{2}$ hours), sterilise the jar tops, bands etc. in boiling water, and prepare a kettle of boiling water. The important thing about the oven method is speed when you bring the jars out of the oven. As the tomatoes will shrink considerably it may be necessary to use one jar to fill up the others. This should be done while the jars are still in the oven. Bring out one jar at a time, stand it on a wooden surface and pour in the boiling water, tapping the jar as you do so until it overflows. Then quickly fasten or screw down the top. Do not handle the jars for 24 hours, then test for a seal as before. Tomatoes need sterilising very carefully, particularly when skinned, and it is not easy to tell when they are done. *Always allow the full time at the given temperature.*

Tomato purée

To make a purée, first cook the halved tomatoes in hardly any water in a covered pan until they feel quite soft. Rub the softened tomatoes carefully and gently through a sieve fine enough to retain the pips as well as the outer skins. Then reheat this purée and add sufficient salt and sugar to taste. Pour the purée into bottling jars, put the lids on and sterilise by immersion in boiling water for 10 minutes.

It is not really necessary to remove the tomato skin first, but if desired this can easily be done by dipping the tomatoes, first in hot water, then in cold.

Granny's quick tomato soup

IMPERIAL · METRIC	AMERICAN
4 oz./100 g. porridge oats	generous 1 cup rolled oats
12 small tomatoes	12 small tomatoes
6 spring onions	6 scallions
4 cloves garlic	4 cloves garlic
3 oz./75 g. butter	6 tablespoons butter
2½ pints/1¼ litres beef stock	3 pints beef stock
1 teaspoon salt	1 teaspoon salt
pinch grated nutmeg	pinch grated nutmeg

Lightly brown the oats in a large heavy saucepan but do not burn. Set the toasted oats aside. Toss the sliced tomatoes, spring onions and crushed garlic in the butter for 1 minute. Add the stock, salt, nutmeg and oats. Boil for 5 minutes over a medium heat and serve hot.

Fresh tomato soup

IMPERIAL·METRIC	AMERICAN
1 lb./450 g. tomatoes	1 lb. tomatoes
1 pint/6 dl. stock	2½ cups stock
1 small onion	1 small onion
bay leaf, parsley and thyme	bay leaf, parsley and thyme
1½ oz./40 g. butter	3 tablespoons butter
1½ oz./40 g. flour	6 tablespoons all-purpose flour
¼ pint/1½ dl. milk	⅔ cup milk
1 teaspoon sugar	1 teaspoon sugar
salt and pepper	salt and pepper
double cream	whipping cream

Cut up the tomatoes and put them into a saucepan with the
stock, onion and herbs. Simmer for 1 hour, until the tomatoes
and onion are tender. Rub through a fine sieve. Melt the butter
and work in the flour. Gradually add the tomato purée. Stir
until boiling and then add the milk, sugar, salt and pepper to
taste. Reheat and serve with a spoonful of cream in each bowl.

Tomato and onion casserole

IMPERIAL·METRIC	AMERICAN
1 lb./450 g. onions	1 lb. onions
salt and pepper	salt and pepper
½ teaspoon marjoram or basil	½ teaspoon marjoram or basil
2 lb./1 kg. tomatoes	2 lb. tomatoes
3 oz./75 g. fresh breadcrumbs	1½ cups fresh soft bread crumbs
3 oz./75 g. cheese, grated	¾ cup grated cheese
1 oz./25 g. butter or bacon fat	2 tablespoons butter or bacon drippings

Peel and slice the onions and boil in salted water for 20 minutes.
Drain well and season with salt, pepper and herbs. Put half in the
bottom of a greased casserole. Skin and slice the tomatoes and put
half of them on top of the onions. Next put a layer of crumbs and
grated cheese mixed. Repeat these layers and pour the melted
butter or bacon fat over the top. Bake in a hot oven (425°F.,
220 °C., Gas Mark 7) for about 20 minutes.

Tomato and onion salad

IMPERIAL · METRIC	AMERICAN
4 large tomatoes	4 large tomatoes
1 onion	1 onion
1 teaspoon basil	1 teaspoon basil
salt and pepper	salt and pepper
pinch sugar	pinch sugar
4 tablespoons oil and vinegar dressing	$\frac{1}{3}$ cup oil and vinegar dressing
lettuce leaves	lettuce leaves

Peel and slice tomatoes and onion thinly and place in a basin.
Sprinkle with the basil, a little salt and pepper and the sugar.
Pour on the dressing and leave for 30 minutes. Serve on lettuce.

Baked tomatoes

IMPERIAL · METRIC	AMERICAN
6 large tomatoes	6 large tomatoes
1 tablespoon chopped parsley	1 tablespoon chopped parsley
1 tablespoon chopped fresh marjoram	1 tablespoon chopped fresh marjoram
salt and pepper	salt and pepper
1 oz./25 g. butter	2 tablespoons butter

Skin the tomatoes by dropping them into boiling water. Slice
them thickly and put into a greased ovenproof dish. Sprinkle
with herbs, salt and pepper. Dot with flakes of butter and bake in
a moderate oven (350°F., 180°C., Gas Mark 4) for 20 minutes.

Baked tomatoes with garlic

IMPERIAL · METRIC	AMERICAN
6 tomatoes	6 tomatoes
4 tablespoons olive oil	$\frac{1}{3}$ cup olive oil
salt and pepper	salt and pepper
1 clove garlic	1 clove garlic
3 tablespoons chopped parsley	4 tablespoons chopped parsley
2 oz./50 g. fine fresh breadcrumbs	1 cup fresh soft bread crumbs

Cut the tomatoes in half, and cook (cut side down) in the oil for 10 minutes. Turn and cook other sides for 5 minutes. Put into an ovenproof dish and sprinkle with salt and pepper, finely chopped garlic, parsley and breadcrumbs. Sprinkle with the oil left in the frying pan. Bake in a moderate oven (350°F., 180°C., Gas Mark 4) for 30 minutes.

These tomatoes are very good served with roast or grilled lamb, or with a plain omelette.

Watercress

Don't think of watercress as just a garnish for roast poultry or game, or grilled fish, because it is delicious cooked in all sorts of ways. If you are a traditionalist, you will enjoy those favourite Victorian sandwiches made with thin brown bread and butter, plenty of watercress and salt, and a sprinkling of vinegar.

Watercress soup

IMPERIAL · METRIC	AMERICAN
1 small leek	1 small leek
2 bacon rashers	2 bacon slices
½ oz./15 g. butter	1 tablespoon butter
1 pint/6 dl. water	2½ cups water
salt and pepper	salt and pepper
2 bunches watercress	2 bunches watercress
1 lb./450 g. potatoes	1 lb. potatoes
½ pint/3 dl. milk	1¼ cups milk
single cream	half-and-half
watercress to garnish	watercress to garnish

Gently fry the chopped leek and bacon in the melted butter, but do not allow the leek to colour. Add the water, seasoning and watercress. Peel and quarter the potatoes and add to the soup. Simmer for 30–40 minutes. Cool slightly, then sieve or liquidise. Add the milk, adjust the seasoning if necessary and heat through. To serve, pour over a little cream in the bottom of each bowl, then pour in soup and garnish with watercress.

Jellied ham and watercress

IMPERIAL·METRIC	AMERICAN
1¼ lb./550 g. cooked ham in one piece	1¼ lb. cooked smoked ham in one piece
¾ pint/4 dl. chicken stock	scant 2 cups chicken stock
freshly ground black pepper	freshly ground black pepper
grated nutmeg	grated nutmeg
1 bunch watercress, chopped	1 bunch watercress, chopped
½ oz./15 g. gelatine	2 envelopes gelatin
2 tablespoons water	3 tablespoons water
1 tablespoon tarragon vinegar	1 tablespoon tarragon vinegar

Dice the ham roughly and place in a pan with the stock, black pepper and nutmeg to taste. Simmer gently for about 5 minutes. Strain and reserve the stock. Wet a glass bowl (individual dishes may be used instead) and coat the inside with some of the watercress. Place the ham in the bowl. Place the gelatine in a cup with the water and heat gently over boiling water. Add the hot stock, remaining watercress and the vinegar. Leave to cool and when almost setting, pour over the diced ham. Leave to set overnight. Serve with a mixed salad.

Watercress butter

IMPERIAL·METRIC	AMERICAN
1 bunch watercress	1 bunch watercress
4 oz./100 g. butter	½ cup butter
2 teaspoons grated onion	2 teaspoons grated onion
salt and freshly ground black pepper	salt and freshly ground black pepper

Chop the watercress finely. Soften the butter and mix in the remaining ingredients with a fork. Place the mixture on wet greaseproof paper and form into a roll 1 inch (2·5 cm.) in diameter. Wrap the greaseproof paper around roll and place in the refrigerator until firm. Cut into slices and use to garnish grilled meat or fish.

Savoury watercress pudding

IMPERIAL · METRIC	AMERICAN
6 oz./175 g. self-raising flour	1½ cups all-purpose flour sifted with 1½ teaspoons baking powder
3 oz./75 g. shredded suet	generous ⅓ cup shredded suet
pinch salt	pinch salt
1 bunch watercress	1 bunch watercress
8 oz./225 g. pork sausages	½ lb. pork sausage links
4 oz./100 g. bacon	¼ lb. bacon slices
1 onion	1 onion
salt and pepper	salt and pepper
½ pint/3 dl. chicken stock	1¼ cups chicken stock

Mix the flour, suet, salt and enough water to make a firm paste. Chop the watercress, sausages, bacon and onion. Using two-thirds of the pastry line a 1½-pint (1-litre) basin. Mix the other ingredients together and place in lined basin. With remaining pastry make a lid and seal. Cover with greaseproof paper and steam for 2 hours.

Eggs in a blanket

IMPERIAL · METRIC	AMERICAN
4 bunches watercress	4 bunches watercress
6 hard-boiled eggs	6 hard-cooked eggs
½ pint/3 dl. cheese sauce	1¼ cups cheese sauce
1 oz./25 g. white breadcrumbs	½ cup fresh soft bread crumbs
1 oz./25 g. cheese, grated	¼ cup grated cheese

Cook the watercress in ½ inch (1 cm.) of boiling salted water for 5 minutes. Drain well and place in a greased ovenproof dish. Halve the eggs and place on top of the watercress. Pour over the cheese sauce and sprinkle with the breadcrumbs and cheese. Brown in a moderately hot oven (400°F., 200°C., Gas Mark 6) for 30 minutes.

Tasty watercress pie

IMPERIAL · METRIC	AMERICAN
6 oz./175 g. Cheddar cheese	1½ cups grated cheese
2 bunches watercress	2 bunches watercress
8 oz./225 g. cooked potatoes	1 cup cooked potato
1 small onion	1 small onion
2 carrots	2 carrots
12 oz./350 g. shortcrust pastry	basic pie dough made with 3 cups all-purpose flour etc.
milk or egg to glaze	milk or egg to glaze

Grate the cheese. Chop the watercress and potatoes. Chop and cook the onion and carrots. Using two-thirds of the pastry line a 9-inch (23-cm.) deep pie plate. Place the watercress in the pastry-lined dish. Mix together the cheese, onion, potato, carrots and seasoning and place on top. Make a lid from remaining pastry, brush the edges with water and seal. Brush with milk or egg and bake in a moderately hot oven (400°F., 200°C., Gas Mark 6) for 30 minutes.

Sauces, pickles, chutneys and sweet preserves

Tomato barbecue sauce

IMPERIAL · METRIC	AMERICAN
4 lb./2 kg. ripe tomatoes	4 lb. ripe tomatoes
2 tablespoons salt	3 tablespoons salt
8 oz./225 g. sugar	1 cup sugar
½ teaspoon cayenne pepper	½ teaspoon cayenne pepper
2 tablespoons ground ginger	3 tablespoons ground ginger
2 cloves garlic, chopped	2 cloves garlic, chopped
1½ teaspoons dry mustard	1½ teaspoons dry mustard

Place all the ingredients in an enamel pan. Bring to the boil and simmer slowly until the mixture has reduced to half, stirring frequently. (This will take 1–1½ hours.) Strain and reheat just to boiling. Pour into hot preserving jars and seal.

Tomato sauce

IMPERIAL · METRIC	AMERICAN
4 lb./2 kg. ripe tomatoes	4 lb. ripe tomatoes
4 large onions	4 large onions
1 lb./450 g. Demerara sugar	2 cups brown sugar
1 oz./25 g. salt	4 teaspoons salt
2 oz./50 g. peppercorns	$\frac{1}{2}$ cup peppercorns
$\frac{1}{2}$ oz./15 g. cloves	3 tablespoons cloves
2 teaspoons cayenne pepper	2 teaspoons cayenne pepper
1 pint/6 dl. vinegar	$2\frac{1}{2}$ cups vinegar

Slice tomatoes and onions and mix with the other ingredients.
Simmer gently for 2 hours, stirring occasionally. Rub through a
fine sieve, leaving nothing but spice, seeds and skins in the
strainer. Bring to the boil and boil for 5 minutes. Bottle when cold.

This sauce will keep well and improves with keeping.

Green tomato jam

IMPERIAL · METRIC	AMERICAN
rind of 1 orange	rind of 1 orange
2 lb./1 kg. green tomatoes	2 lb. green tomatoes
$1\frac{1}{2}$ lb./$\frac{3}{4}$ kg. sugar	3 cups sugar

Cut the orange rind into thin shreds and simmer in a very little
water until tender. Cut up the tomatoes and add to the rind.
Simmer for 45 minutes. Stir in the sugar. Dissolve the sugar and
then boil fast for 20 minutes, until setting point is reached. Put
into small warm jars and cover.

Ripe tomato chutney

IMPERIAL · METRIC	AMERICAN
1 lb./450 g. ripe tomatoes	1 lb. ripe tomatoes
4 oz./100 g. apples	¼ lb. apples
8 oz./225 g. onions	½ lb. onions
1 lb./450 g. stoned raisins	3 cups pitted raisins
4 oz./100 g. soft brown sugar	½ cup brown sugar
¼ oz./10 g. salt	1 teaspoon salt
¼ oz./10 g. ground ginger	1 tablespoon ground ginger
pinch cayenne pepper	pinch cayenne pepper
½ pint/3 dl. vinegar	1¼ cups vinegar

Skin the tomatoes and peel and core the apples. Chop the tomatoes, onions, apples and raisins. Mix all the ingredients and simmer for 1 hour or more, until thick and brown. Pour into small jars and cover.

Military pickle

IMPERIAL · METRIC	AMERICAN
1 marrow	1 summer squash
1 cauliflower	1 cauliflower
1 lb./450 g. beans	1 lb. green beans
1 lb./450 g. onions	1 lb. onions
cooking salt	cooking salt
1 lb./450 g. Demerara sugar	2 cups brown sugar
4 pints/2¼ litres vinegar	5 pints vinegar
7 chillies	7 chili peppers
1 oz./25 g. turmeric powder	¼ cup turmeric powder
1 oz./25 g. ground ginger	4 tablespoons ground ginger
4 oz./100 g. plain flour	1 cup all-purpose flour

Cut the vegetables into small pieces and cover with salt. Leave to stand overnight, then drain. Put into a saucepan, add sugar, vinegar and chillies and boil for 5 minutes. Mix the dry ingredients to a smooth paste with a little cold water. Add to the pan, stirring. Boil for 30 minutes, stirring to prevent burning. Bottle when cold.

Spicy green tomato chutney

IMPERIAL · METRIC	AMERICAN
4 lb./2 kg. green tomatoes	4 lb. green tomatoes
1 lb./450 g. apples	1 lb. apples
1½ lb./¾ kg. shallots	1½ lb. shallots
8 oz./225 g. stoned raisins	scant 1½ cups pitted raisins
½ oz./15 g. root ginger	1 small piece root ginger
12 red chillies	12 red chili peppers
1 lb./450 g. brown sugar	2 cups brown sugar
½ oz./15 g. salt	2 teaspoons salt
1 pint/6 dl. vinegar	2½ cups vinegar

Cut up the tomatoes, peel and cut up the apples and shallots and chop the raisins. Bruise the ginger and chillies and tie in a muslin bag. Place all the ingredients in a pan, bring to the boil and simmer until the chutney is the desired consistency. Remove the bag of spices and bottle the chutney.

Runner bean chutney

IMPERIAL · METRIC	AMERICAN
2 lb./1 kg. runner beans	2 lb. green beans
1½ lb./¾ kg. onions	1½ lb. onions
1½ pints/scant litre vinegar	3¾ cups vinegar
1½ tablespoons cornflour	2 tablespoons cornstarch
1 tablespoon turmeric	1 tablespoon turmeric
1½ tablespoons dry mustard	2 tablespoons dry mustard
1 lb./450 g. Demerara sugar	2 cups brown sugar

Slice the beans and chop the onions. Cook the beans in well salted water until tender. Cook the onions in ½ pint (3 dl., 1¼ cups) of the vinegar. Mix the cornflour, turmeric and dry mustard to a smooth paste with some of the remaining vinegar. Strain the beans, then add to the rest of the vinegar and cook for 10 minutes. Add the sugar and the remaining ingredients and boil for a further 15 minutes. Bottle and cover.

Pickled onions

IMPERIAL · METRIC	AMERICAN
small button onions	small button onions
to each 2 pints/generous litre vinegar allow 2 teaspoons allspice	to each 5 cups vinegar allow 2 teaspoons allspice
2 teaspoons peppercorns	2 teaspoons peppercorns

Peel the onions and place in clean, dry jars. Boil the vinegar with the spices and when cold pour it over to fill the jars completely. Cover and store in a dry place.

The pickled onions will be ready in 2 weeks.

Pickled red cabbage

IMPERIAL · METRIC	AMERICAN
1 large firm red cabbage	1 large firm red cabbage
salt	salt
cayenne pepper	cayenne pepper
vinegar	vinegar

Cut the cabbage into quarters and remove the stalk. Slice the cabbage very thinly; put it on a large flat dish and sprinkle with plenty of salt and some cayenne pepper. Leave overnight, stir the mixture well and then drain. Fill preserving jars or screw-topped jam jars with the drained cabbage. Cover with cold vinegar. Cover tightly. The cabbage will be ready to eat in 3–4 days.

Marrow jam

IMPERIAL · METRIC	AMERICAN
6 lb./2¾ kg. prepared marrow	6 lb. prepared summer squash
4 lemons	4 lemons
3 oz./75 g. root ginger	3 medium pieces root ginger
6 lb./2¾ kg. sugar	12 cups sugar

Cut the peeled marrow into cubes and steam until just tender. Put into a bowl with the grated rind and juice of the lemons, the bruised root ginger, tied in a muslin bag, and the sugar. Leave for 24 hours. Put into a pan and heat carefully until the sugar has dissolved. Cook until the marrow is transparent and the syrup is thick. Pour into hot jars and cover.

Candied marrow

IMPERIAL · METRIC	AMERICAN
2 lb./1 kg. prepared marrow	6 cups diced summer squash
2 lb./1 kg. sugar	4 cups sugar
1 oz./25 g. root ginger	1 piece root ginger
pinch cayenne pepper	pinch cayenne pepper
2 lemons	2 lemons
castor sugar	granulated sugar
bicarbonate of soda	baking soda
cream of tartar	cream of tartar

Cut the marrow into neat cubes. Cover with water and leave for 12 hours. Strain, mix with the sugar and leave for a further 12 hours. Tie the bruised root ginger, cayenne and the grated rind of the lemons into a muslin bag. Heat the marrow with the sugar and lemon juice until the sugar has dissolved. Put in the muslin bag, and simmer until the marrow is clear and the syrup is thick. Pour into a covered bowl and leave for 7 days. Strain off the syrup and put the marrow on waxed paper on a wire rack in a warm place to dry. Roll the cubes in castor sugar containing a pinch of bicarbonate of soda and cream of tartar.

Herbs

You don't need a stately home or a huge garden to grow a few popular herbs, because many of them fit in beautifully with flowers or vegetables. They grow accommodatingly in an herbaceous border, in a tub or window box, and even in flower pots. You can grow them from seed, from cuttings or from small plants which you can get at most nurseries, garden centres or health food shops.

The shrubby kinds like sage, thyme, rosemary, marjoram and bay stay green for most of the year, or you can cut a few pieces and dry them for winter use. The tender-leaved varieties like mint, parsley, chives and basil can be frozen in two ways. The leaves can be packed in polythene bags or foil packets, and they can then be crumbled into dishes while still frozen. They can also be chopped finely and packed into ice-cube trays, then each cube removed to a bag or piece of foil for storage. One cube of herbs will be enough for a sauce or casserole.

Many recipes mention 'bouquet garni', 'fines herbes' and 'mixed herbs', and it is worth freezing small quantities of these mixtures for use when supplies of some of the individual herbs may be in short supply.

Bouquet garni This usually consists of parsley, thyme and bay leaf, but sometimes marjoram is added. Tie together 2 or 3 stalks of parsley, a sprig of thyme and a bay leaf with a piece of strong thread, and put each little bunch into a piece of fine muslin, leaving a long thread end. Pack into polythene bags or packets of foil. Use one 'bouquet' suspended in a casserole.

Fines herbes Chop fresh parsley, chervil and chives, and a little tarragon if available. Freeze in ice-cube trays, or in small foil packets. Use to sprinkle on salads, or to add to omelettes or scrambled eggs.

Mixed herbs A mixture of sage, parsley, thyme and marjoram for use in stuffings, and many meat and fish dishes. Chop the sage, parsley and marjoram and mix with the small leaves of thyme. Freeze in ice-cube trays or in small foil packets.

Here are the herbs you are most likely to use.

Basil

A bit difficult to start as it is half-hardy. Sow the seed under glass in March or April and plant out in May in a well drained and sunny bed, or a large earthenware pot. Two kinds are usually offered called bush and sweet, and their flavour is similar, rather like that of cloves. Use basil to flavour soups, tomato dishes and sausages.

Bay leaves
An evergreen shrub which can be damaged by very cold
weather. It can be grown in a large tub. Use to flavour salmon,
pickled fish and meats, stews, soups, milk puddings and custards.

Chervil
This hardy annual looks rather like parsley, but is used for its
fine flavour rather than for garnishing. Use for soup, salads, egg
and fish dishes.

Chives
These look like a cluster of little onions, and grow best in moist
places. The finely chopped tops give a mild onion flavour to
salads, soups, egg and cheese dishes.

Dill
An annual plant which is easy to grow, and the flavour is
delicious with new potatoes, fish and cucumber.

Fennel
A perennial which can be grown from seed or bought as a plant.
Good with fish dishes, especially mackerel and salmon.

Marjoram
Choose from sweet or pot marjoram. The latter is easy to grow in
ordinary soil and can be propagated by divisions or seeds.
Use with chicken dishes, and Italian-type tomato dishes (e,g.
spaghetti sauce and pizza).

Mint
This herb spreads all over the place, so try to keep it confined.
There are many different kinds, and it is best known as a
flavouring for sauce to use with lamb, but try it chopped on a
tomato or fresh fruit salad.

Parsley
The seeds are slow to germinate, but the herb is worth growing.
Use it in white sauce to serve with ham or broad beans and, of
course, as a garnish.

Rosemary
A pretty small shrub which likes sun and a well-drained soil.
Very good with rabbit dishes and for roasting lamb and pork.

Sage
A woody evergreen which likes a light soil and plenty of sun.
A strongly flavoured herb which is good with onions, pork, duck,
goose and sausages.

Savory
Summer and winter savory can be grown. The summer variety is
an annual, and the winter savory is an almost evergreen
perennial; it thrives in poor soil. The flavours are similar and
particularly good with lentil and bean dishes, and with eggs and
poultry.

Tarragon
Buy a French tarragon plant, not a Russian one, which is
hardier but lacks the fine flavour of the French variety. The
plant is perennial but not really hardy and needs shelter. Use in
salads, when cooking chicken, and in many classic sauces.

Thyme
Many varieties can be grown, but common and lemon thymes
are best for cooking. This perennial herb likes well-drained soil
and sunshine. Use in stuffings, stews and with hare dishes.

Winter mint sauce
Fill a glass jar with chopped young mint leaves, cover them with
cold vinegar and seal the jar. Keep it in a cool dry, dark place.
Whenever you want to make mint sauce remove as much mint
as you require from the jar (re-seal it again), cover the mint with
a generous sprinkling of sugar and pour a little boiling water
over to dissolve the sugar, then dilute to taste with cold vinegar.

Mint relish

IMPERIAL · METRIC	AMERICAN
$\frac{3}{4}$ pint/4 dl. cider vinegar	scant 2 cups cider vinegar
1 lb./450 g. sugar	2 cups sugar
2 teaspoons dry mustard	2 teaspoons dry mustard
1 lb./450 g. eating apples	1 lb. dessert apples
2 medium onions	2 medium onions
8 oz./225 g. fresh mint leaves	$\frac{1}{2}$ lb. fresh mint leaves
3 tablespoons seedless raisins	4 tablespoons pitted raisins
$\frac{1}{4}$ teaspoon salt	$\frac{1}{4}$ teaspoon salt

Scald the vinegar in an enamel pan and then add the sugar and dry mustard. Stir well and remove from the heat and allow to cool slightly. Chop the apples, onions and mint finely. Place in a bowl with the raisins and salt. Pour over the vinegar and sugar, mix well and spoon into hot glass jars. Seal immediately.

Herb cheese

IMPERIAL · METRIC	AMERICAN
8 oz./225 g. Cheddar cheese, grated	2 cups grated Cheddar cheese
2 teaspoons each chopped parsley, chives, thyme, sage and summer savory	2 teaspoons each chopped parsley, chives, thyme, sage and summer savory
2 tablespoons whipped cream	3 tablespoons whipped cream
4 tablespoons sherry	$\frac{1}{3}$ cup sherry

Blend the grated cheese, herbs, cream and sherry together. Put into small pots and chill.

Herb butter

IMPERIAL · METRIC	AMERICAN
1 teaspoon chopped parsley	1 teaspoon chopped parsley
½ teaspoon chopped mint	½ teaspoon chopped mint
½ teaspoon chopped chives	½ teaspoon chopped chives
¾ teaspoon chopped tarragon	¾ teaspoon chopped tarragon
¼ teaspoon chopped marjoram	¼ teaspoon chopped marjoram
4 teaspoons lemon juice	4 teaspoons lemon juice
4 oz./100 g. butter, softened	½ cup softened butter

Mix together all the herbs and let them soak in the lemon juice.
Let the butter soften at room temperature, then work in the
herbs. Put into a covered jar and chill. Use in sandwiches, or on
meat or fish.

Minted fruit fingers

IMPERIAL · METRIC	AMERICAN
4 oz./100 g. butter	½ cup butter
8 oz./225 g. plain flour	2 cups all-purpose flour
pinch salt	pinch salt
½ oz./15 g. sugar	1 tablespoon sugar
water to mix	water to mix
Filling	*Filling*
1½ oz./40 g. butter	3 tablespoons butter
1 oz./25 g. sugar	2 tablespoons sugar
4 oz./100 g. currants	scant 1 cup currants
1 teaspoon chopped mint	1 teaspoon chopped mint

Rub the fat into the sieved flour and salt and add the sugar.
Mix to a stiff dough with cold water. Melt the butter, add the
sugar, currants and mint and mix well. Roll the pastry thinly,
divide into four and sandwich with alternate layers of the fruit
mixture and pastry. Place on a baking sheet and cook in a
moderately hot oven (400°F., 200°C., Gas Mark 6) for 25
minutes. Cut into slices and cool on a wire rack.

Fruit

Apples
Cooking apples can be used when they are not fully mature –
their slight acidity makes them useful for savoury dishes. They
are also excellent for sauces, chutneys and (because they contain
a lot of pectin) are excellent for jams and jellies. Eating apples
are good for cooking in dishes which need firm slices. Apples are
nicer if stewed in cider rather than water, and apple slices are
delicious cooked in fresh butter and lightly sweetened. Apple
sauce has a better flavour if the apples are baked, rather than
boiled – just bake the apples and scoop out the pulp. Beat it
until smooth before serving.

Apricots
Fresh apricots are perfect for puddings and pies, but they are
also delicious simply poached in a sugar and water syrup. For
extra flavour, add a little liqueur when the syrup is cold.
Apricot brandy, kirsch or crème de noyau are all suitable. To
prepare fresh apricots, dip them in boiling water, then in cold,
and slip off the skins. Crack a few of the stones, and shred the
kernels into apricot dishes to give a slight almond flavour.

Blackberries
Large sweet cultivated blackberries are good served fresh with
sugar and cream, and these are the best kind to use for open
tarts. The wild blackberry, which has an excellent flavour for
preserves, often needs sieving, as the pips can be irritating. The
flavour of blackberries is enhanced by a little rose water, or a
couple of rose geranium leaves. A little cinnamon gives a good
flavour to hot blackberry dishes.

Cherries
Cherries come in a number of varieties, and each has its
advantages. The whiteheart cherries are good when eaten fresh

but are rather insipid for cooking. Blackhearts can be cooked and are particularly delicious in cakes, but the morello cooking cherry is best for bottling and for pies and puddings. A little lemon juice helps bring out their flavour. For jam making, lemon juice or redcurrant juice should be used to help setting.

Currants

Redcurrants are invaluable in the kitchen for their setting qualities and for their sharp flavour. Redcurrant jelly forms the basis of a number of sauces which are good with ham and pork, game and poultry, and lamb. The fruit is rather pippy and not often cooked, but currants combine well with raspberries in cold puddings, and may be mixed with other fruit in jams and jellies.

Blackcurrants are sweeter and more richly flavoured than redcurrants. They are delicious in puddings and flans, and make excellent jam and syrup.

Gooseberries

Gooseberries are versatile and can be made into hot and cold puddings, jams and chutneys. Gooseberry jelly can be flavoured with herbs for a variety of savoury jellies to serve with meat or fish. Elderflowers are in season at the same time as gooseberries and give a muscat flavour to jam, jelly and syrup. An elderflower head trailed in the cooked fruit and sugar for a few minutes gives the fruit a grape flavour.

Pears

Pears are ready to eat when they develop a scent and yield to a slight pressure at the stalk end. Dessert varieties can be used for cooking. Pears are nicest cooked in cider or wine, or in butter like apples. Hard winter pears may be peeled but left whole complete with stalk for cooking. Pears combine well with other flavours, particularly chocolate and rum, and with liqueurs.

Plums

Plainly cooked plums (and that includes greengages and damsons) are best if cooked in an ovenproof dish with sugar and very little water, rather than being stewed in a lot of water on top of the cooker. They all take to a little extra flavouring, such as a

dash of cinnamon, a little lemon or orange rind and juice, a
sprinkling of almonds, a little cherry brandy or red wine.

Raspberries
Raspberries are perfect on their own with sugar and cream, but
they also combine well with red or blackcurrants. Try putting
fresh raspberries through a sieve and sweetening the purée to
serve as a sauce with apricots, peaches, bananas or strawberries.
A little lemon juice helps keep the colour of the fruit.

Rhubarb
Early rhubarb need not be peeled, but only washed before
cooking. Later outdoor-grown rhubarb is stronger in flavour
and needs peeling, and it is excellent for jam and chutney. Use
rhubarb when it is fresh and firm, and don't overcook it or it
will be mushy. For the best flavour, cut rhubarb in small pieces
and cook without water, but with raspberry jam or marmalade,
which gives a rich colour and taste. Cinnamon and ginger are
good with rhubarb, and so is the juice and rind of oranges or
lemons. If you find rhubarb rather acid, eat cream, custard or
cheese at the same meal.

Strawberries
A few strawberries can be mixed with other summer fruit as well
as eaten on their own with sugar and cream, but they are also
excellent in tarts, cakes and puddings. For a change from plain
strawberries, leave the fruit to soak in orange juice, or in red
wine, champagne, or an orange-flavoured liqueur before serving
with cream.

Storing apples and pears
As a general rule, apples which ripen latest store best. An apple
is ripe when it falls easily into the hand if lifted gently on its
stalk. Do not put into store immediately after picking. Let the
apples cool and sweat in an airy place before storing. The store
should be dark, cool and very slightly moist.

Keep separate different varieties with varying keeping
qualities. Store in trays in a frostproof shed, cellar or attic.
Greengrocers' boxes, which can be stacked with space between,
make useful trays. Special eating apples can be wrapped

individually in sheets of newspaper and stored in boxes. Pears tend to ripen suddenly. Inspect the fruit regularly and remove any unsound fruit.

Dried apples and pears

This is a useful way to keep apples if the freezer is full, or there is not the time or equipment for bottling. Pears can be dried but the juicy varieties are rather difficult to handle. Apples should be ripe but not over-ripe. Using a silver or stainless steel knife, peel and core the apples and cut into rings about $\frac{1}{4}$ inch ($\frac{1}{2}$ cm.) thick. Immediately put into a basin of salt water ($\frac{1}{2}$ oz. (15 g., 1 tablespoon) salt to 2 pints (generous litre, 5 cups) water) and leave for 10 minutes. The rings should be threaded on a stick which can rest on the runners of the oven; the rings should not touch each other. Dry out in a very cool oven (150°F., 70°C., Gas Mark $\frac{1}{4}$) for several hours. The apples should be like dry, chamois leather – moist and pliable. Cool in the air before packing tightly in paper bags, or in dry jars or tins. Store in a dry, dark place.

It is best to soak fruit for 24 hours before cooking, and to use the soaking water, flavoured with a little lemon or vanilla, a clove or a piece of ginger, for cooking.

Dried plums

Ripe plums can be dried too. Halve and stone them. Stretch muslin on sticks to replace oven shelves, and dry the plums on these. Dry slowly, as for apples. Plums can also be dried whole.

Bottling

Oven method

Wash and drain the jars and lids. Pack tightly with the prepared fruit to the tops of the jars. Place in a very cool oven (150°F., 70°C., Gas Mark $\frac{1}{4}$) on a piece of cardboard or several thicknesses of paper. The jars should be covered with the lids, to prevent the fruit from charring. Leave in the oven for about 45 minutes to 1 hour, until the fruit appears cooked and has shrunk a little. Remove the jars one at a time, place them on a mat or folded newspaper and cover the fruit with boiling water or syrup. Seal immediately with a rubber ring, lid and clip, or screw-band. As the jars cool, the screw-bands will need further tightening. Test the following day. Remove the screw-band or clip; if the seal is perfect it should be possible to lift the jar by the lid. If the lid comes off, the seal is imperfect and the fruit should be eaten within a few days or re-sterilised. Store in a cool, dark place.

Deep pan method

Wash and drain the jars and lids. Pack the jars tightly with the prepared fruit. Apples and pears should be peeled with a stainless knife and put immediately into brine; use 1 teaspoon of salt to 1 pint (6 dl., 2½ cups) of water and pack into the jars after rinsing. Shake soft, juicy fruits down; for hard fruits the handle of a wooden spoon is useful for arranging the fruit in layers and for packing tightly. Pack the fruit almost to the tops of the jars. Cover the fruit with cold water, filling the jars to overflowing. When a screw-band is used it should be given a half-turn back to allow for expansion.

Put some straw, newspaper, or cloth in the bottom of a deep pan or steriliser; place in the jars and completely cover with cold water. A large fish kettle, bucket (not polythene) or any container which is deep enough can be used. The jars should not touch each other, or the sides of the container. Bring the water slowly to simmering point. This should take 1½ hours, then maintain at this temperature for 15 minutes. (Pears require 30 minutes.) Remove the jars one at a time from the steriliser; place on a wooden table or board and tighten the screw-bands. As the jars cool, the screw-band will need further tightening. Test the following day. Remove the screw-band; if the seal is perfect it should be possible to lift the jar by the lid. If the lid comes off, the seal is imperfect and the fruit should be eaten within a few days or re-sterilised. Store in a cool, dark place.

Freezing

Most fruits freeze well, and it is worth preserving them. Try freezing without sugar, with dry sugar or syrup, or in the form of a purée. For a free-flow pack, freeze the fruit on open trays before packing in bags or boxes.

Apples

Use crisp, firm apples for freezing as pie slices. Apples which burst and fluff in cooking are good to freeze as a purée or as apple sauce.

Peel and core apples and drop them into a basin of cold water. Slice medium-sized apples into twelfths, large ones into sixteenths. Apples are best packed with sugar For a dry sugar pack, use a proportion of 8 oz. (225 g., 1 cup) sugar to 2 lb. (1 kg.) fruit, and leave a ½-inch (1-cm.) headspace. For a syrup pack, use 40% syrup (11 oz. (300 g., scant 1½ cups) sugar to 1 pint (6 dl., 2½ cups) water) quarter-filling the pack with syrup and slicing apples into containers. Finish with more syrup if necessary and seal leaving a ½-inch (1-cm.) headspace.

Apricots

Apricots may be frozen in halves without peeling, or in peeled slices for use fresh or cooked. Use small quantities to avoid discolouration. If apricots are to be left unpeeled, dropping the halves into boiling water for 30 seconds will stop the skins toughening in the freezer.

To freeze half apricots, wash them under cold running water, cut into halves and remove stones, and drop into boiling water for 30 seconds. Chill in iced water and drain. Pack in dry sugar, using 4 oz. (100 g., ½ cup) sugar to each 1 lb. (450 g.) of fruit, or use 40% syrup (11 oz. (300 g., scant 1½ cups) sugar to 1 pint (6 dl., 2½ cups) water).

To freeze slices, peel apricots quickly, then slice directly into container quarter-full of 40% syrup (11 oz. (300 g., scant 1½ cups) sugar to 1 pint (6 dl., 2½ cups) water). Top up with syrup to keep the fruit covered; put Cellophane on top, allowing a ½-inch (1-cm.) headspace.

Blackberries

Use fully ripe blackberries that are dark and glossy, avoiding those with woody pips, or any which have green patches. Wash in small quantities in iced water and drain. Pack dry and unsweetened, or in dry sugar (8 oz. (225 g., 1 cup) sugar to 2 lb. (1 kg.) fruit) or in 50% syrup (1 lb. (450 g., 2 cups) sugar to 1 pint (6 dl., 2½ cups) water) leaving headspace.

Cherries
Cherries should be firmed in iced water for 1 hour before processing, then thoroughly dried and stones removed as these may flavour the fruit during storage. Use glass or plastic containers as the acid in cherry juice tends to remain liquid during freezing and may leak through cardboard. Cherries for pie-making are best in a dry sugar pack, allowing 8 oz. (225 g., 1 cup) sugar to 2 lb. (1 kg.) pitted cherries. For sweet cherries a 40% syrup (11 oz. (300 g., scant 1½ cups) sugar to 1 pint (6 dl., 2½ cups) water) is best, and for sour cherries 50% syrup (1 lb. (450 g., 2 cups) sugar to 1 pint (6 dl., 2½ cups) water).

Currants
Black, red and white currants are all frozen in the same way. They should be stripped from the stem with a fork and washed in iced water, then dried gently. For later use in jam-making, pack dry into polythene bags. For a dry sugar pack, use 8 oz. (225 g., 1 cup) sugar to 1 lb. (450 g.) prepared berries, mixing until most of the sugar is dissolved. Use 40% syrup (11 oz. (300 g., scant 1½ cups) sugar to 1 pint (6 dl., 2½ cups) water) if preferred.

Gooseberries
Wash in iced water and dry. For pies, they should be frozen when fully ripe in bags or containers without sweetening. For jam-making, the fruit can be frozen slightly under-ripe. Purée can be made by stewing the fruit in very little water, sieving and sweetening to taste. This is useful at a later date for making gooseberry fools.

Pears
Pears do not freeze very well owing to their delicate flavour, and their flesh does not keep its paleness.

Choose ripe, but not over-ripe pears with strong flavour. Peel and quarter them, remove the cores and immediately dip the pieces in lemon juice. Make up 30% syrup (7 oz. (200 g., scant 1 cup) sugar to 1 pint (6 dl., 2½ cups) water) and poach pears in this for 1½ minutes. Drain and cool and pack into the cold 30% syrup.

Plums, greengages and damsons

Wash the fruit in iced water and dry well. Cut in halves, removing stones, and pack in 40% syrup (11 oz. (300 g., scant 1½ cups) sugar to 1 pint (6 dl., 2½ cups) water). As with all stone fruit, the stone tends to flavour the fruit during freezing, and skins toughen, so unsweetened dry pack is unsuitable.

Raspberries

Raspberries should be picked over very carefully, discarding any hard or seedy ones, then washed in iced water and dried very carefully. Freeze dry in cartons, or with sugar, allowing 4 oz. (100 g., ½ cup) sugar to 1 lb. (450 g.) raspberries. They may also be packed in 30% syrup (7 oz. (200 g., scant 1 cup) sugar to 1 pint (6 dl., 2½ cups) water).

Rhubarb

The early crop of young pink sticks is best for freezing. Sticks may be frozen unsweetened for pies after washing in cold running water and trimming to the desired length. They can be packed in cartons, in polythene bags or in foil. To make packing easier, stalks may be blanched for 1 minute, which makes them slightly limp and easier to pack. The colour and flavour will also be better by this method. The fruit may also be packed in 40% syrup (11 oz. (300 g., scant 1½ cups) sugar to 1 pint (6 dl., 2½ cups) water), or stewed rhubarb can be sieved and sweetened and frozen as purée.

Strawberries

Strawberries are best frozen dry without sugar when they tend to be less pulpy on thawing. Husks should be removed from berries which are fully ripe and mature, but firm. For a dry sugar pack, use 4 oz. (100 g., ½ cup) sugar to each 1 lb. (450 g.) fruit. Sieved, sweetened strawberries may be frozen as a purée.

Fruit syrups

Fruit syrups are useful as a basis for fruit drinks, as sauces for puddings, or to flavour mousses and ices. The usual problem is with sterilising and storage, since bottles tend to burst. The best ones to use are the lever-stoppered type with a china cap and rubber washer; second choice is the traditional sauce bottle with screw cap. Syrups should be stored in a cool, dark place, or the colour will fade. A little vegetable colouring may be added for a more attractive appearance.

The latest answer to the storage problem is to use the freezer. Make the syrup in the usual way. Cool and pour into containers, leaving room for expansion, then freeze. An even better way is to pour the syrup into ice-cube trays, freeze, then wrap each cube in foil, and put them together in labelled, transparent bags. Each cube will be enough for one portion, to dilute with water.

Mixed fruit syrups

Syrups can be made from raspberries, strawberries, elderberries, blackberries, loganberries, and blackcurrants or a mixture of fruit. Use clean ripe fruit, and avoid washing it if possible. Add a little water to the fruit (about ¼ pint (1½ dl., ⅔ cup) to 3 lb. (1½ kg.) raspberries or strawberries, but ½ pint (3 dl., 1¼ cups) to the same amount of blackcurrants). Cook gently for about 1 hour, crushing the fruit at intervals. Drain through a jelly bag overnight then measure and add 12 oz. (350 g., 1½ cups) sugar to each pint (6 dl., 2½ cups) of juice. Stir until dissolved. Strain and pour into bottles, or into freezing containers. Make sure the bottles are securely topped and tied down.

Stand the bottles in a steriliser and fill with cold water to cover. Heat slowly so that the water reaches 175°F. (80°C.) (simmering point) in 1 hour. Keep at this temperature for 30 minutes. Remove the bottles, cool, label and store.

Fruit cordials

These can be made from many fruits and form the basis of summer drinks or winter cures. The most suitable fruits are blackberries, biackcurrants, loganberries, raspberries and strawberries.

This is the basic method. Put the fruit into a large earthenware basin and break it up with a wooden spoon. No water need be added, except to blackberries and blackcurrants. For these, add just enough water to start the flow of juice. Put the basin of fruit over a pan of hot water on the cooker. Keep the water in the bottom pan on the boil and crush the fruit occasionally. When all the juice has been extracted put the fruit into a double muslin bag and leave to strain overnight.

Add 12 oz. (350 g., 1½ cups) sugar to each pint (6 dl., 2½ cups) of juice and stir until thoroughly dissolved. Strain again into clean bottles, filling to within 1 inch (2·5 cm.) of the top of the bottle. Cork securely, using new corks each year. Secure the corks with string, then sterilise. Put the bottles into a pan of cold water. The water must reach to within 1 inch (2·5 cm.) of the tops of the bottles. Bring the water to the boil and simmer for 20 minutes. Dip the corks in melted paraffin wax and store the bottles in a cool dark place.

Sweet preserves

It is always a pleasure to see a shelf full of gleaming jam jars packed with fruit goodness in the form of jams and jellies. As well as making the traditional one-fruit jams, try mixing fruits and turn some of them into butters, cheeses and fruit conserves. These are useful of course to spread on toast or bread and butter, but they are also delicious as cake and tart fillings and as sauces for puddings and ices. Some of them make marvellous emergency puddings when served in pretty glasses with plenty of thick cream. For a special treat, try turning small quantities of fruit into after-dinner candies.

To produce a jam or jelly that will keep, with a good colour flavour and a firm set, the balance of pectin, acid and sugar must be in the correct ratio. Apples being so rich in pectin, may be used alone or mixed with other fruits to make perfect jams and jellies. Weigh and measure your ingredients accurately and follow these basic rules.

Jams

Wash the fruit, which must be firm and ripe, remove any damaged parts and drain in a colander. Prepare as for stewing. Weigh and put into a clean, dry preserving pan greased with butter to prevent the fruit sticking and a scum forming. Simmer gently with water, to release the pectin, until the fruit is soft and pulpy. Add the sugar, previously warmed in a cool oven (275°F., 140°C., Gas Mark 1). Stir until dissolved. (The pan should not be more than half full.) Bring to the boil and boil rapidly. Do not stir but draw a wooden spoon, from time to time, across the bottom of the pan to prevent sticking. Test for a set by the wrinkle method. (Put a teaspoonful of the jam on a plate and leave to cool for 1 minute. If the skin wrinkles on the surface the setting point is reached.) Skim if necessary. Pour into clean, dry, warm jars filling to the brim. Press a waxed circle on the jam whilst still hot, cover with Cellophane and secure with a rubber band. Label the jars. Store in cool, dry atmosphere, preferably in the dark – light causes loss of colour and dampness the growth of mould.

Jellies

Wash and cut up fruit roughly without peeling and coring. Simmer with a measured quantity of water until cooked. Strain overnight through muslin or a jelly bag. To each 1 pint (6 dl., 2½ cups) of juice add 1 lb. (450 g., 2 cups) preserving sugar and follow the rules for making and testing jam.

Purées and cheeses

After cooking the fruit as in jelly making, rub it through a hair or nylon sieve and to each 1 pint (6 dl., 2½ cups) of pulp add 1 lb. (450 g., 2 cups) preserving sugar and proceed as for jam. A blender may be used instead of a sieve, in which case the fruit must be peeled and cored. Tie the peel and cores, which are rich in pectin, in a muslin bag and cook with the fruit. Remove before adding the sugar.

Apple ginger

IMPERIAL · METRIC	AMERICAN
4 lb./1¾ kg. apples	4 lb. apples
4 lb./1¾ kg. sugar	8 cups sugar
3 pints/1½ litres water	7½ cups water
2 oz./50 g. ground ginger	½ cup ground ginger

Peel and core the apples and cut them into slices. Dissolve the sugar in the water and boil the syrup until thick. Add the apple slices and boil until transparent. Stir in the ginger and boil for 5 minutes. Pour into jars and cover.

Apple butter

IMPERIAL · METRIC	AMERICAN
6 lb./2¾ kg. apples	6 lb. apples
2 pints/generous litre water	5 cups water
2 pints/generous litre cider	5 cups cider
granulated or soft brown sugar	granulated or brown sugar
1 teaspoon ground cloves	1 teaspoon ground cloves
1 teaspoon ground cinnamon	1 teaspoon ground cinnamon
1 teaspoon nutmeg	1 teaspoon nutmeg

Do not peel the apples, but cut them into large pieces. Simmer in the water and cider until soft, then put through a sieve. Weigh the pulp and simmer until thick. Add 12 oz. (350 g., 1½ cups) sugar to each lb. (450 g., 2 cups) weighed pulp. Stir the sugar and spices into the apple pulp and cook gently, stirring frequently, until no surplus liquid remains. Pour into hot jars and cover.

Apples in wine

IMPERIAL · METRIC	AMERICAN
8 lemons	8 lemons
1 pint/6 dl. white wine	2½ cups white wine
4½ lb./2 kg. sugar	9 cups sugar
5 lb./2¼ kg. apples	5 lb. apples
2 tablespoons brandy	3 tablespoons brandy

Peel the lemons thinly and pour on 1 pint (6 dl., 2½ cups) boiling water and the wine. Leave for 30 minutes. Put the lemon peel and liquid into a pan with the juice of the lemons and the sugar. Boil for 10 minutes. Strain the liquid and return to the pan. Peel, core and slice apples, add to liquid. Simmer until apples are soft and the syrup is thick. Stir in the brandy, heat and pour into hot screw-topped jars.

This is very good served with cream, and is worth keeping to serve as an emergency pudding.

Apricot conserve

IMPERIAL · METRIC	AMERICAN
10 lb./4½ kg. ripe fresh apricots	10 lb. ripe fresh apricots
apricot kernels	apricot kernels
8 lb./3¾ kg. sugar	16 cups sugar
juice of 1 lemon	juice of 1 lemon

Wipe the apricots gently with a fine cloth, then split in halves and remove the stones. Put the apricot halves, cut sides up, on a dish and sprinkle over the sugar. Leave until the following day. Crack open the stones and remove the kernels. Place the fruit and sugar in a pan and bring very slowly to the boil. Add the lemon juice and simmer for about 1 hour, until the preserve sets when a little is tested on a cold plate. Add the kernels just before removing pan from heat. Pour into warm jars and cover.

Blackberry and apple jam

IMPERIAL · METRIC	AMERICAN
1½ lb./¾ kg. blackberries	1½ lb. blackberries
1½ lb./¾ kg. apples	1½ lb. apples
½ pint/3 dl. water	1¼ cups water
3 lb./1½ kg. sugar	6 cups sugar

Prepare the fruit and simmer gently with the water until soft. Add the sugar and cook rapidly until setting point is reached. Pour into warm jars and cover.

Blackcurrant and cherry jam

IMPERIAL · METRIC	AMERICAN
2 lb./1 kg. blackcurrants	2 lb. blackcurrants
1 pint/6 dl. water	2½ cups water
2 lb./1 kg. black cherries	2 lb. black cherries
3 lb./1½ kg. sugar	6 cups sugar

Simmer the blackcurrants in the water for 1 hour, then put through a jelly bag. Simmer the stoned cherries in the strained blackcurrant juice for 20 minutes. Stir in the sugar and heat until dissolved, then boil hard to setting point. Pour into hot jars.

Blackberry cheese

IMPERIAL · METRIC	AMERICAN
4 lb./1¾ kg. ripe blackberries	4 lb. ripe blackberries
2 teaspoons citric or tartaric acid	2 teaspoons citric or tartaric acid
sugar	sugar

Wash the blackberries and put into a pan with just enough water to cover, and the acid. Bring to the boil, and simmer gently until the fruit is soft. Put through a sieve and weigh the pulp. Allow 1 lb. (450 g., 2 cups) sugar to each 1 lb. (450 g., 2 cups) of pulp. Stir in the sugar until dissolved, then boil and stir until the mixture is thick. Pour into hot jars and cover.

Blackcurrant and apple jelly

IMPERIAL · METRIC	AMERICAN
4 lb./1¾ kg. blackcurrants	4 lb. blackcurrants
2 lb./1 kg. cooking apples	2 lb. baking apples
4 pints/2¼ litres water	5 pints water
sugar	sugar

Put the blackcurrants into a pan with the apples cut into slices but not peeled and cored. Simmer with the water for 1 hour, until the fruit is very soft. Strain through a jelly bag and measure the juice. Allow 1 lb. (450 g., 2 cups) sugar to each 1 pint (6 dl., 2½ cups) of juice. Heat the juice gently, stir in the sugar and heat until dissolved. Boil hard to setting point, then pour into hot jars.

Damson jelly

IMPERIAL · METRIC	AMERICAN
6 lb./2¾ kg. damsons	6 lb. damsons
3 pints/1½ litres water	7½ cups water
sugar	sugar

Simmer the damsons in water until pulpy. Leave to drain through a jelly bag overnight. For each 1 pint (6 dl., 2½ cups) of juice, allow 1 lb. (450 g., 2 cups) sugar. Add the sugar, heat until dissolved, then boil rapidly until the jelly sets when tested.

Damson cheese

IMPERIAL · METRIC	AMERICAN
damsons	damsons
sugar	sugar

Wash the damsons, cover with water and simmer until soft. Put through a sieve and measure the pulp. Allow 12 oz. (350 g., 1½ cups) sugar to each 1 lb. (450 g., 2 cups) of fruit pulp. Cook the pulp and sugar in a thick pan, stirring frequently, for 1 hour, until the pulp is thick enough to hold the impress of a spoon. Put into small straight-sided jars and cover.

When cold, damson cheese can be used as a spread, or turned out and cut into slices to serve with cream.

Gooseberry cheese

IMPERIAL · METRIC	AMERICAN
3 lb./1½ kg. green gooseberries	3 lb. green gooseberries
½ pint/3 dl. water	1¼ cups water
sugar	sugar

Top and tail the gooseberries and simmer in the water until soft. Put through a sieve and weigh the pulp. Allow 12 oz. (350 g., 1½ cups) sugar to each 1 lb. (450 g., 2 cups) pulp. Stir in the sugar and heat until dissolved. Bring to the boil. Cook gently, stirring all the time, until the mixture is thick. Pour into hot jars and cover.

Gooseberry cheese is very good as a spread, or eaten with cold meat, particularly lamb.

Gooseberry curd

IMPERIAL · METRIC	AMERICAN
3 lb./1½ kg. green gooseberries	3 lb. green gooseberries
¾ pint/4 dl. water	2 cups water
1½ lb./¾ kg. castor sugar	3 cups granulated sugar
4 oz./100 g. butter	½ cup butter
4 eggs	4 eggs

Top and tail the fruit and cook in the water until soft. Put through a sieve. Cook in a double saucepan with the sugar, butter and well beaten eggs, stirring until the mixture thickens. Pour into hot jars and cover.

This gooseberry curd will keep for 1 month only.

Pear and cider marmalade

IMPERIAL · METRIC	AMERICAN
2 pints/generous litre cider	5 cups cider
6 lb./2¾ kg. eating pears	6 lb. dessert pears
4 lb./1¾ kg. sugar	8 cups sugar

The pears should be ripe but sound.

Boil the cider for 30 minutes until reduced by half. Peel the pears, remove the cores, and cut the pears into eighths. As each one is prepared, drop the pieces into the hot cider. Simmer until tender. Add the sugar and stir until dissolved, and then boil fast until thick. Put into warm jars and cover.

Pear and cider marmalade is delicious with toast, but it can also be used with steamed puddings or vanilla ice cream.

Plum rum jam

IMPERIAL · METRIC	AMERICAN
3½ lb./1½ kg. plums	3½ lb. plums
¼ pint/1½ dl. lemon juice	⅔ cup lemon juice
3½ lb./1½ kg. sugar	7 cups sugar
4 tablespoons dark rum	⅓ cup dark rum

Chop the plums finely, and put into a preserving pan with the lemon juice and sugar. Bring to the boil and boil hard for 3 minutes, stirring constantly. Add the rum and simmer for 5 minutes, stirring well. Pour into warm jars and seal.

Redcurrant and raspberry preserve

IMPERIAL · METRIC	AMERICAN
3 lb./1 kg. 400 g. redcurrants	3 lb. redcurrants
3 lb./1 kg. 400 g. sugar	6 cups sugar
4 lb./1¾ kg. raspberries	4 lb. raspberries

Remove the stalks from the redcurrants. Wash and drain the redcurrants and mash them in a preserving pan. Cook gently for 1 hour then strain through a jelly bag. Return the juice to the preserving pan, add the sugar and stir over a gentle heat until the sugar has dissolved. Bring to boiling point and add one-quarter of the raspberries. Skim them out and put them into a screw-topped jar. Add another 1 lb. (450 g., 4 cups) of raspberries to the pan and repeat the process. Use all the raspberries in this way. Bring the syrup to the boil, pour over the fruit to fill the jars, and screw on the tops.

Summer four-fruit jelly

IMPERIAL · METRIC	AMERICAN
1 lb./450 g. redcurrants	1 lb. redcurrants
1 lb./450 g. raspberries	1 lb. raspberries
1 lb./450 g. strawberries	1 lb. strawberries
1 lb./450 g. black cherries	1 lb. black cherries
1 teaspoon tartaric acid	1 teaspoon tartaric acid
1 pint/6 dl. water	2½ cups water
sugar	sugar

Use firm fruit which is just ripe.

Put all the fruit into a pan with the acid and water. Simmer until the fruit is soft. Strain through a jelly bag and measure the juice. Allow 1 lb. (450 g., 2 cups) sugar to each 1 pint (6 dl., 2½ cups) of juice. Heat the juice gently and stir in the sugar until dissolved. Boil hard to setting point, then pour into hot jars.

Rhubarb and fig jam

IMPERIAL · METRIC	AMERICAN
2 lb./1 kg. rhubarb	2 lb. rhubarb
8 oz./225 g. dried figs	1¼ cups dried figs
2 lb./1 kg. sugar	4 cups sugar
juice of 1 lemon	juice of 1 lemon

Cut the rhubarb into pieces and the figs into small chunks. Mix with the sugar and lemon juice and leave to stand for 24 hours. Bring to the boil and boil rapidly to setting point. Leave to cool for 15 minutes, stir well, then pour into jars.

Rhubarb and ginger jam

IMPERIAL · METRIC	AMERICAN
3 lb./1 kg. 400 g. rhubarb	3 lb. rhubarb
3 lb./1 kg. 400 g. sugar	6 cups sugar
juice of 3 lemons	juice of 3 lemons
1 oz./25 g. root ginger, bruised	1 large piece root ginger, bruised

Layer the chopped rhubarb and sugar in a basin. Pour over the lemon juice, cover and leave to stand for a few hours if possible. Turn the mixture into a large pan and add the root ginger tied in a muslin bag. Bring to the boil slowly until the sugar has dissolved, then boil rapidly until a little sets on a plate. Remove the ginger before pouring the jam into warm jars. Cover.

Sloe and apple jelly

IMPERIAL · METRIC	AMERICAN
1 lb./450 g. sloes	1 lb. sloes
6 lb./2¾ kg. cooking apples	6 lb. baking apples
peel of 2 lemons	peel of 2 lemons
sugar	sugar

Put the sloes in a pan with the apples, cut up, but not peeled and cored. Add the lemon peel and just enough water to cover. Simmer for 1 hour, until the apples are tender. Strain through a jelly bag and measure the juice. Allow 1 lb. (450 g., 2 cups) sugar to each 1 pint (6 dl., 2½ cups) of juice. Heat the juice gently and stir in the sugar until dissolved. Boil hard to setting point, then pour into hot jars.

Strawberries in syrup

IMPERIAL·METRIC	AMERICAN
strawberries	strawberries
sugar	sugar

Weigh an equal quantity of strawberries and sugar, and put them in layers in a bowl. Leave for 24 hours, and then boil for 5 minutes. Leave in a cool place for 24 hours, and on the second day boil for 5 minutes. Leave for 24 hours and boil for 7 minutes. Put into small, warm jars and cover.

This is very good to serve with all kinds of puddings and ices. Its flavour keeps well during the winter.

Autumn four-fruit jelly

IMPERIAL·METRIC	AMERICAN
3½ lb./1½ kg. elderberries	3½ lb. elderberries
1 lb./450 g. apples	1 lb. apples
1 lb./450 g. damsons	1 lb. damsons
1 lb./450 g. blackberries	1 lb. blackberries
2 pints/generous litre water	5 cups water
1 teaspoon ground cloves	1 teaspoon ground cloves
1 teaspoon ground allspice	1 teaspoon ground allspice
½ teaspoon ground ginger	½ teaspoon ground ginger
pinch cinnamon	pinch cinnamon
2 lb./1 kg. sugar	4 cups sugar

Pick the elderberries from their stalks. Mix with the apples, cut in pieces but not peeled or cored, damsons and blackberries. Add the water and spices and simmer for 1 hour, until the fruit is soft. Strain through a jelly bag and measure the juice. Allow 1 lb. (450 g., 2 cups) sugar to each 1 pint (6 dl., 2½ cups) of juice. Heat the juice gently and stir in the sugar until dissolved. Boil hard to setting point, then pour into hot jars.

Four-fruit jam

IMPERIAL · METRIC	AMERICAN
8 oz./225 g. blackcurrants	2 cups blackcurrants
8 oz./225 g. redcurrants	2 cups redcurrants
8 oz./225 g. raspberries	1¾ cups raspberries
8 oz./225 g. strawberries	1¾ cups strawberries
2 lb./1 kg. sugar	4 cups sugar

Put the blackcurrants in a pan with a very little water and simmer until tender. Add the other fruits and simmer for 10 minutes. Stir in the sugar until dissolved, then boil hard to setting point. Pour into hot jars.

Cherry brandy

IMPERIAL · METRIC	AMERICAN
1 lb./450 g. morello cherries	1 lb. morello cherries
6 oz./175 g. castor sugar	¾ cup granulated sugar
brandy	brandy

Wash the cherries and drain them thoroughly. Use a clean, dry preserving jar and fill it three-quarters full with layers of cherries and sugar. Fill up with brandy, screw on the top firmly, then store in a dark place for 14 weeks. Strain and bottle the flavoured brandy. Use the drained cherries with cream as a pudding.

Candied cherries

IMPERIAL · METRIC	AMERICAN
2 lb./1 kg. firm black cherries	2 lb. firm black cherries
2 lb./1 kg. sugar	4 cups sugar
1 pint/6 dl. water	2½ cups water
icing sugar	confectioners' sugar
bicarbonate of soda	baking soda

The cherries should be weighed after stoning.

Dissolve the sugar in the water over a low heat without boiling. When the syrup is clear put in the cherries. Simmer very gently until the cherries are almost transparent. Drain the fruit and put on flat trays. Dry thoroughly in the sun, or in a very cool oven (225°F., 110°C., Gas Mark ¼) with the door slightly open. Dust with icing sugar containing a pinch of bicarbonate of soda and store in a box between layers of waxed paper. Cubes of fresh pineapple can be treated in the same way.

Candied plums

IMPERIAL·METRIC	AMERICAN
4 lb./1¾ kg. sugar	8 cups sugar
4 pints/2¼ litres water	5 pints water
4 lb./1¾ kg. plums	4 lb. plums

Dissolve half the sugar in half the water and boil to 240°F. (115°C.) (soft ball stage). Put the firm ripe plums into a stone jar and pour over the syrup. Cover and leave in a very cool oven (225°F., 110°C., Gas Mark ¼) overnight. Repeat this process twice more, then drain the plums. Make up another batch of syrup with the remaining sugar and water and take it to the soft ball stage. Put the plums into the second batch of syrup, remove from the heat and leave until cold. Drain the plums and place on a wire rack. Keep in a warm room until dry and firm. Store in a tin between layers of waxed paper.

Redcurrant or blackberry paste

IMPERIAL·METRIC	AMERICAN
2 lb./1 kg. redcurrants or blackberries	2 lb. redcurrants or blackberries
½ pint/3 dl. water	1¼ cups water
castor sugar	granulated sugar

Heat the redcurrants or blackberries in the water until they burst and are soft. Drain through a jelly bag and weigh the juice. Take an equal quantity of sugar and heat slowly, stirring all the time until the mixture is thick and dry. Put the paste into a roasting tin and sprinkle with castor sugar. When cold and hard, cut into pieces with a knife. Dip in more castor sugar and store in a wooden box lined with greaseproof paper.

This is delicious to eat with coffee after dinner.

Spiced fruits and chutneys

Surplus fruits can be made into spicy relishes which are useful in the winter to brighten up heavy meals, and are on hand all the year round to accompany cold meat, poultry and cheese. Spiced fruits are best packed in screw-topped preserving jars, but chutney can be packed into smaller jars so long as no vinegar comes in contact with the metal tops.

Chutneys

Vinegar is used as the preservative as it contains acetic acid which prevents the growth of bacteria, yeasts and moulds. The fruit should be minced or finely chopped and the onion cooked first with a very little water until it is soft. Salt, pickling spices tied in muslin, sugar and vinegar are all added and the chutney cooked slowly until the ingredients are well blended and no surplus liquid is left. It should be poured into clean, dry, warm jars while it is still hot and the consistency of jam. Cover at once with a plastic cover, or a vinegar-resisting ceresin disc. Paper or transparent covers alone are not suitable as they allow evaporation of the vinegar. The flavour of the chutney is improved if kept for 2–3 months before using.

Pickled pears

IMPERIAL · METRIC	AMERICAN
4 lb./1¾ kg. pears	4 lb. pears
lemon juice	lemon juice
2 lb./1 kg. granulated sugar	4 cups granulated sugar
1 pint/6 dl. malt vinegar	2½ cups malt vinegar
2 teaspoons whole cloves	2 teaspoons whole cloves
2 teaspoons whole allspice	2 teaspoons whole allspice
3 pieces stick cinnamon	3 pieces stick cinnamon
1 piece root ginger	1 piece root ginger
2 pieces lemon rind	2 pieces lemon rind

Peel, quarter and core the pears and place in a bowl of cold water with a little lemon juice to prevent browning. Place the sugar and vinegar in a large saucepan. Tie the remaining ingredients in a muslin bag and add to the pan. Stir over a low heat to dissolve the sugar. Bring to the boil and add the pears. Cover the pan and simmer gently until the pears are tender. Remove the pears and pack into clean, warm preserving jars. Remove the spices from the syrup and boil rapidly until the syrup is reduced by half. Cover the pears with syrup and seal. Store for 4 months before use.

Pickled pears are delicious with cold meat, especially ham and pork.

Spiced apple slices

IMPERIAL·METRIC	AMERICAN
1 lb./450 g. granulated sugar	2 cups granulated sugar
1 pint/6 dl. white vinegar	2½ cups white vinegar
1 teaspoon salt	1 teaspoon salt
4 fl. oz./1 dl. water	½ cup water
6-inch/15-cm. stick cinnamon	6-inch stick cinnamon
2 teaspoons whole cloves	2 teaspoons whole cloves
few drops red food colouring	few drops red food coloring
3 lb./1 kg. 400 g. eating apples	3 lb. dessert apples

Put the sugar and vinegar into a saucepan with the salt and water. Tie the spices in muslin and hang them in the pan. Stir over a low heat until the sugar has dissolved. Add a little food colouring and stir to colour evenly. Peel and core the apples and slice them thickly. Drop the slices into the hot spiced syrup and cook gently until the slices are tender but still keep their shape. Skim out the slices and pack them into warm preserving jars. Heat the syrup to boiling point and pour into the jars, covering the fruit slices. Cover tightly.

Spiced apple slices are delicious with cold lamb, ham and pork, or with cold goose or duck.

Spiced plums

IMPERIAL·METRIC	AMERICAN
1½ lb./¾ kg. black plums	1½ lb. black plums
1½ lb./¾ kg. sugar	3 cups sugar
1 pint/6 dl. malt vinegar	2½ cups malt vinegar
¼ oz./10 g. mace	1 tablespoon mace
¼ oz./10 g. allspice	1 tablespoon allspice
¼ oz./10 g. stick cinnamon	¼ oz. stick cinnamon

Prick each plum several times with a needle. Boil the sugar, vinegar and spices together for 10 minutes. Pour over the fruit and set aside for 24 hours. Pour off the vinegar and boil for another 10 minutes. Pour on to the fruit again and leave until the next day. On the third day, boil all together gently for 5 minutes. Pour into warmed preserving jars, removing cinnamon, and seal tightly. Keep for 3 months before using.

Spiced plums are particularly good with cold poultry, pork and ham.

Spiced redcurrants

IMPERIAL·METRIC	AMERICAN
3½ lb./1½ kg. redcurrants	3½ lb. redcurrants
2½ lb./generous kg. brown sugar	5 cups brown sugar
½ pint/3 dl. vinegar	1¼ cups vinegar
2 teaspoons cloves	2 teaspoons cloves
2 teaspoons allspice	2 teaspoons allspice
2-inch (5-cm.) stick cinnamon	2-inch stick cinnamon

Remove the stalks from the redcurrants. Wash and drain the fruit and put it in a preserving pan with the sugar and vinegar. Tie the spices in a piece of muslin and hang in the pan. Bring to boiling point and then simmer for 1½ hours. Take out the spice bag and pour the fruit into small screw-topped jars.

Spiced redcurrants are very good with cold ham, pork and poultry.

Sweet spiced damsons

IMPERIAL · METRIC	AMERICAN
4 lb./1¾ kg. large damsons	4 lb. large damsons
1 pint/6 dl. vinegar	2½ cups vinegar
1½ lb./¾ kg. sugar	3 cups sugar
1 oz./25 g. mixed pickling spice	¼ cup mixed pickling spice

Prick the damsons with a large needle. Put the vinegar, sugar and spice in a pan and heat until the sugar has dissolved. Add the damsons, cook until soft but not broken and then lift carefully into jars. Reduce the vinegar to a syrup by boiling. Remove the spices and pour the reduced syrup over the fruit. Cover tightly.

Serve with poultry, particularly goose, or cold meat.

Plum sauce

IMPERIAL · METRIC	AMERICAN
4 lb./1¾ kg. plums or damsons	4 lb. plums or damsons
8 oz./225 g. onions	½ lb. onions
1 pint/6 dl. vinegar	2½ cups vinegar
1 oz./25 g. salt	4 teaspoons salt
½ oz./15 g. each of ginger, allspice, nutmeg and mustard	2 tablespoons each of ginger, allspice, nutmeg and mustard
8 oz./225 g. sugar	1 cup sugar

Cut up the plums and onions and cook with the vinegar, salt and spices for 30 minutes. Sieve, then stir in the sugar and bring to the boil. Simmer for 1 hour, stirring occasionally. Bottle while still warm.

This is a good way of using up windfalls, or a mixture of odd plums and damsons which are not good enough for table use.

Plum chutney

IMPERIAL · METRIC	AMERICAN
2 lb./1 kg. plums, weight after stoning	2 lb. plums, weight after pitting
1 lb./450 g. carrots	1 lb. carrots
1 pint/6 dl. vinegar	2½ cups vinegar
1 lb./450 g. stoned raisins	3 cups pitted raisins
1 lb./450 g. soft brown sugar	2 cups soft brown sugar
1 oz./25 g. garlic, chopped	2 cloves garlic, chopped
1 oz./25 g. chillies	¼ cup chili peppers
1 oz./25 g. ground ginger	4 tablespoons ground ginger
1½ oz./40 g. salt	6 teaspoons salt

Mix the prepared plums with the minced carrots and the vinegar and simmer until soft. Add the remaining ingredients and simmer until the mixture is thick. Put into jars and cover tightly.

Apple chutney

IMPERIAL · METRIC	AMERICAN
5 lb./2¼ kg. apples	5 lb. apples
1 tablespoon salt	1 tablespoon salt
scant 1 tablespoon ground ginger	1 tablespoon ground ginger
6 chillies	6 chili peppers
1 lb./450 g. Demerara sugar	2 cups brown sugar
½-1 pint/3-6 dl. vinegar	1¼-2½ cups vinegar
8 oz./225 g. onions	½ lb. onions
8 oz./225 g. stoned dates	1¼ cups pitted dates
8 oz./225 g. raisins or sultanas	1⅓ cups raisins or seedless white raisins

Peel and core the apples. Put the salt, ginger, chopped chillies and sugar into a pan with some of the vinegar. Add the apples and minced onions and bring to the boil. Add the chopped dates and whole raisins or sultanas and simmer until thick and brown, adding more vinegar as required (the apples make a lot of juice, but the chutney should not be runny). Put into warm jars and cover well.

Blackberry chutney

IMPERIAL · METRIC	AMERICAN
6 lb./2¾ kg. blackberries	6 lb. blackberries
2 lb./1 kg. cooking apples	2 lb. baking apples
2 lb./1 kg. onions	2 lb. onions
1 oz./25 g. salt	4 teaspoons salt
2 oz./50 g. dry mustard	½ cup dry mustard
2 oz./50 g. ground ginger	½ cup ground ginger
2 teaspoons ground mace	2 teaspoons ground mace
1 teaspoon cayenne pepper	1 teaspoon cayenne pepper
2 pints/generous litre vinegar	5 cups vinegar
2 lb./1 kg. brown sugar	4 cups brown sugar

Wash the blackberries and put into a pan. Peel and chop the apples and peel and chop the onions. Add to the blackberries with all the spices and the vinegar. Cook gently for 1 hour. Put through a sieve, stir in the sugar, then simmer for 1 hour until thick. Put into warm jars and cover well.

Gooseberry chutney

IMPERIAL · METRIC	AMERICAN
3 lb./1 kg. 400 g. gooseberries	3 lb. gooseberries
8 oz./225 g. onions	½ lb. onions
½ pint/3 dl. water	1¼ cups water
1 lb./450 g. sugar	2 cups sugar
½ oz./15 g. salt	2 teaspoons salt
1 tablespoon ground ginger	1 tablespoon ground ginger
¼ teaspoon cayenne pepper	¼ teaspoon cayenne pepper
1 pint/6 dl. malt vinegar	2½ cups malt vinegar

Cut up the cleaned gooseberries and onions. Simmer in the water until soft. Add the remaining ingredients and simmer for about 2 hours, until the mixture is really thick. Put into jars and cover.

Rhubarb chutney

IMPERIAL · METRIC	AMERICAN
2 lb./1 kg. rhubarb	2 lb. rhubarb
8 oz./225 g. onions	$\frac{1}{2}$ lb. onions
1$\frac{1}{2}$ lb./$\frac{3}{4}$ kg. brown sugar	3 cups brown sugar
8 oz./225 g. sultanas	1$\frac{1}{3}$ cups seedless white raisins
$\frac{1}{2}$ oz./15 g. mustard seeds	1$\frac{1}{2}$ tablespoons mustard seeds
1 teaspoon mixed spice	1 teaspoon mixed spice
1 teaspoon pepper	1 teaspoon pepper
1 teaspoon ground ginger	1 teaspoon ground ginger
1 teaspoon salt	1 teaspoon salt
$\frac{1}{4}$ teaspoon cayenne pepper	$\frac{1}{4}$ teaspoon cayenne pepper
1 pint/6 dl. vinegar	2$\frac{1}{2}$ cups vinegar

Cut the rhubarb into 1-inch (2·5-cm.) lengths and chop the onions finely. Put all ingredients into a heavy pan and simmer gently, stirring frequently until mixture is of consistency of jam. Put into pots and cover tightly.

Spiced redcurrant jelly

IMPERIAL · METRIC	AMERICAN
3 lb./1 kg. 400 g. redcurrants	3 lb. redcurrants
1 pint/6 dl. water	2$\frac{1}{2}$ cups water
$\frac{1}{4}$ pint/1$\frac{1}{2}$ dl. white vinegar	$\frac{2}{3}$ cup white vinegar
3 cloves	3 cloves
$\frac{1}{2}$ stick cinnamon	$\frac{1}{2}$ stick cinnamon
sugar	sugar

Place the redcurrants in a pan with the water and vinegar. Put the spices in a muslin bag and suspend in the pan. Simmer until the fruit is soft; remove the spice bag. Strain through a jelly bag and measure the juice. Allow 1 lb. (450 g., 2 cups) sugar to each 1 pint (6 dl., 2$\frac{1}{2}$ cups) of juice. Heat the juice gently, stir in the sugar until dissolved. Boil hard to setting point and pour into hot jars.

This is excellent served with roast lamb or with game.

Gooseberry mint jelly

IMPERIAL·METRIC	AMERICAN
4 lb./1¾ kg. gooseberries	4 lb. gooseberries
sugar	sugar
fresh mint	fresh mint

Cook the gooseberries with just enough water to cover. Strain
through a jelly bag and measure the liquid. Allow 1 lb. (450 g.,
2 cups) sugar to each 1 pint (6 dl., 2½ cups) of juice. Bring to
the boil, stir until the sugar has dissolved. Tie up a bunch of
fresh mint and hang this in the pan. Boil hard to setting point
then remove the mint. Pour into small hot jars.

Serve with roast lamb.

Hot and cold puddings

Fresh fruit is delicious at the end of a meal, but a hot or cold
fruit pudding makes an even better ending.

Autumn fruits such as apples, pears, plums and blackberries
are excellent for steamed puddings, batters, tarts, sponges,
dumplings, pies and flummeries. Summer berries and currants
are always welcome served simply with sugar and cream, but a
small quantity of fruit can be transformed into delectable fools
and flummeries.

Apple batter

IMPERIAL · METRIC	AMERICAN
2 lb./1 kg. cooking apples	2 lb. baking apples
sugar	sugar
2 tablespoons Calvados or brandy	3 tablespoons Calvados or brandy
8 oz./225 g. plain flour	2 cups all-purpose flour
½ teaspoon salt	½ teaspoon salt
2 eggs	2 eggs
1 pint/6 dl. milk	2½ cups milk

Peel and cut the apples into fairly large slices. Cover generously with sugar and sprinkle on Calvados or brandy. Leave to stand.

Make a batter with the flour, salt, eggs and milk. Grease an ovenproof dish. Mix the apples and batter and pour into the dish. Bake in a hot oven (450°F., 230°C., Gas Mark 8) for 40 minutes, until nicely browned and set. Serve with a good pat of butter on each helping.

Apple crackle cake

IMPERIAL · METRIC	AMERICAN
8 oz./225 g. self-raising flour	2 cups all-purpose flour sifted with 2 teaspoons baking powder
pinch salt	pinch salt
1 teaspoon ground cinnamon	1 teaspoon ground cinnamon
½ teaspoon ground nutmeg	½ teaspoon ground nutmeg
4 oz./100 g. butter or margarine	½ cup butter or margarine
4 oz./100 g. castor sugar	½ cup granulated sugar
8 oz./225 g. cooking apples	½ lb. baking apples
2 eggs	2 eggs
6 tablespoons milk	½ cup milk
Topping	*Topping*
2 tablespoons castor sugar	3 tablespoons granulated sugar
½ oz./15 g. butter or margarine	1 tablespoon butter or margarine

Sift the dry ingredients into a bowl. Rub in the fat, then stir in the sugar and very finely sliced apples. Mix to a thick batter with the eggs and milk and stir until smooth. Turn into a well greased 7–8-inch (18–20-cm.) round cake tin. Bang gently to settle the mixture, then cover the top with sugar and small pieces of butter or margarine. Bake in the centre of a moderately hot oven (375°F., 190°C., Gas Mark 5) for 45 minutes, then lower the heat to moderate (325°F., 160°C., Gas Mark 3) and bake for a further 30 minutes. Turn on to a plate and serve warm with cream, custard or ice cream.

Apple flummery

IMPERIAL · METRIC	AMERICAN
4 tablespoons pearl barley	5 tablespoons pearl barley
2 pints/generous litre water	5 cups water
1½ lb./¾ kg. eating apples	1½ lb. dessert apples
1½ oz./40 g. castor sugar	3 tablespoons granulated sugar
juice of 1 lemon	juice of 1 lemon
3 tablespoons single cream	4 tablespoons half-and-half

Put the barley into the water and bring to the boil. Peel and slice the apples and add to the pan. Simmer until the apples and barley are soft. Put through a sieve and return to the pan. Add the sugar and lemon juice and bring to the boil. Cool and stir in cream. Serve very cold.

Apple snow

IMPERIAL · METRIC	AMERICAN
8 oz./225 g. cooking apples	½ lb. baking apples
½ oz./15 g. sugar	1 tablespoon sugar
grated rind of ½ lemon or orange	grated rind of ½ lemon or orange
1 egg white	1 egg white

Gently cook the peeled, cored and sliced apples with the sugar in a covered pan until soft. Sieve and add the grated rind. When cool, whisk the egg white until stiff and fold thoroughly into the apple purée. Chill and garnish with a twist of orange or lemon peel.

Apple pancakes

IMPERIAL·METRIC	AMERICAN
Batter	*Batter*
2 oz./50 g. plain flour	½ cup all-purpose flour
pinch salt	pinch salt
1 small egg	1 small egg
¼ pint/1½ dl. milk	⅔ cup milk
1 teaspoon melted butter	1 teaspoon melted butter
oil or butter for frying	oil or butter for frying
Filling	*Filling*
1 cooking apple	1 baking apple
1 teaspoon castor sugar	1 teaspoon granulated sugar
1 tablespoon water	1 tablespoon water

Sift the flour and salt into a bowl. Gradually beat in the egg, half the milk and the melted butter until the batter is smooth. Stir in the remaining milk. The batter is ready for use when required – make the pancakes following the instructions on page 57).

For the filling, cook the sliced apple, sugar and water very gently in a covered pan until a soft purée is obtained. Use to fill pancakes, roll up and serve with lemon juice.

Apple sponge

IMPERIAL·METRIC	AMERICAN
fine breadcrumbs or semi-sweet biscuit crumbs	fine bread crumbs or cracker crumbs
4 small eating apples	4 small dessert apples
2 oz./50 g. blanched almonds	½ cup blanched almonds
½ pint/3 dl. milk	1¼ cups milk
1½ oz./40 g. semolina	¼ cup semolina flour
4 oz./100 g. butter or margarine	½ cup butter or margarine
4 oz./100 g. sugar	½ cup sugar
3 eggs	3 eggs
1–2 teaspoons ground cinnamon	1–2 teaspoons ground cinnamon
2 oz./50 g. raisins	6 tablespoons raisins

Butter a small loose-bottomed cake tin (or better still an 8-inch (20-cm.) spring form cake tin) and coat with crumbs. Peel, core and slice the apples. Chop the almonds. Heat the milk, stir in the semolina, and cook gently for 3 minutes, stirring. Set aside to cool. Cream the butter and sugar. Beat in the egg yolks and cinnamon. Add almonds and raisins and stir in the semolina mixture. Fold in the stiffly whisked egg whites and then the apple slices. Pour in the prepared cake tin and bake in a moderate oven (350°F., 180°C., Gas Mark 4) for 1¼ hours. Serve hot or cold with cream.

Apple sauce upside-down pudding

IMPERIAL · METRIC	AMERICAN
2 oz./50 g. butter	¼ cup butter
2 oz./50 g. lard	¼ cup lard
8 oz./225 g. granulated sugar	1 cup granulated sugar
2 eggs	2 eggs
½ pint/3 dl. sweetened apple sauce	1¼ cups sweetened applesauce
4 oz./100 g. raisins, coarsely chopped	scant 1 cup coarsely chopped raisins
4 oz./100 g. walnuts, chopped	1 cup chopped walnuts
12 oz./350 g. plain flour	3 cups all-purpose flour
1 teaspoon baking powder	1 teaspoon baking powder
1 teaspoon salt	1 teaspoon salt
¾ teaspoon bicarbonate of soda	¾ teaspoon baking soda
1 teaspoon ground cinnamon	1 teaspoon ground cinnamon
½ teaspoon ground cloves	½ teaspoon ground cloves
½ teaspoon ground nutmeg	½ teaspoon ground nutmeg
4 eating apples	4 dessert apples
3 tablespoons dark brown sugar	4 tablespoons dark brown sugar

Beat the butter and lard until light and fluffy and then cream in the granulated sugar. Lightly beat the eggs and stir into the creamed mixture. Mix in the apple sauce, raisins and walnuts. Heat the oven to moderately hot (375°F., 190°C., Gas Mark 5).

Sift the dry ingredients and mix with the raisin mixture. Butter an 8- by 12-inch (20- by 30-cm.) tin. Peel, core and slice the apples and arrange the slices in the bottom. Sprinkle with brown sugar and pour in the batter. Bake for 40–50 minutes. Cool for 15 minutes, then turn on to a serving plate. Serve warm with whipped cream.

Apple taffety tart

IMPERIAL · METRIC	AMERICAN
8 oz./225 g. plain flour	2 cups all-purpose flour
pinch salt	pinch salt
4 oz./100 g. mixed lard and butter	½ cup mixed lard and butter
1 egg yolk	1 egg yolk
1 lb./450 g. cooking apples	1 lb. baking apples
1 lemon	1 lemon
4 oz./100 g. castor sugar	½ cup granulated sugar
1 oz./25 g. butter	2 tablespoons butter
Icing	*Icing*
4 oz./100 g. icing sugar	1 cup confectioners' sugar
lemon juice	lemon juice

Sift the flour and salt and rub in the lard and butter. Mix to a
firm pastry with the egg yolk and a little cold water. Chill the
pastry, then roll it into two rounds. Line a pie plate with one
round of pastry. Peel the apples and slice them thinly. Grate the
rind from the lemon and mix it with the sugar and chop the
lemon pulp into small pieces. Fill the pastry case with layers of
apples, sugar and lemon pulp. Dot with butter and cover with
the second piece of pastry. Bake in a moderately hot oven (400°F.,
200°C., Gas Mark 6) for 30 minutes. While the pie is still warm,
cover with a thin glacé icing made with the icing sugar mixed
with a little lemon juice.

Bread and apple spicy pudding

IMPERIAL · METRIC	AMERICAN
8 ¼-inch/½-cm. thick slices white bread from a large loaf	8 ¼-inch thick slices white bread from a large loaf
1½ oz./40 g. butter	3 tablespoons butter
1½ lb./¾ kg. cooking apples	1½ lb. baking apples
3 oz./75 g. Demerara sugar	6 tablespoons brown sugar
1 teaspoon ground cinnamon	1 teaspoon ground cinnamon
3 eggs	3 eggs
½ pint/3 dl. milk	1¼ cups milk
extra Demerara sugar for topping	extra brown sugar for topping

Cut the crusts off the bread and, using 1 oz. (25 g., 2 tablespoons) of the butter, spread each slice on one side only. Cut each slice into four squares. Peel, core and slice apples and put half the quantity into a lightly buttered 3-pint (1½-litre) ovenproof dish. Mix the sugar and cinnamon and sprinkle one-third over the apples. Cover with half the bread and another third of the sugar and cinnamon mixture. Add the remaining apples and sprinkle with remaining sugar and cinnamon. Overlap the rest of the bread, butter-side uppermost, in a circle around the edge of the dish. Beat the eggs and milk together, strain over the top and sprinkle with the extra sugar. Cover and bake in a moderate oven (350°F., 180°C., Gas Mark 4) for 30 minutes. Melt the remaining butter and brush lightly over the apple in the centre and bake uncovered for a further 30 minutes, until the bread is golden brown.

Apricot pie

IMPERIAL · METRIC	AMERICAN
6 oz./175 g. plain flour	1½ cups all-purpose flour
pinch salt	pinch salt
1½ oz./40 g. castor sugar	3 tablespoons granulated sugar
3 oz./75 g. butter	6 tablespoons butter
1 egg	1 egg
1½ lb./¾ kg. apricots	1½ lb. apricots
¾ pint/4 dl. water	scant 2 cups water
4 oz./100 g. sugar	½ cup sugar
castor sugar to sprinkle	granulated sugar to sprinkle

To make the pastry, sift together the flour and salt, stir in the castor sugar and rub in the butter to make fine crumbs. Separate the egg and bind the pastry with the yolk. Chill well. Cut the apricots in half and put them into a pie dish, with one or two kernels from the cracked stones. Make a syrup with the water and sugar and pour this over the fruit. Roll out the pastry lightly as it is very delicate. Cover the fruit with the pastry and brush with stiffly beaten egg white. Sprinkle with castor sugar. Bake in a moderately hot oven (375°F., 190°C., Gas Mark 5) for 40 minutes. Serve just warm, or cold, with cream or ice cream.

Apple sauce biscuits

IMPERIAL · METRIC	AMERICAN
2 oz./50 g. butter	¼ cup butter
2 oz./50 g. lard	¼ cup lard
8 oz./225 g. granulated sugar	1 cup granulated sugar
2 eggs	2 eggs
½ pint/3 dl. sweetened apple sauce	1¼ cups sweetened applesauce
4 oz./100 g. walnuts, chopped	1 cup chopped walnuts
2 oz./50 g. raisins, coarsely chopped	scant ½ cup coarsely chopped raisins
2 oz./50 g. sultanas, coarsely chopped	scant ½ cup coarsely chopped seedless white raisins
12 oz./350 g. plain flour	3 cups all-purpose flour
1 teaspoon baking powder	1 teaspoon baking powder
¾ teaspoon bicarbonate of soda	¾ teaspoon baking soda
1 teaspoon salt	1 teaspoon salt
1 teaspoon ground cinnamon	1 teaspoon ground cinnamon
½ teaspoon ground cloves	½ teaspoon ground cloves
½ teaspoon ground nutmeg	½ teaspoon ground nutmeg

Blend the butter and lard until fluffy and then cream in the granulated sugar. Beat the eggs lightly and beat them into the creamed mixture. Stir in the apple sauce, nuts, raisins and sultanas. Sift the dry ingredients and work into the creamed mixture. Drop the batter by tablespoons on to a buttered baking sheet and bake in a moderately hot oven (375°F., 190°C., Gas Mark 5) for 12–15 minutes. Cool for 1 minute before lifting on to a wire rack.

Apricot fritters

IMPERIAL·METRIC	AMERICAN
4 oz./100 g. plain flour	1 cup all-purpose flour
pinch salt	pinch salt
2 teaspoons salad oil	2 teaspoons salad oil
¼ pint/1½ dl. warm water	⅔ cup warm water
1 egg white	1 egg white
6 whole apricots	6 whole apricots
fat for deep frying	oil for deep frying
castor sugar to sprinkle	granulated sugar to sprinkle

Make a batter with the flour, salt, salad oil and water. Leave
to stand for 1 hour. Just before using the batter, fold in the
stiffly whipped egg white. Dip in the apricots and fry in hot
deep fat for a few minutes. Drain on absorbent paper and serve
at once sprinkled with castor sugar.
Pineapple rings may be treated in the same way.

Apricot dumplings

IMPERIAL·METRIC	AMERICAN
8 large apricots	8 large apricots
sugar	sugar
ground cinnamon	ground cinnamon
4 oz./100 g. butter	½ cup butter
8 oz./225 g. plain flour	2 cups all-purpose flour
1 egg	1 egg
butter	butter
beaten egg or milk to glaze	beaten egg or milk to glaze

Peel the apricots and roll them in a mixture of sugar and
cinnamon. Make the pastry by rubbing the butter into the flour
and binding the mixture with the egg. Chill the pastry well and
roll it out a ¼ inch (½ cm.) thick. Cut into 4-inch (10-cm.)
squares. Put an apricot in the middle of each pastry square and
add a tiny dot of butter. Draw up the corners of the pastry and
seal with a little water. Place on a baking sheet and brush with
a little beaten egg or milk. Prick the tops lightly with a fork and
bake in a moderately hot oven (375°F., 190°C., Gas Mark 5)
for 30 minutes.

Apricot pudding

IMPERIAL · METRIC	AMERICAN
10 fresh apricots	10 fresh apricots
2½ tablespoons Demerara sugar	3 tablespoons brown sugar
5 tablespoons water	6 tablespoons water
2 oz./50 g. butter	¼ cup butter
2 tablespoons sugar	3 tablespoons sugar
2 eggs	2 eggs
3 tablespoons flour	4 tablespoons all-purpose flour

Stone the apricots and put them in an ovenproof dish with the
Demerara sugar and water. Cream the butter and sugar, add the
eggs and continue beating well. When the mixture is creamy,
mix in the flour gradually. Put this mixture on top of the
apricots and bake in a moderate oven (350°F., 180°C., Gas
Mark 4) for 1 hour. Serve with cream.

Blackberry flummery

IMPERIAL · METRIC	AMERICAN
1 lb./450 g. blackberries	3 cups blackberries
8 oz./225 g. sugar	1 cup sugar
2 tablespoons cornflour	3 tablespoons cornstarch
pinch salt	pinch salt
1 teaspoon lemon juice	1 teaspoon lemon juice

Simmer the fruit with sugar and just enough water to cover until
the berries are soft. Put through a sieve and return to the
saucepan. Mix the cornflour and salt with 2 tablespoons water
and add to the blackberries. Simmer for 5 minutes, stirring well.
Add the lemon juice and cool. Serve with sugar and cream.

Blackberry pancakes

IMPERIAL·METRIC	AMERICAN
4 oz./100 g. plain flour	1 cup all-purpose flour
2 tablespoons sugar	3 tablespoons sugar
1 egg	1 egg
½ pint/3 dl. milk	1¼ cups milk
8 oz./225 g. blackberries	1½ cups blackberries
1 tablespoon melted butter	1 tablespoon melted butter
lard or butter for frying	lard or butter for frying

Mix together the flour, sugar, egg yolk, milk and blackberries
to make a batter. Add the butter and fold in the stiffly beaten
egg white. Make small pancakes with this mixture following the
instructions on page 57, browning on both sides. Serve very hot
with ice cream.

Bramble betty

IMPERIAL·METRIC	AMERICAN
1 lb./450 g. cooking apples	1 lb. baking apples
8 oz./225 g. blackberries	1½ cups blackberries
2 oz./50 g. granulated sugar	¼ cup granulated sugar
2 oz./50 g. butter	¼ cup butter
6 oz./175 g. fresh white breadcrumbs	3 cups fresh soft bread crumbs
2 oz./50 g. soft brown sugar	¼ cup brown sugar
fresh blackberries and whipped cream to decorate	fresh blackberries and whipped cream to decorate

Peel, core and slice the apples. Place the apples, blackberries
and granulated sugar in a pan with 1 tablespoon of water,
cover and cook gently until the fruit is tender. Set aside to cool.
Meanwhile, melt the butter in a pan and mix in the crumbs and
soft brown sugar. Turn the mixture well so that the butter is
properly mixed in. Layer the fruit and crumb mixture
alternately in a bowl ending with a layer of crumbs. Set aside
overnight. To serve, decorate with fresh blackberries and
whipped cream.

Blackcurrant flummery

IMPERIAL·METRIC	AMERICAN
1 lb./450 g. blackcurrants	4 cups black currants
1 pint/6 dl. water	2½ cups water
2 teaspoons cornflour	2 teaspoons cornstarch
4 oz./100 g. castor sugar	½ cup granulated sugar
2 teaspoons lemon juice	2 teaspoons lemon juice
2 eggs	2 eggs

Remove the stalks and wash the currants. Stew gently in the water until tender, then sieve. Mix the cornflour to a smooth paste with 1 tablespoon of the blackcurrant purée. Put the rest of the purée on to boil with the sugar. When boiling, add the blended cornflour and the lemon juice, and cook for 2 minutes, stirring all the time to prevent sticking. Leave to cool. Separate the eggs, beat the yolks, and add to the cooled blackcurrant mixture, mixing well. Whip the egg whites to a stiff foam and fold into the mixture when cold. Pour into a bowl and serve with cream or egg custard.

Cherry cream ring

IMPERIAL·METRIC	AMERICAN
1 lb./450 g. morello cherries	1 lb. morello cherries
4 oz./100 g. sugar	½ cup sugar
juice of 1 lemon	juice of 1 lemon
3 tablespoons fine semolina	4 tablespoons semolina flour
1½ tablespoons sugar	2 tablespoons sugar
¼ pint/1½ dl. single cream or top of the milk	⅔ cup half-and-half
1 egg	1 egg
few blanched almonds (optional)	few blanched almonds (optional)

Wash the cherries and remove the stalks. Remove the stones with a cherry pipper or, if one is not available, slit down one side of each cherry and remove the stone using a pointed knife. Put the cherries, the 4 oz. (100 g., ½ cup) sugar and lemon juice in an enamelled pan. Cover and cook slowly until the fruit is tender but not broken. (No water should be needed. This can be done in a casserole in the oven or in a basin placed in a covered pan of

boiling water.) Remove the cherries. Make the syrup up to
$\frac{3}{4}$ pint (4 dl., scant 2 cups) with water. Heat and sprinkle in the
semolina and bring to the boil, stirring. Cook slowly for 5
minutes. Remove from the heat and add the sugar and cream or
top of milk and whip in the beaten egg. Stir over very low heat
for 1–2 minutes without boiling. Pour into a 7-inch (18-cm.) ring
tin rinsed with cold water, or into a fancy mould or serving dish.
Leave in a cool place until firm. Unmould and serve with the
cherries. If liked, decorate with a few blanched almonds.

Blackberry pudding

IMPERIAL · METRIC	AMERICAN
1 lb./450 g. blackberries	3 cups blackberries
$\frac{1}{2}$ pint/3 dl. cider	1$\frac{1}{4}$ cups cider
8 oz./225 g. castor sugar	1 cup granulated sugar
5 slices white bread	5 slices white bread

Simmer the blackberries with the cider and sugar. Take the
crusts from the bread, and use some of the bread to line a
pudding basin. Fill the bread-lined basin with the cooled fruit
mixture and cover with the remaining bread. Put a plate and a
weight on top and leave in a cold place for 24 hours. Turn out
and serve with cream.

Gooseberry fool

IMPERIAL · METRIC	AMERICAN
1 lb./450 g. gooseberries	1 lb. gooseberries
$\frac{1}{4}$ pint/1$\frac{1}{2}$ dl. water	$\frac{2}{3}$ cup water
8 oz./225 g. sugar	1 cup sugar
2 teaspoons orange flower water	2 teaspoons orange flower water
$\frac{3}{4}$ pint/4 dl. double cream	scant 2 cups heavy cream

Simmer the gooseberries with the water and sugar until the fruit
is soft. Cool and whip in the orange flower water and cream.
Serve very cold.

In old recipes for fools, the fruit was never sieved, but if you
prefer a smoother result, sieve the fruit before stirring in the
cream.

Gooseberry flummery

IMPERIAL · METRIC	AMERICAN
1 lb./450 g. gooseberries	1 lb. gooseberries
8 oz./225 g. sugar	1 cup sugar
1 teaspoon lemon juice	1 teaspoon lemon juice
½ pint/3 dl. milk	1¼ cups milk
4 tablespoons fine semolina	5 tablespoons semolina flour
few drops green food colouring	few drops green food coloring

Simmer the gooseberries with the sugar and a very little water until the skins burst and the fruit is pulpy. Take off the heat and add the lemon juice. Warm the milk and sprinkle in the semolina. Bring to the boil and let it simmer for 3 minutes to thicken. Take off the heat, stir in the gooseberries and tint a pale green. Pour into a bowl and leave in a cold place to set.

Gooseberry pudding

IMPERIAL · METRIC	AMERICAN
pinch salt	pinch salt
4 oz./100 g. shredded suet	scant 1 cup shredded suet
8 oz./225 g. self-raising flour	2 cups all-purpose flour sifted with 2 teaspoons baking powder
1 oz./25 g. butter	2 tablespoons butter
1½ lb./¾ kg. gooseberries	1½ lb. gooseberries
4 oz./100 g. sugar	½ cup sugar

Stir the salt and suet into the flour and rub in the butter. Add just enough cold water to make a firm pastry. Roll out the pastry and line a small greased pudding basin, keeping enough for a lid. Top and tail the gooseberries and fill the basin with fruit and sugar. Cover with a pastry lid and seal the edges with a little water. Cover with foil and cook in a pan of boiling water for 2½ hours. Turn out and serve with hot apricot jam and cream.

Gooseberry tansy

IMPERIAL · METRIC	AMERICAN
1 lb./450 g. gooseberries	1 lb. gooseberries
4 oz./100 g. butter	½ cup butter
4 oz./100 g. sugar	½ cup sugar
2 egg yolks	2 egg yolks
¼ pint/1½ dl. double cream	⅔ cup heavy cream
juice of 1 lemon	juice of 1 lemon

Simmer the gooseberries in the butter until cooked. Stir in the sugar and bring to the boil. Remove from the heat and allow to cool slightly. Add the beaten egg yolks and lightly whipped cream and turn into a serving dish. Sprinkle with the lemon juice and a little extra sugar. Serve hot or cold.

Baked pears

IMPERIAL · METRIC	AMERICAN
2 lb./1 kg. cooking pears (or hard eating pears)	2 lb. cooking pears (or hard dessert pears)
4 oz./100 g. castor sugar	½ cup granulated sugar
½ pint/3 dl. cider	1¼ cups cider
½ pint/3 dl. water	1¼ cups water
twist of lemon peel	twist of lemon peel
shredded almonds	shredded almonds

Peel the pears, leaving the stems on, and arrange them upright in a deep casserole. Sprinkle on the sugar and pour over the cider and water and add the lemon peel. Cook in a cool oven (300°F., 150°C., Gas Mark 2) until the pears are tender and can be pierced with a fork. Leave to cool in the juice. Remove the pears and reduce the juice until thick and syrupy. Spike the pears with almonds and serve in the reduced liquid with thick cream. The pears may also be cooked in red wine.

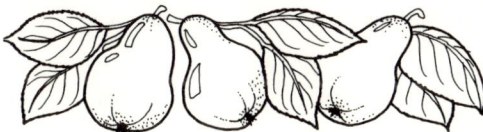

Plum gingerbread pudding

IMPERIAL · METRIC	AMERICAN
1½ lb./¾ kg. yellow plums	1½ lb. yellow plums
6 oz./175 g. castor sugar	¾ cup granulated sugar
2 oz./50 g. butter	¼ cup butter
3 oz./75 g. black treacle	¼ cup molasses
1 oz./25 g. golden syrup	1½ tablespoons corn syrup
5 tablespoons milk	6 tablespoons milk
1 egg	1 egg
4 oz./100 g. plain flour	1 cup all-purpose flour
1 oz./25 g. granulated sugar	2 tablespoons granulated sugar
1 teaspoon mixed spice	1 teaspoon mixed spice
1 teaspoon ground ginger	1 teaspoon ground ginger
½ teaspoon bicarbonate of soda	½ teaspoon baking soda

Mix the plums and castor sugar and put into a buttered ovenproof dish. Warm together the butter, treacle and syrup, then add the milk and beaten egg and leave to cool. In a bowl, mix the sieved flour, granulated sugar, spices and soda, add cooled treacle mixture and blend well together. Pour over the fruit, spreading evenly. Bake in the centre of a cool oven (325°F., 160°C., Gas Mark 3) for 1¼ hours.

Plum sponge

IMPERIAL · METRIC	AMERICAN
1 egg	1 egg
4 oz./100 g. castor sugar	½ cup granulated sugar
4 oz./100 g. plain flour	1 cup all-purpose flour
1 teaspoon baking powder	1 teaspoon baking powder
¼ teaspoon salt	¼ teaspoon salt
4 tablespoons milk	⅓ cup milk
3 tablespoons melted butter	4 tablespoons melted butter
¼ teaspoon lemon essence	¼ teaspoon lemon extract
½ teaspoon vanilla essence	½ teaspoon vanilla extract
1 lb./450 g. plums	1 lb. plums
2 oz./50 g. sugar	¼ cup sugar
1 teaspoon ground cinnamon	1 teaspoon ground cinnamon
4 tablespoons water	⅓ cup water

Beat the egg and gradually beat in the sugar. Add the flour, baking powder and salt, and gradually blend in the milk, butter and essences. Pour into a rectangular tin 7 inches (18 cm.) by 10 inches (26 cm.). Cut the plums in half and arrange them face down on the surface, close together. Sprinkle the fruit with sugar, cinnamon and water. Bake in a moderate oven (350°F., 180°C., Gas Mark 4) for 45 minutes. Cut in squares and serve warm or cold with cream or ice cream.

Raspberry cream

IMPERIAL·METRIC	AMERICAN
3 oz./75 g. castor sugar	6 tablespoons granulated sugar
1 lb./450 g. raspberries	3 cups raspberries
½ pint/3 dl. double cream	1¼ cups heavy cream
2 egg whites	2 egg whites
sponge finger biscuits	ladyfingers

Sprinkle the sugar over the prepared raspberries and leave, covered, in a cool place for at least 1 hour. Rub through a fine sieve. Fold the whipped cream into the fruit pulp and then fold in the stiffly whisked egg whites. Spoon into a large serving bowl, or individual bowls, and chill. Serve with sponge finger biscuits.

Stewed rhubarb

This simple method of cooking and serving is one of the most delicious ways with rhubarb. Prepare the rhubarb and cut into 1-inch (2·5-cm.) pieces. Sprinkle generously with sugar, usually 4 oz. (100 g., ½ cup) to 1 lb. (450 g.) rhubarb. If liked, a few gratings of orange or lemon rind can be added. Add just enough water to prevent catching, about 3 tablespoons. Cover and stew very gently until soft but not mushy, a few minutes. Taste and add more sugar if needed. Serve with fresh cream or custard.

Baked rhubarb

Prepare 1 lb. (450 g.) rhubarb. Mix with about 4 oz. (100 g., ½ cup) sugar. Put into casserole with 4 tablespoons water. Cover and bake in a cool oven (300°F., 150°C., Gas Mark 2) until tender. Serve with fresh cream or custard.

Rhubarb cream betty

IMPERIAL · METRIC	AMERICAN
1 lb./450 g. rhubarb	1 lb. rhubarb
1 tablespoon water	1 tablespoon water
4 oz./100 g. sugar	½ cup sugar
¼ pint/1½ dl. double cream, whipped	⅔ cup heavy cream, whipped
Crumb mixture	*Crumb mixture*
2 oz./50 g. butter	¼ cup butter
6 oz./175 g. fresh white breadcrumbs	3 cups fresh soft bread crumbs
2 oz./50 g. soft brown sugar	¼ cup brown sugar

Cut the rhubarb into 1-inch (2·5-cm.) lengths. Stew gently in the water and sugar in a tightly lidded pan. Cool.

To make the crumb mixture, melt the butter in a pan, remove from the heat and mix in the crumbs and sugar. Fill a glass bowl with layers of rhubarb and layers of crumb mixture. Top with cream and decorate with a couple of pieces of rhubarb.

Rhubarb and orange lattice tart

IMPERIAL · METRIC	AMERICAN
6 oz./175 g. plain flour	1½ cups all-purpose flour
pinch salt	pinch salt
1 oz./25 g. icing sugar	¼ cup sifted confectioners' sugar
3 oz./75 g. butter	6 tablespoons butter
about 2 tablespoons water	about 3 tablespoons water
Filling	*Filling*
1 lb./450 g. rhubarb	1 lb. rhubarb
6 oz./175 g. sugar	¾ cup sugar
1 oz./25 g. plain flour	¼ cup all-purpose flour
1 egg	1 egg
grated rind of 1 orange	grated rind of 1 orange
2 tablespoons orange juice made up to ¼ pint/1½ dl. with water	3 tablespoons orange juice made up to ⅔ cup with water

Sift the flour, salt and icing sugar into a bowl and rub in the butter until the mixture resembles fine breadcrumbs. Mix to a firm dough with water. Roll out and line an 8-inch (20-cm.)

ovenproof plate; save the trimmings for the lattice. Chill. Wipe the rhubarb and cut into 1-inch (2·5-cm.) lengths then put on the pastry. In a basin blend together the sugar, flour, egg and orange rind. Place the juice and water in a pan and bring to the boil. Pour on to the flour mixture and stir briskly. Return to the pan and bring to the boil, stirring all the time. Pour over the rhubarb. Cut strips from the trimmings and place on the filling to form a lattice. Bake in a hot oven (425°F., 220°C., Gas Mark 7) for 35–40 minutes. Serve hot or cold.

Rhubarb hot cake

IMPERIAL · METRIC	AMERICAN
8 oz./225 g. self-raising flour	2 cups all-purpose flour sifted with 2 teaspoons baking powder
pinch salt	pinch salt
¼ teaspoon ground nutmeg	¼ teaspoon ground nutmeg
1 oz./25 g. butter	2 tablespoons butter
1 oz./25 g. sugar	2 tablespoons sugar
1 egg	1 egg
¼ pint/1½ dl. milk	⅔ cup milk
icing sugar to sprinkle	confectioners' sugar to sprinkle
Filling	*Filling*
8 oz./225 g. rhubarb	½ lb. rhubarb
2 oz./50 g. sugar	¼ cup sugar
½ oz./15 g. butter	1 tablespoon butter

Sieve together the flour, salt and nutmeg and rub in the butter until the mixture resembles fine breadcrumbs. Add the sugar. Mix in the egg and milk to form a soft dough. Divide the mixture in half and roll out to two 7-inch (18-cm.) rounds. Put one round on a baking sheet, cover with the chopped rhubarb, mixed with the sugar and dotted with butter. Divide the second round into six or eight triangles with a knife and place these wedges on top of the rhubarb. Bake in a moderately hot oven (375°F., 190°C., Gas Mark 5) for about 40 minutes. Dust with icing sugar and serve hot with cream.

Old-fashioned rhubarb pudding

IMPERIAL·METRIC	AMERICAN
1 oz./25 g. butter	2 tablespoons butter
brown sugar	brown sugar
Suet crust pastry	*Suet crust pastry*
8 oz./225 g. self-raising flour	2 cups all-purpose flour sifted with 2 teaspoons baking powder
1 teaspoon salt	1 teaspoon salt
3 oz./75 g. shredded suet	generous $\frac{1}{2}$ cup shredded suet
$\frac{1}{4}$ pint/1$\frac{1}{2}$ dl. water	$\frac{2}{3}$ cup water
Filling	*Filling*
1$\frac{1}{2}$ lb./$\frac{3}{4}$ kg. rhubarb	1$\frac{1}{2}$ lb. rhubarb
1 oz./25 g. chopped candied peel	3 tablespoons chopped candied peel
2 oz./50 g. currants	scant $\frac{1}{2}$ cup currants
grated rind and juice of $\frac{1}{2}$ lemon	grated rind and juice of $\frac{1}{2}$ lemon
4 oz./100 g. sugar	$\frac{1}{2}$ cup sugar
cinnamon	cinnamon
5 tablespoons water	6 tablespoons water

To make the suet crust pastry, sieve together the flour and salt.
Mix in the suet and add the water. Mix to a soft dough with a
round-bladed knife. Lightly knead on a floured board until the
dough is smooth. Cut off a third of the pastry for a lid.

To make the pudding, butter a 2-pint (1-litre) pudding basin
thickly and sprinkle the inside with plenty of brown sugar and
line it with the pastry. Cut the rhubarb into 1-inch (2·5-cm.)
lengths and put half of them into the basin. Sprinkle over the
chopped candied peel, currants, grated rind and juice of $\frac{1}{2}$ lemon,
half the sugar and dusting of cinnamon. Add the rest of the
rhubarb and the sugar. Add the water. Cover with a pastry lid
and greased paper over that. Bake in a moderate oven (350°F.,
180°C., Gas Mark 4) for 1$\frac{1}{4}$ hours. Turn out and serve with
cream or custard.

Strawberry shortcake

IMPERIAL · METRIC	AMERICAN
4 oz./100 g. butter	½ cup butter
4 oz./100 g. castor sugar	½ cup granulated sugar
2 eggs	2 eggs
grated rind of 1 orange	grated rind of 1 orange
4 oz./100 g. self-raising flour	1 cup all-purpose flour sifted with 1 teaspoon baking powder
¾ pint/4 dl. double cream	scant 2 cups heavy cream
little sugar (optional)	little sugar (optional)
1 lb./450 g. strawberries	1 lb. strawberries

Cream the butter and sugar together until light and fluffy. Beat the eggs with the orange rind and add to the creamed mixture alternately with the flour. Mix thoroughly and spread in two greased and floured 7-inch (18-cm.) sponge tins. Bake in a moderately hot oven (400°F., 200°C., Gas Mark 6) for 25 minutes. Cool on a wire rack. Whip the cream, sweetening slightly to taste, if liked. Reserve a few strawberries for decoration, and crush the rest. Sandwich the two layers together with strawberries and cream, and top with more cream and whole strawberries.

Hot strawberries in wine

IMPERIAL · METRIC	AMERICAN
1 lb./450 g. strawberries	1 lb. strawberries
8 oz./225 g. sugar	1 cup sugar
good pinch cinnamon	good pinch cinnamon
¼ pint/1½ dl. red wine	⅔ cup red wine
2 teaspoons honey	2 teaspoons honey
2 teaspoons lemon juice	2 teaspoons lemon juice

Put the strawberries in an ovenproof dish with the sugar and cinnamon. Cover and cook in a moderate oven (325°F., 160°C., Gas Mark 3) for 30 minutes. Drain off the syrup and mix it with the wine. Pour over the strawberries again and cook for a further 15 minutes. Just before serving, stir in the honey and lemon juice. Serve hot with thick cream.

Honey

Honey has been a natural food and sweetening ingredient for thousands of years. It is still delicious spread on brown bread and butter, but is also of great value in the kitchen. It is easier to digest than sugar and gives a quick lift when you are tired, so try it in coffee, on breakfast cereals and pancakes and for sweetening baby food. Fold a spoonful of honey into whipped cream for a rich flavour, add it to lemon or orange juice to make a glaze for a joint of bacon or ham, and sweeten good-night drinks with honey to suit your own taste.

Honey can be used in syrup for bottling fruit. Dilute with twice as much water for a heavy syrup, and four times as much water for light syrup. In pickles and chutneys, substitute honey for half the sugar in the recipe. In baking, substitute honey for one-quarter of the sugar in cake recipes. The cakes will be a little darker, but will keep longer.

Honey should not be stored in the refrigerator. If it seems a little stiff to use, stand the jar in a saucepan of hot water until the honey is soft enough to pour or spoon out. If you want to weigh it, sprinkle a little flour on the scale pan first, so that the honey will slip off easily. It is easy to measure out spoonfuls if you heat a tablespoon in hot water and dry it quickly before spooning out the honey (1 tablespoon honey equals 1 oz./25 g. honey).

Honey orange roly-poly

IMPERIAL·METRIC	AMERICAN
8 oz./225 g. shortcrust pastry	basic pie dough made with 2 cups all-purpose flour etc.
2 oz./50 g. butter	¼ cup butter
2 oz./50 g. castor sugar	¼ cup granulated sugar
2 oranges	2 oranges
2 tablespoons honey	3 tablespoons honey

Roll out the pastry into a square. Cream the butter and sugar.
Add the grated orange rind and the honey and beat well. Spread
on to the pastry. Arrange the roughly chopped segments of
peeled orange on top. Roll up the pastry like a Swiss roll and
place on a baking sheet. Seal the edges with milk and brush the
top with a little milk. Bake in a moderately hot oven (400°F.,
200 °C., Gas Mark 6) for 20 minutes. Serve with custard or cream.

Alternatively, decorate with some extra orange slices and pour
over hot honey.

Spice pudding and honey cream

IMPERIAL·METRIC	AMERICAN
2 tablespoons honey	3 tablespoons honey
3 oz./75 g. butter	6 tablespoons butter
3 oz./75 g. castor sugar	6 tablespoons granulated sugar
2 standard eggs	2 eggs
6 oz./175 g. plain flour	1½ cups all-purpose flour
1 teaspoon baking powder	1 teaspoon baking powder
½ teaspoon ginger	½ teaspoon ginger
½ teaspoon cinnamon	½ teaspoon cinnamon
pinch allspice	pinch allspice
1–2 tablespoons milk (optional)	1–2 tablespoons milk (optional)
Honey cream	*Honey cream*
¼ pint/1½ dl. double cream	⅔ cup heavy cream
1 tablespoon honey	1 tablespoon honey

Butter a 1½-pint (1-litre) pudding basin and put the honey in the
bottom. Cream the butter and the sugar until light and fluffy.
Add the beaten eggs one at a time. Sieve the flour, baking
powder, ginger, cinnamon and allspice together. Stir into the
creamed mixture gradually and if necessary add the milk to form
a stiff dropping consistency. Turn into the basin, cover and
steam for 1½ hours.

To make the honey cream, pour the cream into a small basin,
add the honey and whisk together until the mixture is thick.
Serve with the pudding.

Honey, apple and almond pudding

IMPERIAL · METRIC	AMERICAN
1 lb./450 g. cooking apples, peeled and cored	1 lb. baking apples, peeled and cored
3 tablespoons honey	4 tablespoons honey
2 oz./50 g. fine breadcrumbs	1 cup fresh soft bread crumbs
3 oz./75 g. butter or margarine	6 tablespoons butter or margarine
4 oz./100 g. castor sugar	½ cup granulated sugar
2 oz./50 g. ground almonds	½ cup ground almonds
1 egg	1 egg

Stew the apples with the honey and a little water until soft. Stir in the breadcrumbs, then turn the mixture into a buttered ovenproof dish. Melt the butter over a low heat and mix together with the sugar, almonds and beaten egg. Spread over the apple mixture. Bake in a moderately hot oven (375°F., 190°C., Gas Mark 5) for 45 minutes. Serve with lightly whipped cream.

Honey rice meringue

IMPERIAL · METRIC	AMERICAN
2½ oz./65 g. round-grain rice	scant ½ cup round-grain rice
1 pint/6 dl. milk	2½ cups milk
1 egg	1 egg
4 tablespoons clear honey	5 tablespoons clear honey
15-oz./425-g. can apricots, drained	15-oz. can apricots, drained

Put the rice and milk into a 1¾-pint (1-litre) pie dish and bake in a cool oven (300°F., 150°C., Gas Mark 2) for 2 hours. Cool slightly. Beat the egg yolk and 2 tablespoons of the honey together until thick. Stir into the rice. Arrange the apricots on top of rice.

To make the meringue, whisk the egg white until slightly frothy then gradually whisk in the remaining honey. Continue whisking until the meringue stands in peaks. Pile on top of the apricots. Bake in a moderate oven (350°F., 180°C., Gas Mark 4) for 20 minutes, or until golden and crisp. Serve hot or cold.

The apricot syrup may be thickened with cornflour or arrowroot and served as a sauce.

Honey and lemon sponge pudding with cinnamon sauce

IMPERIAL · METRIC	AMERICAN
3 oz./75 g. butter	6 tablespoons butter
3 oz./75 g. castor sugar	6 tablespoons granulated sugar
2 eggs	2 eggs
6 oz./175 g. flour	1½ cups all-purpose flour
½ teaspoon baking powder	½ teaspoon baking powder
good pinch of salt	good pinch of salt
juice of ½ lemon	juice of ½ lemon
grated rind of 1 lemon	grated rind of 1 lemon
2 tablespoons honey	3 tablespoons honey
Cinnamon sauce	*Cinnamon sauce*
1 tablespoon flour	1 tablespoon all-purpose flour
¼ teaspoon cinnamon	¼ teaspoon cinnamon
¼ teaspoon salt	¼ teaspoon salt
6 fl. oz./2 dl. water	¾ cup water
3 oz./75 g. honey	4½ tablespoons honey
1 teaspoon butter or margarine	1 teaspoon butter or margarine

Cream the butter and sugar until light and fluffy and beat in the eggs one at a time. Sieve the flour with the baking powder and salt. Stir gradually into the butter and sugar mixture. Mix well and add the lemon juice and rind. (The mixture should be of a stiff dropping consistency; add a little milk if necessary.) Butter a 1½-pint (1-litre) pudding basin. Put the honey at the bottom and spoon the sponge mixture on top. Cover with foil, twist it well over the rim of the basin and steam for 1½ hours.

To make the sauce, sieve the flour, cinnamon and salt. Put the water and honey in a pan over a low heat and allow the honey to dissolve. Pour on to the flour, stirring well. Return the sauce to the pan and cook until thick, stirring all the time. Stir in the butter. Serve with the sponge pudding.

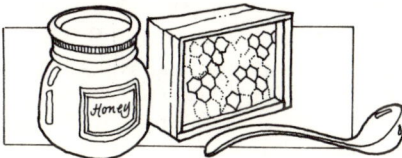

Honey-baked fruit

IMPERIAL · METRIC	AMERICAN
4 eating apples or pears	4 dessert apples or pears
4 tablespoons lemon juice	$\frac{1}{3}$ cup lemon juice
6 oz./175 g. honey	$\frac{1}{2}$ cup honey
1 teaspoon cinnamon or 4 whole cloves	1 teaspoon cinnamon or 4 whole cloves
1 oz./25 g. butter	2 tablespoons butter

Wipe the apples and core them. If using pears, peel and core them and cut them in half. Arrange the fruit close together in a greased shallow ovenproof dish. Mix together the lemon juice and honey and pour over the fruit. Sprinkle with cinnamon, or add cloves, and dot with butter. Bake in a moderate oven (350°F., 180°C., Gas Mark 4) for 25 minutes. Serve hot with cream.

Rhubarb can also be cooked in the same way, using 1½ lb. (¾ kg.) sliced rhubarb and either cinnamon or a pinch of ginger.

Rum and honey fritters

IMPERIAL · METRIC	AMERICAN
4 oz./100 g. plain flour	1 cup all-purpose flour
pinch salt	pinch salt
¼ pint/1½ dl. tepid water	$\frac{2}{3}$ cup tepid water
1 tablespoon cooking oil	1 tablespoon cooking oil
2 egg whites	2 egg whites
3–4 cooking apples	3–4 baking apples
4 tablespoons clear honey	5 tablespoons clear honey
1½ tablespoons rum	2 tablespoons rum
juice and finely grated rind of ½ lemon	juice and finely grated rind of ½ lemon
flour	flour
fat or oil for deep frying	oil for deep frying
¼ pint/1½ dl. double cream	$\frac{2}{3}$ cup heavy cream

To make the batter, sieve the flour and salt. Add the water and oil and beat well until smooth. Leave to stand for 1 hour. Fold in the stiffly beaten egg whites just before using. Peel and core the apples and cut into rings, ⅜ inch (¾ cm.) wide. Heat the honey over a low heat until dissolved. Remove from heat, add the rum, lemon juice and rind and pour over the apple slices. Leave for about 1 hour, turning the slices occasionally. When ready to cook, drain the apples and dust them lightly with flour which helps the batter to stick. Heat the oil in a deep frying pan. (To test if the oil is ready, drop a little of the batter into the oil. This should rise to the surface immediately and begin to brown.) Dip the apple rings in the batter and fry until crisp and golden, turning once. Drain well on absorbent paper. Lightly whip the cream, fold in the remaining honey and rum marinade and spoon over the fritters.

This recipe can also be used with pineapple rings or sliced bananas instead of the apples.

Honey meringue with strawberries

IMPERIAL · METRIC	AMERICAN
5 egg whites	5 egg whites
10 oz./275 g. castor sugar	1¼ cups granulated sugar
¼ pint/1½ dl. double cream	⅔ cup heavy cream
2 tablespoons orange-flavoured liqueur (Cointreau or Orange Curaçao) or fresh orange juice	3 tablespoons orange-flavored liqueur (Cointreau or Orange Curaçao) or fresh orange juice
4 tablespoons clear honey	5 tablespoons clear honey
1 lb./450 g. strawberries	1 lb. strawberries

Draw a 9-inch (23-cm.) circle on a piece of lightly oiled cooking foil placed on a baking sheet, using a plate as a guide.

Whisk the egg whites until stiff. Add 5 teaspoons of the sugar and continue whisking for about 2 minutes. Fold in the remaining sugar. Spread half the meringue over the circle. Put the rest of the meringue into a piping bag and pipe a thick circle around the edge on top of the base to form a wall. Bake in a cool oven (275°F., 140°C., Gas Mark 1) for 1–1½ hours, until lightly coloured and quite dry. Remove to a wire rack, peel off the paper and leave to cool. Whip the cream and fold in the orange liqueur or orange juice and half the honey. Spoon into the meringue case. Place the strawberries on the top. Just before serving, heat the rest of the honey and pour the warm honey over the strawberries.

Honey tart

IMPERIAL · METRIC	AMERICAN
6 oz./175 g. shortcrust pastry	basic pie dough made with 1½ cups all-purpose flour etc.
5 tablespoons clear honey	6 tablespoons clear honey
1½ oz./40 g. fresh breadcrumbs	¾ cup fresh soft bread crumbs
pinch ground ginger or a little lemon juice	pinch ground ginger or a little lemon juice

Roll out the pastry to line an 8- or 9-inch (20- or 23-cm.) ovenproof plate. Trim off the excess pastry and decorate the edge. Mix the honey, breadcrumbs, ginger or lemon juice together and turn into the middle of the pastry. Spread to within 1 inch (2·5 cm.) of the edge. Roll out pastry trimmings and cut into strips. Place the strips to form a lattice on top of tart. Bake in a moderately hot oven (400°F., 200°C., Gas Mark 6) for about 25 minutes. Serve with cream or custard.

Honey syllabub

IMPERIAL · METRIC	AMERICAN
1 pint/6 dl. double cream	2½ cups heavy cream
6 tablespoons clear honey	7 tablespoons clear honey
¼ pint/1½ dl. Marsala or white wine	⅔ cup Marsala or white wine
2 tablespoons lemon juice	3 tablespoons lemon juice

Whisk all the ingredients together until stiff enough to spoon into glasses. Chill and serve with ice cream wafers or shortbread fingers.

Honey junket

IMPERIAL · METRIC	AMERICAN
4 teaspoons clear honey	4 teaspoons clear honey
1 pint/6 dl. milk	2½ cups milk
2 drops vanilla essence	2 drops vanilla extract
3 teaspoons rennet	3 teaspoons rennet
pinch nutmeg	pinch nutmeg

Warm the honey gently until runny. Add the milk and vanilla essence and heat until lukewarm (the milk must not be hotter than 100°F./38°C.). Stir in the rennet and pour into a serving bowl. Leave in a warm kitchen until set, and then chill. Dust with nutmeg before serving.

This junket is particularly delicious if covered completely with a layer of thick, unwhipped cream, lightly flavoured with brandy, just before serving.

Honey posset with lemon sugar

IMPERIAL·METRIC	AMERICAN
½ pint/3 dl. double cream	1¼ cups heavy cream
2 egg whites	2 egg whites
2 tablespoons clear honey	3 tablespoons clear honey
juice of 2 lemons	juice of 2 lemons
finely grated rind of 1½ lemons	finely grated rind of 1½ lemons
1 oz./25 g. castor sugar	2 tablespoons granulated sugar

Whip the cream and egg whites together until the whisk leaves a slight trail. Gently whip in the honey, lemon juice and two-thirds of the lemon rind. Pile into six individual serving dishes and chill. Just before serving, mix the remaining lemon rind with the sugar and sprinkle on top of each serving.

Strawberry fool

IMPERIAL·METRIC	AMERICAN
1 lb./450 g. strawberries	1 lb. strawberries
½ pint/3 dl. double cream	1¼ cups heavy cream
1 tablespoon honey	1 tablespoon honey
1 teaspoon chopped almonds	1 teaspoon chopped almonds

Rub three-quarters of the strawberries through a fine sieve and slice the rest. Pour the cream and honey into a bowl and whisk until thick. Fold in the strawberry purée and the slices. Serve in four individual glasses or dishes and decorate with the almonds.

Honey ice cream

IMPERIAL·METRIC	AMERICAN
1 lb./450 g. raspberries	1 lb. raspberries
¼ pint/1½ dl. double cream	⅔ cup heavy cream
¼ pint/1½ dl. natural yogurt	⅔ cup unflavored yogurt
10 tablespoons clear honey	11 tablespoons clear honey
2 tablespoons lemon juice	3 tablespoons lemon juice
pinch salt	pinch salt
4 egg whites	4 egg whites

Sieve the raspberries. Put the raspberry purée into a mixing bowl and add the cream, yogurt, honey, lemon juice and salt. Mix thoroughly. Pour into ice trays and partially freeze. Put into a mixing bowl and stir until smooth. Fold in the stiffly whisked egg whites. Return the mixture to ice trays and freeze again. Serve in chilled glasses.

Spiced honey cake

IMPERIAL·METRIC	AMERICAN
2 oz./50 g. butter or margarine	¼ cup butter or margarine
5 oz./150 g. honey	scant ½ cup honey
5 oz./150 g. Demerara sugar	⅔ cup brown sugar
10 oz./275 g. plain flour	2½ cups all-purpose flour
pinch salt	pinch salt
1 teaspoon bicarbonate of soda	1 teaspoon baking soda
1 teaspoon baking powder	1 teaspoon baking powder
1 teaspoon mixed spice	1 teaspoon mixed spice
1 teaspoon ginger	1 teaspoon ginger
1 teaspoon cinnamon	1 teaspoon cinnamon
2–4 oz./50–100 g. chopped peel	½–¾ cup chopped peel
1 egg	1 egg
¼ pint/1½ dl. milk	⅔ cup milk
flaked almonds to decorate	flaked almonds to decorate

Slice the butter into a pan and heat gently until melted. Draw the pan off the heat and stir in the honey and sugar. Cool the mixture. Sift the flour, salt, bicarbonate of soda, baking powder and spices into a bowl. Add the peel. Beat the egg and milk together and mix thoroughly with the cooled honey mixture.

Pour into the flour mixture and beat until smooth. Pour into a
1-lb. (450-g.) loaf tin, greased and lined at the bottom with
greased paper. Scatter the flaked almonds on top. Bake in a
moderate oven (350°F., 180°C., Gas Mark 4) for about 1¼ hours,
until firm. (Cover with foil after 1 hour, to prevent becoming too
brown.) Cool on a wire rack. Serve sliced and spread with butter.

Honey bombe

IMPERIAL·METRIC	AMERICAN
4 tablespoons water	⅓ cup water
8 oz./225 g. clear honey	scant ¾ cup clear honey
6 egg yolks	6 egg yolks
¾ pint/4 dl. double cream	scant 2 cups heavy cream

Boil the water and honey and leave to cool. Turn into a basin
placed over a pan of hot water and add the egg yolks. Beat until
thick and creamy. Remove from the heat and beat until cold.
When cold, fold in the whipped cream. Put into a metal pudding
basin and freeze. Turn out of this on to a chilled serving dish.

Honey loaf

IMPERIAL·METRIC	AMERICAN
4 oz./100 g. butter	½ cup butter
4 oz./100 g. castor sugar	½ cup granulated sugar
6 tablespoons honey	7 tablespoons honey
1 egg	1 egg
10½ oz./290 g. plain flour	2½ cups plus 2 tablespoons all-purpose flour
3 teaspoons baking powder	3 teaspoons baking powder
½ teaspoon salt	½ teaspoon salt
¼ pint/1½ dl. milk	⅔ cup milk

Cream the butter and sugar until light and fluffy, then mix in the
honey. Beat in the egg. Sift together the flour, baking powder and
salt and stir into the creamed mixture alternately with the milk.
Put the mixture into a greased 2-lb. (1-kg.) loaf tin and bake in a
moderate oven (350°F., 180°C., Gas Mark 4) for 1¼ hours. Cool
on a wire rack. Serve sliced and spread with butter.

Family honey cake

IMPERIAL · METRIC	AMERICAN
8 oz./225 g. plain flour	2 cups all-purpose flour
3 teaspoons baking powder	3 teaspoons baking powder
pinch salt	pinch salt
4 oz./100 g. butter or margarine	½ cup butter or margarine
3 oz./75 g. sugar	generous ⅓ cup sugar
4 oz./100 g. dates, sliced	generous ½ cup sliced dates
1 oz./25 g. walnuts, chopped	¼ cup chopped walnuts
2 eggs	2 eggs
2 tablespoons honey	3 tablespoons honey
4 tablespoons milk	⅓ cup milk

Sift the flour, baking powder and salt into a bowl and rub in the butter or margarine. Stir in the sugar, dates and walnuts. Mix to a soft consistency with the beaten eggs, honey and milk. Put into a greased, round 7-inch (18-cm.) cake tin and bake in a moderate oven (350°F., 180°C., Gas Mark 4) for 1¼ hours. Cool on a wire rack.

Honey cakes

IMPERIAL · METRIC	AMERICAN
1 lb./450 g. honey	1⅓ cups honey
6 oz./175 g. soft brown sugar	¾ cup brown sugar
4 eggs	4 eggs
1 teaspoon cinnamon	1 teaspoon cinnamon
¼ teaspoon mixed spice	¼ teaspoon mixed spice
12 oz./350 g. wholemeal flour	3 cups wholewheat flour
1 teaspoon baking powder	1 teaspoon baking powder
2 oz./50 g. sultanas	scant ½ cup seedless white raisins
2 oz./50 g. blanched almonds, chopped	½ cup blanched chopped almonds
2 oz./50 g. chopped peel	scant ½ cup chopped peel

Grease and line a 9-inch (23-cm.) square cake tin with greased greaseproof paper.

Melt the honey and sugar over a gentle heat, then cool slightly. Beat in the eggs and spices and stir in the flour and baking powder. Stir in the sultanas, almonds and peel. Turn into the prepared tin and bake in a moderately hot oven (400°F., 200°C., Gas Mark 6) for 45 minutes–1 hour. Cool in the tin then turn on to a wire rack and strip off the paper. Store in an airtight tin and cut into squares to serve.

Honey nut spice cake

IMPERIAL · METRIC	AMERICAN
10 oz./275 g. plain flour	2½ cups all-purpose flour
1½ teaspoons baking powder	1½ teaspoons baking powder
¾ teaspoon bicarbonate of soda	¾ teaspoon baking soda
1 teaspoon mixed spice	1 teaspoon mixed spice
4 oz./100 g. butter	½ cup butter
4 oz./100 g. granulated sugar	½ cup granulated sugar
2 eggs	2 eggs
scant ¼ pint/1¼ dl. milk	scant ⅔ cup milk
6 oz./175 g. honey	½ cup honey
Filling	*Filling*
2 oz./50 g. butter	¼ cup butter
8 oz./225 g. icing sugar	2 cups sifted confectioners' sugar
1 tablespoon lemon juice	1 tablespoon lemon juice
2 oz./50 g. honey	3 tablespoons honey
2 oz./50 g. walnuts, chopped	½ cup chopped walnuts
castor or icing sugar to sprinkle	granulated or confectioners' sugar to sprinkle

Sift the flour, baking powder, bicarbonate of soda and spice together. Cream the butter and sugar until light and fluffy. Gradually beat in the eggs. Fold in the flour alternately with the milk and honey. Divide the mixture between two greased and floured 8-inch (20-cm.) sandwich tins and bake in a moderate oven (350°F., 180°C., Gas Mark 4) for about 35 minutes, until firm. Cool slightly before turning on to a wire rack.

To make the filling, beat the butter until soft then gradually beat in the sifted icing sugar, lemon juice and honey. Add the chopped nuts. When the cakes are cold, sandwich them together with the filling. Before serving, dust the top of the cake with castor or icing sugar.

Honey date bars

IMPERIAL · METRIC	AMERICAN
3 oz./75 g. butter	6 tablespoons butter
6 tablespoons honey	7 tablespoons honey
3 eggs	3 eggs
8 oz./225 g. plain flour	2 cups all-purpose flour
1 teaspoon baking powder	1 teaspoon baking powder
½ teaspoon salt	½ teaspoon salt
6 oz./175 g. dates, chopped	1 cup chopped dates
4 oz./100 g. nuts, chopped	1 cup chopped nuts

Cream the butter and honey together until light and fluffy. Beat in the eggs one at a time. Sift together the flour, baking powder and salt and work into the mixture. Stir in the dates and nuts. Spread the mixture on a greased baking sheet, about 9 inches (23 cm.) by 12 inches (30 cm.). Bake in a moderate oven (350°F., 180°C., Gas Mark 4) for 30 minutes. Cut into bars and cool on a wire rack.

Honey squares

IMPERIAL · METRIC	AMERICAN
4 oz./100 g. plain flour	1 cup all-purpose flour
¼ teaspoon salt	¼ teaspoon salt
½ teaspoon bicarbonate of soda	½ teaspoon baking soda
1 teaspoon ginger	1 teaspoon ginger
1 teaspoon cinnamon	1 teaspoon cinnamon
3 tablespoons salad oil	scant ¼ cup salad oil
2 oz./50 g. honey	3 tablespoons honey
2 oz./50 g. black treacle	3 tablespoons molasses
2 oz./50 g. Demerara sugar	¼ cup brown sugar
1 egg	1 egg
2 tablespoons milk	3 tablespoons milk
2 oz./50 g. sultanas (optional)	½ cup seedless white raisins (optional)
chopped walnuts or almonds (optional)	chopped walnuts or almonds (optional)

Sift the flour, salt, bicarbonate of soda and spices into a bowl. Add the oil, honey, treacle, sugar, beaten egg and milk and the sultanas if used. Beat quickly until smooth. Pour into a 7-inch (18-cm.) square tin, greased and lined at the bottom with greased paper. Sprinkle a few chopped walnuts or almonds over the top, if liked. Bake in a moderate oven (350°F., 180°C., Gas Mark 4) for 30–40 minutes, until firm. Cool on a wire rack. Cut into nine squares to serve.

Honey nibbles

IMPERIAL·METRIC	AMERICAN
2½ oz./65 g. stoned dates	generous ¼ cup pitted dates
2 egg whites	2 egg whites
6 oz./175 g. castor sugar	¾ cup granulated sugar
1 tablespoon honey	1 tablespoon honey
9 oz./250 g. ground almonds	2¼ cups ground almonds

Cut the dates into small pieces. Beat together the egg whites, sugar and honey until the mixture is foamy. Fold in the dates and almonds. Place in small heaps on rice paper on a baking sheet. Bake in a moderate oven (350°F., 180°C., Gas Mark 4) for 15–20 minutes, until golden brown.

Honey treats

IMPERIAL·METRIC	AMERICAN
2 lb./1 kg. loaf sugar	4 cups granulated sugar
¼ pint/1½ dl. water	⅔ cup water
2 oz./50 g. clear honey	3 tablespoons clear honey
⅓ pint/1¼ dl. single cream	generous ¾ cup half-and-half
¼ oz./10 g. butter	½ tablespoon butter
strawberry, lemon or vanilla essence	strawberry, lemon or vanilla extract
pink food colouring	pink food coloring

Place the sugar in a heavy-based pan with the water and stir over a low heat to dissolve the sugar. Stir in the honey, cream and butter and boil until a sugar thermometer registers 290°F. (145°C.). Quickly stir in the flavouring essence and colouring and pour on to an oiled slab. Leave to set, then cut into small squares.

Honey mallow crunchies

IMPERIAL·METRIC	AMERICAN
4 oz./100 g. marshmallows	¼ lb. marshmallows
2 tablespoons honey	3 tablespoons honey
grated rind of 1 small lemon	grated rind of 1 small lemon
grated rind of ½ orange	grated rind of ½ orange
2½ oz./65 g. cornflakes, lightly crushed	2 cups lightly crushed cornflakes
1 oz./25 g. raisins	2 tablespoons raisins

Melt the marshmallows with the honey in a bowl over a pan of boiling water. Stir gently together. Remove from the heat and add lemon and orange rind, crushed cornflakes and raisins. Mix well together. With slightly wet hands, shape the mixture into small balls and place each in a paper sweet case. Leave to set in a cool place.

Glazed fruits

IMPERIAL·METRIC	AMERICAN
1 lb./450 g. granulated sugar	2 cups granulated sugar
¼ pint/1½ dl. water	⅔ cup water
2 tablespoons clear honey	3 tablespoons clear honey

This quick candy glaze can be used for coating fresh fruits, such as grapes, whole apples or pears, orange or tangerine segments, and nuts.

Put the sugar, water and honey into a small pan and stir over a moderate heat until the sugar is dissolved. Put in a sugar thermometer and boil briskly without stirring until the thermometer registers 265°F., (135°C.). Reduce the heat and boil gently to 310°F. (151°C.). (If you have no thermometer, test the syrup by dropping a little into cold water. It should form a crisp hard ball. Check this by biting a piece to make sure it is crisp and not chewy.) When the syrup is ready, stand the pan in a roasting tin of boiling water to prevent syrup setting too quickly. Have the fruit ready, peeled or wiped, and using skewers for the larger fruits or tongs for the smaller ones, dip in the syrup to cover completely, lift out and drain off surplus syrup. Leave on a greased tray until set.

Honey lemonade

IMPERIAL · METRIC	AMERICAN
6 lemons	6 lemons
4 oz./100 g. sugar	½ cup sugar
4 tablespoons honey	5 tablespoons honey
2 pints/generous litre water	5 cups water

Peel the lemons thinly and put the peel into a bowl with the juice of the lemons, the sugar and honey. Boil the water, pour over the lemon juice and stir well. Cool and strain. Serve chilled with water, soda or tonic water.

Honey orange punch

IMPERIAL · METRIC	AMERICAN
6 oranges	6 oranges
3 lemons	3 lemons
½ pint/3 dl. water	1¼ cups water
9 tablespoons clear honey	10 tablespoons clear honey
cloves	cloves

Squeeze the juice from five of the oranges and from all the lemons. Add the water and honey and heat to boiling point. Meanwhile, slice the remaining orange (leaving the skin on) and stick one or two cloves into the centre of each slice. Pour the hot drink into mugs and float an orange slice on the top of each serving.

Honey cold cure

IMPERIAL · METRIC	AMERICAN
1 tablespoon clear honey	1 tablespoon clear honey
juice of ½ lemon	juice of ½ lemon
1 tablespoon whisky	1 tablespoon whisky
1 lemon slice	1 lemon slice

Put the honey, lemon juice and whisky into a mug. Top up with boiling water and stir well. Float the lemon slice on top and drink while very hot.

Honey egg nog

IMPERIAL·METRIC	AMERICAN
1 teaspoon clear honey	1 teaspoon clear honey
1 egg	1 egg
½ pint/3 dl. milk	1¼ cups milk

Beat the honey and egg together and then pour on the milk
which can be hot or cold, stirring all the time.

Invalids and small children like this drink very much. It makes
a quick and nourishing meal-in-a-glass. To make the drink look
more special, whisk the honey with the egg yolk only, then pour
on the milk, and finally stir in the stiffly whisked egg white.

Honey nightcap

IMPERIAL·METRIC	AMERICAN
½ pint/3 dl. milk	1¼ cups milk
2 teaspoons clear honey	2 teaspoons clear honey
2 teaspoons rum	2 teaspoons rum

Heat the milk and honey until almost boiling. Pour into a warm
mug, stir in the rum and drink at once.

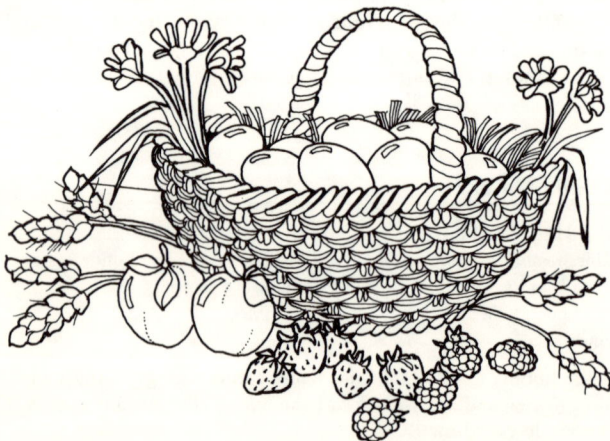